INTERNATIONAL NIETZSCHE STUDIES

Richard Schacht, series editor

Editorial Board
Ruediger Bittner (Bielefeld)
Eric Blondel (Paris-Sorbonne)
Maudemarie Clark (Colgate)
David Cooper (Durham)
Arthur Danto (Columbia)
Kathleen Higgins (Texas-Austin)
R. J. Hollingdale (London)
Bernd Magnus (California-Riverside)
Wolfgang Mueller-Lauter (Berlin)
Alexander Nehamas (Princeton)
Martha Nussbaum (Brown)
Joerg Salaquarda (Vienna)
Gary Shapiro (Richmond)
Robert Solomon (Texas-Austin)
Tracy Strong (California-San Diego)
Yirmiyahu Yovel (Jerusalem)

T0373468

*A list of books in the series appears
at the back of this book.*

International Nietzsche Studies

Nietzsche has emerged as a thinker of extraordinary importance, not only in the history of philosophy but in many fields of contemporary inquiry. Nietzsche studies are maturing and flourishing in many parts of the world. This internationalization of inquiry with respect to Nietzsche's thought and significance may be expected to continue.

International Nietzsche Studies is conceived as a series of monographs and essay collections that will reflect and contribute to these developments. The series will present studies in which responsible scholarship is joined to the analysis, interpretation, and assessment of the many aspects of Nietzsche's thought that bear significantly upon matters of moment today. In many respects Nietzsche is our contemporary, with whom we do well to reckon, even when we find ourselves at odds with him. The series is intended to promote this reckoning, embracing diverse interpretive perspectives, philosophical orientations, and critical assessments.

The series is also intended to contribute to the ongoing reconsideration of the character, agenda, and prospects of philosophy itself. Nietzsche was much concerned with philosophy's past, present, and future. He sought to affect not only its understanding but also its practice. The future of philosophy is an open question today, thanks at least in part to Nietzsche's challenge to the philosophical traditions of which he was so critical. It remains to be seen—and determined—whether philosophy's future will turn out to resemble the "philosophy of the future" to which he proffered a prelude and of which he provided a preview, by both precept and practice. But this is a possibility we do well to take seriously. International Nietzsche Studies will attempt to do so, while contributing to the understanding of Nietzsche's philosophical thinking and its bearing upon contemporary inquiry.

—Richard Schacht

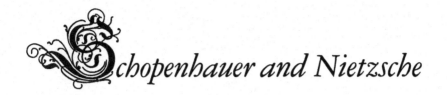

Schopenhauer and Nietzsche

Georg Simmel

Translated by Helmut Loiskandl,

Deena Weinstein,

and Michael Weinstein

University of Illinois Press
Urbana and Chicago

First Illinois paperback, 1991
© 1986 by the University of Massachusetts Press
Manufactured in the United States of America
P 8 7 6 5 4

This book is printed on acid-free paper.

Library of Congress Cataloging-in-Publication Data
Simmel, Georg, 1858–1918.
    [Schopenhauer and Nietzsche. English]
    Schopenhauer and Nietzsche / Georg Simmel ; translated by Helmut
Loiskandl, Deena Weinstein, and Michael Weinstein. — Illini Books
ed.
        p.   cm.
    Translation of: Schopenhauer und Nietzsche.
    Reprint. Originally published: Amherst : University of
Massachusetts Press, 1986.
    ISBN 0-252-06228-0/ISBN 978-0-252-06228-5
    1. Schopenhauer, Arthur, 1788–1860. 2. Nietzsche, Friedrich
Wilhelm, 184–1900. I. Title.
    B3148.S518   1991
    193—dc20   91-9804
                                                      CIP

CONTENTS

TRANSLATORS' PREFACE

THE PRESENT TRANSLATION OF GEORG SIMMEL'S *Schopenhauer und Nietzsche: Ein Vortragszyklus* (1907), which is the first to appear in English, was undertaken for several reasons. The project was originally inspired by sheer intellectual curiosity: What did Simmel have to say about the two great nineteenth-century German philosophers of life? Each of this project's collaborators had cultivated a longstanding appreciation for Simmel's work and its significance to both the study of social relations and, more important, to the understanding of twentieth-century philosophy. Although he was the major German representative of mature vitalistic thought, Simmel had not been given due recognition for his contributions. Thus, it seemed that presenting his reflections on Schopenhauer and Nietzsche to a wider audience would help to enhance his stature as a leading philosopher. During the preliminary work on the translation it became clear that not only was Simmel a first-rank philosopher, but also that *Schopenhauer und Nietzsche* was crucial in his canon, representing a mediation between his early positivism and his later metaphysics, and constituting the seedbed of his considered observations on human existence and reality—that is, life. In *Schopenhauer und Nietzsche*, Simmel for the first time ventured beyond the analysis of society and a critique of culture to reveal their grounds in individuated life, and he did so through a novel deconstructionist approach to the thought of the founders of *lebensphilosophie*. The translators were determined to make Simmel's analytical criticism of Schopenhauer and Nietzsche as accessible as possible, and thereby focused their efforts on making the work clear and intelligible, targeting a wide reading audience in the humanities and social sciences.

The major difficulty encountered in the translation involved Simmel's style, not the substance of his thought. First, Simmel's syntax is idiosyncratic and, unfortunately, does not conform to any models of German prose. Second, his sentence construction is highly complex; he often compacts diverse themes into a single sentence and sometimes leaves these themes incompletely developed, only to have their resolution appear later on. Third, his examples and metaphors are frequently dated and obscure. In light of their goal of enhancing this work's accessibility, the translators confronted these stylistic problems by choosing to present *Schopenhauer und Nietzsche* in a contemporary English version. They employed English syntax, shortened sentences and sorted out themes, and updated examples and metaphors, all without sacrificing any of Simmel's meaning. Thus, the translation strives to be faithful, though it is not literal. Inquiry into Simmel's intellectual career provides some explanation for the stylistic vicissitudes of *Schopenhauer und Nietzsche*. In this work Simmel is struggling to gain a purchase on the major problem of his thought—the meaning of life—and his method is to assess the ideas of his great predecessors. He is tentative and probing, adopting the aporetic approach of Aristotle, which involves shuttling between contesting propositions, first upholding one of them and then its opposite, and finally limiting both of them mutually. His mind is not confused, but its development is in process. It appears that he was thinking too quickly to present his reflections in as systematic a form as they actually take when the text is studied carefully. The translators did not reorder or rework Simmel's argumentation, and have preserved the flavor of open and fresh inquiry characteristic of the work. But they strove to clear up any obscurities due to style. Fortunately Simmel is a sufficiently trenchant thinker to allow for a clear distinction of style from substance.

Schopenhauer und Nietzsche went through three editions, the first of which was published in 1907. The others appeared after Simmel's death, in 1920 and 1923, all under the imprint of the Leipzig House of Duncker und Humblot. The 1923 edition was used for the present translation, but there are no substantial differences among the editions. The translation took three years to complete, occupying the major scholarly efforts of the collaborators, who passed copies to one another and sometimes worked together, translating and revising on the spot. The contemplated result is a work that is more accessible than the original, but true to it, a vehicle for enlightening current opinion on Schopenhauer and Nietzsche, for broadening the contemporary Simmel revival in the English language, and for enhancing the understanding of twentieth-century philosophy. The following philosophical introduction provides a frame for appreciating the work in the contexts of the history of ideas, Simmel interpretation, and Simmel's intellectual career.

1985   HELMUT LOISKANDL
                                                University of Queensland
                                          DEENA WEINSTEIN
                                                DePaul University
                                          MICHAEL WEINSTEIN
                                                Purdue University

INTRODUCTION

GEORG SIMMEL (1858–1918) BELONGED TO THE CRUCIAL generation in Western intellectual history whose members' task was to assimilate, interpret, and try to fashion positively the ideas that had matured in the nineteenth century. That generation, which included Max Weber, Henri Bergson, Emile Durkheim, Samuel Alexander, Edmund Husserl, and Sigmund Freud, reviewed and evaluated the mixed results of nineteenth-century thought: a dominant optimism based on the expansion of industrialization and democratization, and a subordinate pessimism warning of the corrosive effects of the rationalism that expressed and presided over the great processes of social change. In its confrontation with its ambivalent legacy—Hegel and Schopenhauer, Marx and Nietzsche, Darwin and Dostoevsky—the turn-of-the-century generation put the brakes on intellectual progressivism, but fought not to give up on life, though the myth of rationalism, in both its spiritualist and materialist forms, had been shattered. Its members continued to attack progressivism, completing Weber's "disenchantment of the world," but they also attempted to rescue civilization from the effects of that disenchantment: the loss of meaning for life, the attendant dispersion of meanings and incipient despair, and the social disorganization and conflict that grounded and reflected cultural variety and disunity. In general, members of the turn-of-the-century generation began on the progressive side, while striving, under Darwinian influence, to remove all vestiges of idealism through some sort of naturalism, realism, or empiricism. But in the 1890s they questioned progress, faced spiritual crisis, and encountered the problematic consequences—for society and the individual—of their destruction of objectivized meanings. When they emerged from their crises they attempted to restore meaning to culture and society, while remaining thoroughly critical, scientific, and modern. Their efforts essentially ended in frustration, paving the way intellectually for the dispersed and specialized thought of the twentieth century, in which there is no general discourse, but merely isolated discourses. That is, they proved to be too rigid in their criticism to permit a redogmatization of meanings and purposes; though their wish was to be constructive, their will was deconstructionist.

Simmel was typical of his generation and was one of its most productive and insightful members, his thought anticipating in many respects that of the present. He criticized the Kantian form of rationalism and grappled with the disenchantment of the world according to the specific cultural and individual crises revealed by his deconstruction of critical philosophy. Fundamentally, Simmel opposed that form of *a priorism* which holds that the ideas that regulate cultural pursuits—for example epistemological categories and moral principles—are objective, in the sense that they have being independent of the vicissitudes of individual experience and social process. His criticism of what he called "conceptual realism" left him with the logical options of reducing cultural meanings to historical dynamics, as interpreted psychologically and sociologically, or of devising a new status for regulative forms. As did the other leading members of his generation, Simmel opted to attempt to ground the forms of culture on a new basis. His new foundation was "objectivization," the doctrine that when human reality emerges from the flux of life, the pressures of adaptation to circumstance are projected into realms of form which stand over and against more spontaneous adaptation, guiding it as though from without. Thus, Simmel preserves a phenomenological independence of cultural meaning from individual and social experience, while deriving such meaning ontologically and genetically from the process of life. This is his variant of the double project of his generation: he destroys an eternalistic interpretation of cultural meaning and form, and then tries to rescue the objectivity of meaning and form even as he refers it to the flux. Simmel's destiny was to have revealed the skepticism lurking beneath Kantian *a priorism*, and then to have struggled against the spirit of gravity in order to continue to uphold the objectivity of guiding ideas.

There is a deep tension in Simmel's project that pulls it toward a tragic conclusion. The enchantment or mystification of conceptual realism consists in its legitimation of the experienced independence of form from content (for example, the sense of the constraint of moral duty), by appeal to an independent realm of eternalistic categories or principles (the rational necessity of the moral law). Once such forms, that relate the contents of life to finalities, are referred for their genesis to the processes of individual and social life, they lose their legitimation and are interpreted initially as phases of temporal process. Thus, form is made relative to content, and its constraining character is interpreted merely as a psychological impulse projected from the self and then read back into it. The particular form of relativism expressed here sows the seeds of a legitimation crisis: Can one respond to the regulative ideas of civilized activity as though they were objective, when one interprets them as objectivizations which result from the specific circumstances of the life process? For the individual this question appears as a deeply personal perplexity—that is, as a way to the absurd, to the problems of the meaning of a life void of a transpersonal purpose, and of a slackness of the will to go beyond oneself into a world of merely finite and transient accomplishments. Culturally this question exposes the problems of social unity in a disenchanted world: of mobilizing commitment to live together in pursuit of common aims and, at the limit, to engage in mutual relations at all. Simmel's project was to vindicate cultural form as objectivization, but the drift toward relativism and skepticism impelled him to quest for something beyond the "as if," for a real *a priori* anchored somehow in the life process rather than in a return to the transcendental. At the end of his career he seemed to find that *a priori* in the structure of life, but it turned out to be a broken and tragic structure. Up until the final stage of his thinking, Simmel searched restlessly for a way to undo the damage of disenchantment. That is the drama of his thought.

Simmel will be interpreted here primarily as a philosopher, but though he began and ended his intellectual career with philosophy, he is best understood as a model of the French *penseur*, one who employs a variety of modes of thought to express a critical vision of life and culture. That he was not a specialist but a cultural critic explains, in great part, why only late in his career did he gain a professorship and why he has been characterized as unsystematic and an "impressionist."[1] If one,

1 For this line of interpretation, see particularly David Frisby, *Sociological Impressionism: A Reassessment of Georg Simmel's Social Theory* (London: Heinemann, 1981). For other commentaries see Peter Lawrence, *Georg Simmel: Sociologist and European* (New York: Barnes and Noble, 1976) and Donald N. Levine, *Georg Simmel: On Individuality and Social Forms* (Chicago: University of Chicago Press, 1971).

however, considers his work in light of its central problematic, that work appears as an intelligible intellectual process, characterized by a basic thematic unity that is varied by different genres of thought and content. Always struggling to restore the *a priori* on a new ground, Simmel first attempts to establish a positive moral science in the early phase of his career (1892), then regroups and produces an impressive body of cultural theory based on his notion of objectification (1900–1910), and finally expounds a tragic ontology of life in his waning years (1918). His project and quest take him through sociology, aesthetics, the literary essay, art criticism, philosophical commentary, and philosophy of life. In his period of intense work he produces studies of: the role of money in civilization; the grounds of sociology; various social relations; Goethe, Kant, and Schopenhauer and Nietzsche; religion; and philosophy as a cultural activity. Although his greatest intellectual impact has been as one of the leading classical sociologists, and although his dominant pursuit was that of the philosopher, neither role exhausted him; both are informed by his project and quest, which run beyond any single form of cultural activity to a reflection on cultural activity and its personal dimensions. These reflections are undertaken not from the viewpoint of a new form but, paradoxically, through the deconstruction of the forms in which Simmel deploys his thought.

As a major thinker of his generation, Simmel has enjoyed a lasting influence on twentieth-century thought, primarily in the United States, but also in Germany, France, and, more recently, Great Britain. In America, he has gone through three stages of appropriation. He was first brought to the attention of American intellectuals by Albion Small, one of the founders of sociology in the United States. After World War I, through the work of Robert Park, Simmel became an important influence on the Chicago School of sociology, which incorporated his interactionist approach. In this first period, Simmel's insights into the forms and dynamics of social relations were taken as a basis for a significant movement in American sociology, which continues today in symbolic interactionism. But the distinctive pattern of his thought was not a matter of concern. After World War II, through the efforts of Lewis Coser and Kurt Wolff, Simmel enjoyed a small revival, not by virtue of the dissemination of some of his ideas, but as one of the founders of classical sociology. His sociology and its philosophical grounds were considered as a whole and, as sociological theorist, his reputation was secured. Beginning in 1960, with the publication of Rudolph Weingartner's major study of Simmel's philosophy, but maturing only in the late 1970s, a third phase of Simmel's influence has broadened the appreciation of his work as a whole. Translations have been published of his *Problems of the Philosophy of History* (1977), *Philosophy of Money* (1978), essays on interpretation in social science (1980), and essays on women, sexuality, and love (1984). Peter Lawrence (1976) and David Frisby (1981) have produced books on Simmel as a sociologist, and Donald Levine (1971) has contributed important work on the philosophical grounds of Simmel's sociology. The following translation of Simmel's *Schopenhauer und Nietzsche* is meant as a contribution to the current wave of interest in his thought. It reveals his confrontation with the great philosophers of life, who conditioned the debate over optimism and pessimism that overarched the special concerns of his generation. This work thus provides a privileged glimpse of Simmel as an integral thinker.

Rudolph Weingartner has provided the leading interpretation of Simmel's philosophy for the American audience. Weingartner's *Philosophy of Georg Simmel* considers the anatomy of Simmel's philosophical ideas.[2] Weingartner's interpretative approach uses Simmel's late philosophy of life as a key for organizing the thought of his middle period, proceeding by a method of reconstruction or assemblage. For Weingartner, Simmel was guided by a single philosophic vision throughout his intellectual career, but only brought it to more-or-less coherent expression in his tragic life-philosophy. Weingartner's treatment of Simmel, therefore, has a somewhat static character, in that both his thesis and method press for systematization, for a philosophic position that Simmel never stated "in so many words."[3] Although Weingartner's contribution has been to show how Simmel's final reflections illuminate his earlier struggles, in so doing he has made Simmel's career appear to be far more unitary than it actually was. A reading of *Schopenhauer und Nietzsche*, which was Simmel's first important confrontation with modern philosophy of life, reveals that in his middle period he was not a metaphysician of life but rather a relativist and pragmatic humanist. Weingartner is correct that there are not two Simmels, a culture-

2 Rudolph H. Weingartner, *Experience and Culture: The Philosophy of Georg Simmel* (Middletown: Wesleyan University Press, 1960).
3 Ibid., p. x.

philosopher and a life-philosopher, but that observation does not mean
that there is one Simmel. The unity of Simmel's thought proceeds not
from a single vision but from a project, his quest to reground form in a
real *a priori*. That search ended in a tragic vitalism based on intuition,
but the result was not prefigured; it was merely an intelligible development. Weingartner's stress on systematization takes much of the real
drama out of Simmel's intellectual life and renders him almost a dog-
matist of paradox, rather than a man who struggled to resolve the great
personal and cultural problematic of his generation. This emphasis is,
perhaps, also responsible for Weingartner's estimation that Simmel "is
not a philosopher of the first rank" because he neither "succeeded in fus-
ing disparate elements into a single, unified, all-encompassing system
that is vulnerable to major criticism only from outside it," nor "relentlessly pushed some original insight without allowing 'foreign' elements to obscure [the] vision."[4] Based on another criterion, that of serious and profound engagement with a fundamental problem, Simmel
can be judged to be a philosopher of the first rank. He, along with
William James and Henri Bergson, closed the discourse of philosophy
of life. Inheriting the problem of optimism and pessimism from the
nineteenth century, each showed a possibility for its resolution, and together exhausted those possibilities.

A worthy counterpoint to Weingartner's interpretation is the only
other major study of Simmel's philosophy as a whole, A. Mamelet's *Le
Relativisme Philosophique Chez Georg Simmel* (1914).[5] Mamelet, who
could consider only Simmel's early and middle periods, argued, like
Weingartner, that Simmel's work evinced a single position, but understood that position to be a kind of skeptical humanism rather than a
tragic vision of the dialectic of life and form. Mamelet's interpretative
approach was straightforwardly chronological, moving through Simmel's works and illustrating how each of them evinced a relativistic account of the forms of culture through the process of the objectification
of personal life. He insisted upon the sharp difference between Bergson's
intuitionism, which promised immediate knowledge of nonegological
reality, and Simmel's critical approach, which confined knowledge
to forms that grew out of an unanalyzed and perhaps unanalyzable
ground. He argued that Simmel was surely tempted by intuitionism,

4 Ibid., p. 188.
5 Albert Mamelet, *Le Relativisme Philosophique chez Georg Simmel* (Paris: Alcan, 1914).

but that his intellectual probity prevented him from succumbing to it. In his late period Simmel did turn toward classical vitalism, but Mamelet's study shows that in his middle period, Simmel was not yet guided by that position. Instead he was skirting and even actively avoiding it, maintaining a much more flexible and tentative view. The subtlety and probity of Simmel's philosophic thought prompted Mamelet to conclude, in contrast to Weingartner, that it had earned its "proper rank among the great doctrines that honor human thought."[6] This judgment has not withstood the test of time, but it points to Simmel's significance in the history of modern thought.

The interpretation of Simmel's philosophy presented here differs from those of Weingartner and Mamelet by attending to project and problematic rather than to doctrine. Both of Simmel's major commentators present static views, Mamelet reading forward and Weingartner reading back. Each provides a different snapshot, which is valuable for fixing a structure of thought, a guidepost, but neither offers a moving picture of the life of a mind. By considering Simmel's work as indicative of an intellectual career, one is able to appreciate its tension and subtlety, its character of an intelligible development—which is not preordained by certain static ideas, but which is in constant ferment in response to the struggle to find ground to guide living in a fragmented world. The following discussion will trace Simmel's philosophic odyssey beginning with brief remarks on its early stages, which focused on the possibility of a positive moral science, through its middle period of skeptical humanism, to its final period of classical philosophy of life. The primary concern will be to place *Schopenhauer und Nietzsche* within this career, specifically to show how it captures Simmel at his most open moment, when he confronts the leading ideas of his generation and has not yet resolved his response to them. He is an integral thinker here, not in the sense of displaying a system, but in containing within his thought his past struggles and the germs of his future conclusions. He appears as the master of speculative possibility and psychological fact, a privileged vantage point from which to view the rest of his contributions.

Simmel's intellectual career opens in the early 1890s with his encounter with the two major streams of nineteenth-century thought: idealism and evolutionary naturalism. Through the second half of the nineteenth century the influence of Darwin's theory of evolution had

6 Ibid., p. 207.

widened and deepened, and had begun not only to undermine the idealistic tendencies of thought inherited from Kant and Hegel, but also to spread into the interpretation of society and of the cultural forms in which social relations are mediated. The challenge presented to Simmel's generation was to judge the contributions of evolutionary naturalism, especially the progressivist assumptions of its social applications—and to consider whether there was any lasting value to be learned from the idealist legacy. It was nearly impossible for an advanced thinker of Simmel's time to ignore the idea of evolution or even to criticize it profoundly, at least in his early stages of thought. The category of "life"—as Simmel noted in his late essay, "The Conflict in Modern Culture"—was becoming the master conception of the modern era and had to play a key role in any emergent philosophy or, as William James called it, "conception of the frame of things." Yet as the evolutionary interpretation was extended to culture and society, the seeds of a cultural crisis began to germinate. What was to be the fate of the cultural forms that integrated social and cultural life if they became instruments of a temporal process based on the struggle for survival? The objectivity of cultural standards was at stake, which is why Simmel's generation turned back to contemplate and draw sustenance from the idealist tradition. The protagonist in the conflict of nineteenth-century systems was evolutionary naturalism. The specific project that informed turn-of-the-century thinkers in their early stages of thought was to save the objectivity of form while remaining within the frame of life: form would somehow have to express, yet regulate, life.

As representative of his generation Simmel placed himself firmly in the modernist camp. Similar to his contemporaries Samuel Alexander in Great Britain and Emile Durkheim in France his early work was devoted to interpreting morals on the basis of positive science. The declared purpose of his major early work, *Einleitung in die Moralwissenschaft*, was to advance the study of morality beyond its philosophical stage of speculation about concepts and to base it on psychological, historical, and sociological facts; that is, Simmel attempted to found a science of morals. The ground for that science was to be cleared by a criticism of the realism of moral concepts, the doctrine that the principles regulating moral conduct are independent of the practical life of evolving desires and their changing fulfillments. Specifically, Simmel engaged Kant, whose ethical theory was based on the separation of the moral law, interpreted as a universal principle of reason, from the inclinations that shape practical life. Having deprived moral ideas, through his criticism, of any status outside the process of life, his task was to show their precise relation to experience and, in particular, to account for their apparent objectivity. That objectivity had been secured for Kant by his doctrine of the *a priori*, that is, of rational form that could be analyzed out of the manifold of life through a transcendental critique. Eschewing speculative philosophy, Simmel had to reject Kant's *a priorism*, but he also sought to find a way in which the function served by the *a priori*, that of regulating conduct in the case of morals, could still be retained.

Simmel's strategy in his attempt to found a moral science was, in the language of contemporary criticism, deconstructionist: he undertook simultaneously a genealogy of morals after the manner of Marx and Nietzsche, and a criticism of the rational unity of Kantian moral theory. The criticism of Kant was the key to Simmel's moral reflections. As Mamelet puts it, Simmel took the concept of duty, voided it of all logical content, and reduced it to a simple and purely subjective form, a structure of individual experience that could hold indifferently a multitude of contents.[7] By making duty the sentiment of obligation, Simmel was free to show that what was obliged varied according to historical circumstance, both social and psychological. And here he inserted his genealogy: not only was the content of duty relative to historical circumstance, but that relativity was grounded in "the practical requirements of the species," that is, in the struggle for survival. Simmel, however, was not content to reduce moral concepts to the status of other facts. Though he had deconstructed duty to a sentiment that interiorized the external pushes and pulls of social discipline, he had to contend with the psychological fact that obligation appears as a binding constraint; that is, he sought to reconcile the genetic order of historical development with the order of meaning, the latter which appears as atemporal. Simmel's gambit here is to introduce the notion of objectivization, which is the hallmark of all of his succeeding thought. Extending his genealogy, he argues that the small number of practical requirements which constitute the moral life are condensed and combined in the social and individual consciousness through the action of

7 Ibid., p. 36.

tradition and the synthesizing processes of the mind. These requirements become crystallized into principles of conduct that reciprocally unite form and content. However, although form springs historically from content, the in-formation of content presumes some form, some *a priori*. As Mamelet comments: "If all *a priori* form in some way springs from matter, all content supposes, in order to be lived, an *a priori* form and then raises itself into a new form that is ruled by the first one. But, in turn, this new form becomes a new *a priori* for other contents that are lived later on, and so on to infinity." The progress of moral life, therefore, becomes "an incessant displacement of *a prioris* and forms on one side, and of matter and empirical contents on the other."[8]

The necessity of an *a priori*, albeit a transient one, provides Simmel with his lever for objectivization. He argues that repeated subjective representations which harmonize with habits and tendencies naturally take on the form of objectivity. In the case of morals the "transformation of our subjective ideal into an objective ideal is facilitated by the effacement of the 'me'" when it confronts the totality of subjects and human interests, which cancels individual inclination and leaves only the "reality of the species."[9] This is Simmel's first resolution of the conflict in modern culture between the dynamism of life and the unifying function of cultural form: form springs from the life process, but appears to individual experience as independent of it and regulative over it. It is a troubling resolution because by making the *a priori* relative to life and continually in flux, it destroys its objectivity. Obligation is here fundamentally based on a natural illusion, or at least on an "as if." But the moral consciousness cannot interpret it in that way if it is to be embraced as binding; that consciousness cannot judge its adherence to principles to be at the discretion of the temporal self, but must experience them as imperatives for that self. For all of his efforts to restore and reinterpret the *a priori*, Simmel has failed to revive its function. He is left drifting toward the tragic view of his late period, in which a paradoxical life process continually engenders its formal antithesis without ever completing itself, and individuals are increasingly hedged in by their unique vital contents, deprived of an objective exit to the wider world once provided by the illusion of objectivity.

For eight years after the issue of his *Einleitung*, Simmel did not pub-

8 Ibid., p. 37.   9 Ibid., p. 45.

lish a major work. Then, beginning in 1900 with his magisterial *Philosophie des Geldes*, and ending in 1910 with his reflections on philosophy in *Hauptprobleme der Philosophie*, Simmel passed through a period of intense productivity, deepening his problematic and, despite many continuities with his early work, giving it a new resolution. The works of his middle period evince a new tone and attitude. He is no longer concerned with criticizing philosophical speculation or founding the study of cultural forms as a positive science. Rather, he vindicates the integrity of these forms as authentic expressions of individual and social life and especially justifies philosophical thought. In *Philosophie des Geldes*, Simmel's announced aim is to demonstrate the legitimacy of philosophical speculation as a grounding for and provider of significance to political economy. In *Hauptprobleme*, he attempts to defend philosophy in and through itself while simultaneously deconstructing it. Simmel now is less interested in deriving cultural form from evolutionary process, in providing a genetic account or genealogy of culture, than he is in identifying and defining the significance of various cultural forms such as value, goodness, truth, and beauty. Thus, his ground shifts from that of a general life process supposed by evolutionism, toward an individualism, although a more general interpretation of a wider life remains as a counterpoint. His overall procedure is to focus on the link between sentiment and form, perceived in the *Einleitung* as the relation between the subjective sentiment of duty and its object, excluding any interpretation of the natural basis for this relation or of its metaphysical significance. Simmel's new turn in his middle period is, perhaps, more a shift in emphasis than in substance. He persistently acknowledges the necessity of a circumstantial and historical analysis of cultural form alongside his interpretation of meaning. However, the foundation for his own philosophizing becomes ambivalent, moving between the dynamics of the personal self, of conscious and individuated life, and life as more generally and impersonally construed. Simmel seems to be straining to shift his order of priority from life to self, but he never completes that process.

The roots of Simmel's ambivalence lie in his conception of philosophy, and the reflections on philosophy that close his middle period are the clearest expression of the tensions that mark this stage of his intellectual career. Metaphysics, which is the concern of *Hauptprobleme*, is, for Simmel, the most personalized of cultural pursuits, the activity that places the greatest emphasis on the initiative of the self. Simmel begins *Hauptprobleme* with an observation on the uniqueness of philosophy:

> Philosophy, and perhaps only philosophy, moves in the following vicious circle: It determines the presuppositions of its method of thinking and of its purposes by the use of its own method of thinking and in accordance with its own purposes. There is no access to the concept of philosophy from the outside; for only philosophy can decide what philosophy is—indeed, whether it is at all, or whether perhaps its name merely conceals a worthless phantasm.[10]

The peculiar circularity of philosophy is bound up with its project of trying to "think without presuppositions," that is, without *a prioris*, a quest Simmel believes is doomed to frustration. There is, then, no way to logically break philosophy's vicious circle; it can only be broken from outside itself through a substantive presupposition proceeding either from self or world, through a real *a priori*. In *Hauptprobleme*, Simmel moves to the self for a ground—the philosophizing self is the foundation of philosophy: "Only in philosophy does every thinker who is at all original determine not only what he wants to answer but also what he wants to ask."[11] Philosophy is here the freest of activities, the determination by the individual of a standard of importance. However, such freedom eludes any principle of determination. Is philosophy merely the arbitrary declaration of a self? As such existentialists as Nicholas Berdyaev later discovered, the ground of self is a "meonic freedom," a groundless ground, an in-determination. Simmel does not embrace this conclusion, but claims, instead, that the philosopher "not only determines what to ask in the sense of special problems but what it is that he must ask at all in order to be in accord with the concept of philosophy."[12] Yet here the circularity breaks out again: the philosopher is the one who defines the concept of philosophy.

Simmel can only escape from the circle by defining his own conception of philosophy, for he does not try to make philosophy a positive science, as he did for morals in the *Einleitung*. He defines philosophy through a description of its special project, which takes away the free-

---

10 Georg Simmel, "On the Nature of Philosophy," in *Georg Simmel, 1858–1918: A Collection of Essays, with Translations and a Bibliography*, ed. Kurt H. Wolff. (Columbus: Ohio State University Press, 1959), p. 282.

11 Ibid., p. 284.   12 Ibid.

dom he first accorded it. The "principle that underlies the form of the philosophical image of the world" is "the achievement of the *unity* that the mind needs in the face of the immeasurable multiplicity, the variegated and unreconciled shreds of the world." [13] The unity sought by the philosopher in the face of the dispersion of life, however, cannot be discovered in that life. Rather, unity is found in subjectivity: "For the psyche knows itself as a unity; in it—and at first *only* in it—the rays of existence intersect, as it were, at one point." [14] Here, similar to the account in the *Einleitung*, a variety of impressions and strains are internalized around a subjective sentiment, in this case the need for unity. But, as Simmel points out, the more the philosopher strives to include in his ambit, the more "the necessity of reacting in a way that is equally valid for all individuals approaches the limit of zero." [15] That is, the variegated whole cannot be expressed univocally. In order to ground the possibility of any particular philosophy, Simmel resorts once again to the process of objectivization:

> The very image of the *whole*, which seems to imply the fullest and purest objectivity, reflects the peculiarity of its possessor much more than the objective image of any *particular* thing usually reflects it. If art is, as it is said to be, an image of the world seen through a temperament, then philosophy is a temperament seen through an image of the world. [16]

It follows from this interpretation of philosophy that "in philosophical assertions there is no question of correspondence (however understood) with an 'object'; the question is whether the assertions are an adequate expression of the being of the philosopher himself or of the human type that lives within him." [17] The real *a priori* of philosophy is the philosopher's psyche, his temperamental response to his sense of the whole.

Simmel's account of philosophy illuminates the depth of the cultural crisis to which he sought to respond constructively. One might query whether he would be ready to define his own philosophizing as merely the expression of his temperament, or whether philosophy could perform its cultural function of unification if it were to be understood as a sort of inverted poetry. Just as the moral consciousness is structured by

13 Ibid., p. 302.   14 Ibid.
15 Ibid., p. 294.   16 Ibid.
17 Ibid., p. 297.

the objectivity of the imperative, so the metaphysical consciousness is formed by the sense that one actually is describing the nature of things or, at least, is trying to describe them. The personal dimension of the crisis revealed here is what Albert Camus called "the absurd": lurking beneath the theory of objectification is the insight that the demand of the self for unity with its circumstances goes unmet. One may create one's own cosmic poem, but it is a song of the self, not the poetry of Being. Philosophizing self-consciously would be one kind of absurd life. This is the source of Simmel's ambivalence, why he seeks to ameliorate the radically personal character of philosophy through the notion of human types which dwell within thinkers. But he does not move beyond the brink of the absurd. The cultural aspect of the crisis is the loss of any unity for the varied phases of cultural activity, an absence of any wider significance for social relations. And now there is not even the foundation of an objectivized idea of evolutionary process that guided the reflections of the Einleitung. Simmel's deconstruction of philosophy leaves it nerveless: if the self is the real *a priori*, there is no exit to objectivity.

The implications for metaphysics of Simmel's philosophy of philosophy were grasped by an American, J. Loewenberg, a student of Josiah Royce, a Hegel scholar, and one of the few explicit followers of Simmel's line of thinking. Confronted with the conflicting demands of pragmatic naturalism and idealism—the "strife of systems" that preoccupied American philosophers of the generation succeeding that of the great classical thinkers—Loewenberg strove for a way to embrace the scientific spirit and yet not destroy the humanities by immersing them in a tide of naturalism. His response to his problematic was to articulate a "metaphysics of skepticism," metaphysical in the sense of proclaiming that there is a reality independent of the one who seeks to know it as a whole, and skeptical by virtue of a refusal to accept that any definition of that reality could be adequate. Loewenberg claimed to have derived his doctrine's "pragmatic element" not from James or Dewey, who taught him "the spirit of rebellion against the pretensions of absolutism," but from Simmel, who introduced him to "a constructive humanism, not enmeshed in exclusively psychological or biological terms." In his account of philosophy Loewenberg followed Simmel closely, arguing that though "we long to be cosmocentric, . . . it is a longing that cannot be satisfied." The results of "our cognitive efforts to lay bare the inherently problematic nature of being" must be "perennially precarious" in light of "the composite character of judgment whose cosmocentric direction can be distinguished but not separated from its anthropocentric (or egocentric) source and origin." Loewenberg sought to defend himself from the radically subjectivist conclusions of Simmel's pragmatism through appending a realism to it, involving "the most complete avowal of cosmomorphism, since it recognizes the disparity between the intrinsically qualitied real and the real as humanly qualified."[18] Reality thus became for him the obscure background against which the strife of systems was illuminated. This resolution acknowledged the deep problem in the philosophic position of Simmel's middle period, but it could not save metaphysics, which in any particular manifestation was philosophical poetry, or worse, because of the realism, ideology.

In his move to declare existence a surd rather than the absurd, Loewenberg also recognized the more general culture crisis revealed by Simmel. It was through Simmel's books that he "first came to understand the positive implications of the perennial strife of systems." There could be no metaphysical, religious, or political harmony, because "all the 'humanities' exhibit incomparable responses to the same 'problematic reality.'"[19] From Simmel's tragic view, rooted in the inherent solipsism of life, this crisis of the humanities could only indicate a loss of mediating cultural forms. But for Loewenberg realism became an exit to the wider world, a way to vindicate the humanities on a new ground. He held that his doctrine of "problematic realism" was "on its positive side a philosophy of liberalism and tolerance: Just because the nature of reality is so everlastingly problematic every human effort to sound its depths becomes invested with indelible worth."[20] By shifting the focus of skepticism from subject to object, Loewenberg is able to generate an integral response to existence that is lacking in Simmel's middle period. He is, in short, able to be a metaphysician in the classical sense, by providing a bare minimum of an objectivity outrunning objectification. One might say that Loewenberg highlights the radically deconstructionist tendencies of Simmel's middle period by carrying reconstruction

18 J. Loewenberg, "Problematic Realism," in *Contemporary American Philosophy: Personal Statements*, ed. George P. Adams and William Pepperell Montague, vol. 2 (New York: Macmillan, 1930), pp. 80, 65.
19 Ibid., p. 80.   20 Ibid.

only so far as a minimalist metaphysics, which provided the unification of an arena for the conflicts of life. Following Dewey's humanism, he declared us all to be in the same boat and, like Dewey, responded to that judgment with a reverence for humanity, a variant of the "common faith." Far more of a modernist than Loewenberg, when Simmel finally turned to metaphysics he produced it in full strength and gave it a tragic, not a harmonic, turn. From the radical skepticism of *Hauptprobleme*, Loewenberg's problematic realism is a step back from the modern dynamic.

Hauptprobleme provides a privileged look at the structure of Simmel's thought in its middle period. It is the last of four philosophical books Simmel published between 1900 and 1910, the others being *Philosophie des Geldes* (1900), *Vorlesungen Ueber Kant* (1904), and *Schopenhauer und Nietzsche* (1907). *Philosophie des Geldes* is a continuation of the project of the *Einleitung* applied to the problem of value theory, with the difference that philosophy provides epistemological criticism and metaphysical significance to the positive study of value, and is not, as in the early period, debunked as "speculation." By placing epistemology as the terminus *a quo* of science, and metaphysics as its terminus *ad quem*, Simmel splits philosophy into two distinctive pursuits. This split had first been opened by Kant, in his sharp distinction between pure and practical reason. Simmel does not heal the scission but deepens it, thereby casting metaphysics adrift from theory of knowledge. Between 1900 and 1910, he worked toward analyzing the *Hauptprobleme*, first by taking up the problem of epistemology in his study of Kant, and then turning to the problem of conduct and life's meaning in the work on Schopenhauer and Nietzsche. Simmel's epistemology is subjectivist, taking from Kant the notion that "objective knowledge is the product of the synthetic and unifying activity of the ego, which is conceived not as a substantial reality, but as a pure form."[21] He illustrates this variant of his theory of objectification in his more specialized work on philosophy of history, *Probleme der Geschichte philosophie* (1907). However, metaphysics, which provides significance rather than criticism, was far more central to the cultural crisis and its resolution. In recurring to Schopenhauer and Nietzsche, Simmel for the first time confronted philosophy

21 Mamelet, *Le Relativisme*, p. 92.

of life directly, paving the way for the conclusions of *Hauptprobleme* and
for his late vitalistic metaphysics.

From the interpretative approach taken here, *Schopenhauer und Nietzsche*, which has been neglected by Simmel's commentators, should be
considered as one of his three most important philosophical works, the
others being *Hauptprobleme* and *Lebensanschauung*. As the first of his
metaphysical ventures, it shows Simmel grappling with the sources he
will use first to define the nature of metaphysics and then, after the
outbreak of World War I, to attempt to articulate a substantive metaphysics that moves beyond the skeptical and subjective impasse of
Hauptprobleme. In terms of his career, *Schopenhauer und Nietzsche* may be
considered a germinal philosophy, a work that contains all of the ideas
that Simmel will later deploy in more explicit and systematic fashion.
By placing the contrasting standpoints of Schopenhauer and Nietzsche
in confrontation with each other, he moves toward the doctrine of
Hauptprobleme: that the metaphysical world picture is a projection of
temperament, of the psyche. Indeed, nineteenth-century philosophy
of life is a variant of metaphysics that lends itself admirably to Simmel's
interpretation, because it explicitly cultivates a sense of life. And by
encountering the substance of the two opposed world views, optimism
and pessimism, Simmel gains the intellectual resources he will need to
construct his own philosophy of life.

In *Schopenhauer und Nietzsche*, Simmel examines the problem of the
meaning of life, and addresses that issue in terms of both its cultural
and personal dimensions. Indeed, though he supported the nineteenth-
century division between pure and practical reason, he synthesized another and perhaps more important split between culture and personal
existence. It is not merely that there are two crises of modernity—the
loss of objective cultural forms to unify society, and the agony of the
individual confronting the task of living without stable transpersonal
meaning—but that both of these are expressions of the same problematicity of the objectivity of form. In *Schopenhauer und Nietzsche*, Simmel
treats both dimensions of the crisis: the first chapter grounds the problem of meaning in social and cultural history, and the remaining seven
chapters are concerned with the ways in which the two thinkers responded to that problem in terms of their personal existence. Schopenhauer concerns him the most, because he offered a metaphysics, the

form of which was paradigmatic for *Hauptprobleme* and the content of which was transposed into the dominant motif of *Lebensanschauung*. Nietzsche is a counterpoint, substituting evolution for metaphysics but providing added dimensions for the later vitalism. Parallel to his concern with fundamental philosophical issues, Simmel is also interested in evaluating the two sides of the more general cultural debate in nineteenth-century Germany, between optimistic and pessimistic stances toward a life devoid of transpersonal meaning. Because he takes this debate—symbolized by Schopenhauer the pessimist and Nietzsche the optimist—to be rooted in the more general cultural-personal crisis, he does not commit the distortion of taking a stand and then basing his philosophical interpretation on it. That is, he does not project his own temperament into the analysis, but instead remains on the level of criticism by transferring his approach to epistemology to philosophy of life. He seeks to discover the presuppositions of the metaphysics of the will.

Simmel's account of the social and cultural patterns that conditioned the emergence of philosophy of life anticipate his late reflections in "The Conflict in Modern Culture" and is strikingly contemporary. Simmel begins sociologically by defining man as the "indirect being," that is, as the being who expands the simple triad of practicality, desire-means-end, by compounding the means between desire and its fulfillment. As higher cultures evolve, chains of means become ever more complex and far-flung until the point is reached at which "our consciousness is bound up with the means, whereas the final goals which impart sense and meaning into the intermediate steps are pushed toward our inner horizon and finally beyond it" (pp. 3–4). Foreshadowing Heidegger, Simmel declares that "technology, which is the sum total of the means of civilized existence, becomes the essential object of struggle and evaluation" (p. 4). It is when technical interests become "transparent in their character of being just means" that "the anxious question about the sense and meaning of the whole" is broached. Simmel notes that the problem of meaning is not a uniquely modern phenomenon. At the beginning of the Christian era, Greco-Roman culture also suffered from hypercomplexity of society, and responded with hedonism, mysticism, and philosophy of conduct. Only Christianity restored finality to life, but in the nineteenth century it, too, lost its power to unify, setting off the modern cultural crisis. Simmel notes that the failure of Christianity has not been attended by loss of the need for a final goal in life, because "every need develops deep roots if it is satisfied for long periods of time." Nineteenth-century man was left with "a need for a definitivum of life's movement, which has continued as empty urge for a goal which has become inaccessible" (p. 5). Simmel is not clear here or in the rest of the work about whether the need for final meaning, for Camus's unity, is central to human life; he is not an absurdist, at least explicitly. Instead he remains open to the possibility that the flow of experienced life itself might hold within it the prospect of its own satisfying transcendence, whether that transcendence is active or passive. It is this openness or hope that guides Simmel to turn back to Schopenhauer and Nietzsche, rather than move forward to the existential thinking of Heidegger and Ortega, who found the real *a priori* not in life but in the structure of temporalized personal existence. The results of his inquest into Schopenhauer and Nietzsche led Simmel away from existentialism and toward his late metaphysical vitalism.

Schopenhauer is crucial for Simmel because his philosophy is the "absolute expression of this inner condition of modern man," that of ever-frustrated yearning for meaning. This frustration is peculiarly acute because it is not the result of a content being temporarily out of reach or, as for Loewenberg, even permanently unattainable, but the consequence of a content being excluded from a "form of inner existence." Here Simmel reaches the most incisive interpretation of the cultural-personal crisis that the terms of his thought will permit, an existential agony conceived of epistemologically rather than ontologically, form straining in its own vacancy. Schopenhauer indicates this agony through his doctrine that will rather than any of its objects or satisfactions is the "essential metaphysical essence of the world" which "has its total and only decisive expression in our will" (p. 5). As will by itself is condemned to eternal dissatisfaction, so are all individual wills doomed to temporal frustration. Schopenhauer announces the end of metaphysical optimism. But then Nietzsche appears as a counterpoint of hope, bearing the possibility that through its evolutionary process of successive individuations, "life can become the goal of life" (p. 6). He is not a metaphysician but a moralist, offering the individual a challenge, not a final harmony. Thus, the subtext of *Schopenhauer und Nietzsche* is the conflict between the metaphysical and the moral forms of inner existence, the testing of Simmel's own metaphysical will against its moral alternative.

Schopenhauer und Nietzsche follows a dramatic structure of argumentation that reflects the form of philosophical activity analyzed by Simmel in *Hauptprobleme*. After his opening discussion of the social and cultural context of the emergence of the problem of meaning, he moves to a critical account of Schopenhauer's metaphysics of the will (chapters 2 and 3), that is, he examines metaphysics as a cultural object and provides a critique of its presuppositions. From there he turns back to subjectivity (chapter 4), examining Schopenhauer's pessimism as a sentiment of life, the temperamental ground of the metaphysical objectification. Chapters 5 and 6 turn outward once again to examine, respectively, Schopenhauer's aesthetics and his moral and religious ideas as objectifications of his pessimism, and to show how that pessimism biases them. Thus, Simmel's analysis at first reverses the movement of *Hauptprobleme* by beginning with the object and moving to its subjective ground, but afterwards follows the systematic order of his thought. Chapters 7 and 8 continue in the systematic order, addressing Nietzsche's moral interpretation of life as an objectification of his optimistic temperament. The work concludes with a very brief statement of Simmel's own resolution of the problem of meaning, a kind of vital and skeptical individualism. But this sketchy statement of his position may be supplemented by observations on the various questions of philosophy that are scattered throughout the critical analysis. In one sense, *Schopenhauer und Nietzsche* is Simmel's critique of philosophy.

The method by which Simmel treats the doctrines of Schopenhauer and Nietzsche may be denominated usefully as an analytic critique. This critique has three moments, positive, negative, and positive, which are often reflected in a chapter's sequential order of argumentation. It is analytic in a fundamental sense, by virtue of its first moment which is to start from the philosopher's "own center," that is, to understand the philosopher as presenting an intelligible response to a genuine problematic. Simmel, then, does not initially bring any external perspective to bear on the thought he is discussing, but instead presupposes its authenticity and attempts to describe its internal meaning. He does as little synthetic reconstruction as possible, stating major doctrines clearly and avoiding efforts to reconcile contradictions while correcting the misinterpretations of other critics. As Mamelet puts it,

"*Schopenhauer und Nietzsche* is inspired by the . . . tendency to illuminate, independently of the historical circumstances in which they emerge and in their relation to human life and its subjective conditions, the fundamental ideas [of] these philosophers."[22] Once Simmel has taken up the philosopher's position, however, he proceeds to a second and more deconstructionist analysis, illustrating that the very assumptions of the position permit at least one substantive alternative, other than the one asserted by it, to follow logically from it. Here Simmel adopts a flexible form of Kant's procedure of setting up antinomies in order to stalemate competing metaphysical doctrines. The generation of alternative speculative possibilities within the assumptions of the system he is studying permits Simmel to relate the possibility chosen by that system to the philosopher's temperament and to relieve it of the pretension to objective truth. As a subsidiary procedure he also appeals to "psychological facts," the phenomenological integrity of which seem to be irreducible to their metaphysical interpretation. Having deconstructed the position, Simmel moves to the third moment of critique, which is a statement of what he has found to be tenable and significant in it. The third moment contains the germinal philosophy within the work, and anticipations of the late philosophy of life.

Simmel begins his analytic critique at the center of Schopenhauer's thought, his metaphysics of the will. That metaphysics arises from a conjunction of Schopenhauer's "basic vital sentiment" (which remains unclarified in chapters 2 and 3), and the Kantian categories of phenomena and things-in-themselves. These categories, "which allow one to grasp the multiplicity of phenomena in a unity, gave Schopenhauer the most perfect technical possibility for changing his basic vital sentiment into a world-view" (pp. 16–17). Simmel argues that far from deproblematizing metaphysics, Kant had incited a "philosophical desire for the thing-itself . . . for being beyond imagination." According to Simmel, whereas Kant gave the thing-itself only the status of an idea, finding his unity in the subjective categories of knowledge, Schopenhauer deemed it the essence of being and defined it as unitary will, inaccessible to intellectual cognition and articulation. Simmel first shows that Schopenhauer's sharp division between the inessential but cognizable world of representation, and the essential but inapprehensible world of will, is

22 Ibid., p. 89.

but one way of reinterpreting the Kantian legacy. As Hegel and Schelling demonstrated, the absolute could also be conceived of as the very structure of appearance, thereby eliminating the effacement of multiplicity demanded by Schopenhauer's approach. Simmel remarks that Schopenhauer and Hegel fall on different sides of "the great dividing line between the two main human types." For the type represented by Hegel, "the substance and definite meaning of existence fills every point appearing in a pantheistic unity," whereas for the type exemplified by Schopenhauer, "a harsh dividing line is drawn through the cosmos making space for the absolute, for being-as-such" (p. 18). Simmel completes his initial deconstruction by concluding that the basic "temperamental opposition [is] not rooted in philosophical speculation, but in the total breadth of the soul's life" (p. 19).

Having relativized the foundations of Schopenhauer's system by exhibiting an alternative response to his problematic, Simmel works his way into the metaphysics of will through successive deconstructions. The most important of these deconstructions shows that by making the thing-itself inaccessible to intellectual cognition, Schopenhauer has no grounds to call it will, inasmuch as human knowledge is only privy to specific acts of will, each with an object, that appear in the imagination. Though this criticism reveals that the substance of the metaphysics of the will is merely one speculative possibility among many others, Simmel is sympathetic with Schopenhauer's intent, because of the psychological fact that "there is a 'more-than-that' which can be sensed alongside and beyond any particular 'that.'" Of course, "what we feel as the inexhaustibility of our essence, as something 'beyond' that is the source of all our singular phenomena" could also lie in logical connection, the unity of the ego, or the ego's potentialities in relation to existence (p. 26). Yet Schopenhauer's thought is significant because it insists that "our total being is not exhausted by the sequence and sum of our singular acts." Here Simmel indicates that the intent of his deconstruction is to criticize metaphysics as objective knowledge, yet vindicate the lived experiences that impel its pursuit. The sense of a dynamism enfolding the experience of a self-conscious ego is the first of Simmel's appropriations of Schopenhauer. It provides him with the ground for his *Lebensanschauung*, not a metaphysical experience—which would be impossible for Simmel's critique to allow—but an experience that makes the metaphysical project intelligible.

Simmel's greatest interest in Schopenhauer, however, concerns his denial that man is a rational being:

> Schopenhauer destroyed the dogma that rationality is the deep-seated and basic essence of man that lies beneath the other ripples of life. It does not matter whether or not one accepts what he puts in reason's place; he must in any case be added to the company of great philosophical creators who have discovered new potentialities for the explication of existence. [P. 28]

Schopenhauer "had the deep insight that the contents of an idea and the logical connection of ideas, in their status as activities of the soul, presuppose a moving force existing beyond the merely ideal or logical relations to contents" (p. 28). By extending this insight into an interpretation of being as an eternally frustrated and objectless will, Schopenhauer provided a speculative alternative to the entire Western tradition of philosophy, effectively stalemating rationalism and, in Ortega's sense, "dehumanizing" metaphysics, making it no longer a secure repository for human aspirations for harmony. Henceforth, in Simmel's view, life and not reason would have to be the touchstone of philosophy, and philosophy's personal and cultural import would have to rest on the interpretation one would be able to give to life. Simmel's appropriation of Schopenhauer's antirationalism proved to be a mixed blessing. Although he was under no logical compulsion to accept Schopenhauer's conclusion that "the absolute One does not have anything outside itself to quench its thirst and to put an end to its ceaseless quest," and did not embrace it in *Schopenhauer und Nietzsche*, it is just this tragic view of will that Simmel later transposes into his conception of "absolute life."

The culmination of Simmel's analytical criticism of Schopenhauer's metaphysics is a fully developed speculative possibility of metaphysical individualism which he offers as an alternative to holism. Throughout his succeeding substantive discussions, Simmel sets up an antinomy between holism and individualism, taking whichever side is opposed to the thinker he is considering. He does not explicitly take a stand in favor of one of these positions, but remains open to whatever significant "psychological facts" they illuminate, and does not attempt to gather those facts under a single interpretation. Simmel generates the holism-individualism duality through criticizing Schopenhauer's deduction of monism from the plurality of phenomena. Even if one claims that phe-

nomenal diversity is appearance and not reality, Simmel argues that it
does not follow that reality is unitary. It is equally possible to assert a
"metaphysical individuality," which is "beyond empirical imagination,"
and "must be conceived of in terms of absolute units, the life and life-
forms of each one of which express its innermost essence, and the elements of each one of which are internally related to the whole" (p. 38).
Just as Schopenhauer's doctrine of will was reflected in the transego-
logical experience of human will, so is metaphysical individualism's
tenet—that "in absolute individuality there is an ultimate element of
being"—paralleled experientially in "the feeling of freedom and being-
for-itself of a single soul" (p. 38). Simmel views these basic experiences
as functions of temperament that cannot harmonize with each other.
They express the two directions of the vital self, toward that in which it
finds itself and toward its distance from its environment, respectively.
And this is the specific form in which Simmel, in his middle period,
struggles with the problem of the meaning of life: Should the ego transcend itself into the whole or sharpen its separation? Should it deliver
itself or stand on its freedom?

   In Chapter 4, Simmel moves from analysis of the objectification,
metaphysics, to the temperament that sustains it, specifically Schopenhauer's pessimism. This is the book's crucial chapter because in it,
Simmel must confront most directly the problem of the meaning of
life, which, for him, cannot be resolved by rational cognition. Schopenhauer's pessimism is based on the premise that "happiness is pacified
will," that it is negative, relative to will, and, therefore, never satisfying. Simmel's strategy in engaging this doctrine is twofold. First, he
argues that Schopenhauer has been inattentive to psychological fact,
that pleasure cannot be merely negative, but must be a positive quality,
or else it could not be cognized as the pacification of will. Empirically
all that one can say is that "pacified will is happiness," that one of the
contexts in which happiness is experienced is the fulfillment of desire.
Having shown the independence of pleasure and pain from will and
imagination, Simmel derives Schopenhauer's pessimism from his temperament, contrasting it to the temperament that finds joy in any
happiness, however small or fleeting. Having relativized pessimism,
Simmel reverses field and argues for the depth of its psychological insight that no amount of happiness can redeem a single instance of suffering. So, two polar temperaments confront each other, one offering

suffering as a background against which happiness appears as mar-
velous, and the other making happiness the context in which failure is
ever more sharply etched. Simmel concludes by looping back to metaphysics and showing that Schopenhauer's monistic doctrine of identification with the suffering of the will can be matched by an individualistic principle, that the form of distributing pleasure and pain to
individuals is decisive in determining a stance toward life. He therefore
proceeds from metaphysical doctrine, to psychological fact, to temperament, and then back to speculative possibility as a projection of
temperament, carrying through a complete deconstruction.

Schopenhauer's root failure, according to Simmel, is to impose his
metaphysical interpretation of will on lived experience. The form of
metaphysical will is a duality between possession and nonpossession,
which is ever renewed because will has no proper object and, indeed, is
objectless. Schopenhauer reads this duality into human will, which is
relative to objects, and concludes that happiness is merely the transient
moment of possession between states of nonpossession, or desire. For
Simmel this procedure ignores the psychological fact that in most human activities there is as much or more happiness gained from moving
toward the objective as in achieving it. Happiness is a quality that
characterizes process, not the name for extinguished desire. Freeing
happiness from will allows Simmel to show that the basis for Schopenhauer's pessimism is the judgment that "no quantity of suffering is acceptable to man and no quantity of happiness would satisfy him after a
short period of adjustment" (p. 63). This is the same judgment that
actuated Ivan Karamazov when he related the "Legend of the Grand
Inquisitor" to Alyosha. It is one of the great responses to life, deeply
rooted in the biblical accounts of Job and Jonah. But it must, for
Simmel, be counterposed to the judgment that "rare and humble joys"
are transcendent, the view of both Alyosha and the biblical prophet
Habakkuk. Thus, Simmel concludes, "the stand for the value or lack of
value of existence depends in resolute and principled natures on the
specific reaction that their innermost soul exhibits to happiness or suffering" (p. 65).

Although Simmel refuses to choose between the two temperaments
that respectively ground optimism and pessimism, he illustrates their
limitations in terms of each other. Schopenhauer's insight into the
"identity of I and Thou" in suffering is "based on an unerring homing

instinct," which highlights the relativity of the ego to a wider life. But just that insight threatens to void individuality and with it the possibility of the moral viewpoint, in this case the idea of justice. The positivity of happiness and suffering, their independence of will, may be correlated with the speculative possibility of metaphysical individualism, the presupposition that "individuality has absolute reality and significance" (p. 72). Having failed to acknowledge this possibility, Schopenhauer "cannot understand that, in a thoroughly objective sense indicative somehow of some ultimate, the existence of a plurality of people could be of greater or lesser value, not only because the sum of their happiness might increase or decrease, but according to a criterion governing the distribution of a fixed quantum" (p. 72). Justice requires that finite completions or satisfactions be taken seriously, that the differential quality of the individual's experience matters, and that life is not exhausted by its failure. The outcome of pessimism is the deprecation of the will and the attempt to negate it, whereas the outcome of optimism is the affirmation of the will through ethical form. Each of these attitudes is based on a temperament and projected into a world picture, and each has a special insight into psychological fact. Simmel does not reconcile this duality, though in this work he leans toward optimism as he moves through his analytic critique of Schopenhauer's thought, defending individuality, differentiation, and the ego. The counterpoint of the wider life, of fundamental passivity, becomes the dominant theme in his later reflections.

In Chapter 5, Simmel turns outwards from the ground of philosophy of life in temperament to discuss the objectivization of the sense of life in philosophy of culture, specifically art and the aesthetic experience. He deems Schopenhauer one of the few German philosophers with an aesthetic temperament and, so, finds the root of his response to pessimism—the denial of the will—to be rooted in the experience or psychological fact of aesthetic contemplation. Simmel shares with Schopenhauer the view that the aesthetic experience fosters a suspension of the practical viewpoint of everyday life, which is always caught up in a temporal flux of contingency and the impulsion to prolong itself. Their contemplation of the aesthetic object momentarily fuses the split between subject and object in what Husserl and Santayana called an intuition of essence, which is timeless. Indeed, Simmel may be conceived here as presenting a phenomenology of the aesthetic dimension. He

parts, however, with Schopenhauer when the latter carries his description of aesthetic experience into metaphysical interpretation, and when
he joins that experience to his pessimism. In criticizing Schopenhauer,
Simmel follows the strategy of relieving psychological fact from metaphysical and temperamental interpretation, and then of posing an alternative interpretation of fact based on the independence of art from
philosophy and from the hedonic process. He offers an aesthetic individualism in opposition to Schopenhauer's holism.

Simmel's first task is to relieve aesthetic experience of metaphysical
interpretation. He argues that Schopenhauer, who declared the independence of art from any utility, actually drew art into the service of the
metaphysical intention to subordinate variety to a single intellectual
interpretation. The aesthetic experience, which was at the core of Schopenhauer's response to life, became his means to salvation from the will
by virtue of its fusion of subject and object in the contemplation of
essence, and its nontemporal form. According to Simmel, "the decisive
motif of Schopenhauer's thought is revealed as the redemption from individuality and from the determination of the moving elements of life
by spatial, temporal, and causal relations" (p. 78). Schopenhauer's metaphysical intention resulted in his depriving the art object of any of its
particularity and materiality, and making it a mere vehicle for a Platonic "idea," and aesthetic "vision," that informed it. As Simmel notes,
this realm of "eternal objects," as Whitehead called them, had no place
in Schopenhauer's metaphysics, which allowed only will and phenomenal representation, but it was necessary to posit for supporting the
project of liberation from will, which could not be achieved through
particulars. In the process Schopenhauer deprived art of any claim to
autonomy, because it could be replaced by any other means by which
the split between subject and object could be healed. Simmel does not
deny that aesthetic experience is intuition of essence, but he rejects a
static realm of ideas that give the art object its significance.

Having performed his analytical critique of Schopenhauer's interpretation of the art object, Simmel moves to his own account of that
object, which emphasizes its specificity. He remarks that "the formula
l'art pour l'art . . . directs us to the unique importance of the form of
art itself, regardless of historical, psychological, metaphysical, or other
meanings" (p. 85). Then he poses the decisive question: "Is the meaning
and value of a work of art constituted by the presentation of *this* content

or by *this* presentation of the content?" (p. 86). Schopenhauer took the former alternative, making the particular presentation an excuse for the exemplification of the "idea." Simmel argues for the latter alternative, that the meaning of art is "bound up with an interest in the transformation of the content itself, thereby vindicating the existence of art without having to appeal to any specific content." Here Simmel anticipates the influential theory of Roger Fry, that art is "significant form." He opposes Schopenhauer's degradation of art "to the status of a tool for the expression of the idea" with the "alternative thesis . . . that the essential happiness involved in art lies not only in expressing ideas, but in the *expression* of ideas" (p. 88). Thus, for Simmel, the materiality of the art object becomes of equal importance to its meaning. He does not deny significance, but argues that rather than beauty residing in the idea, it is "what with varying degrees of success makes the idea visible clearly and perfectly, and allows us to accept it with certitude" (p. 88). He prepares the way here for interpreting aesthetic experience as a special form of contemplation with intrinsic limits.

The second prong of Simmel's critique of Schopenhauer's aesthetics is to question the bond in the metaphysics of will between aesthetic contemplation and happiness. Here, following in the path laid out in his criticism of pessimism, Simmel argues that the negative definition of happiness as pacification of the will leads Schopenhauer to misinterpret the very aesthetic experience that forms his temperament. He asserts that "even if we granted that all happiness could be basically negative, the difference among kinds of happiness could not be merely quantitative and grounded in various mixtures with pain, but would have to be explained by positive causes that a pessimistic system cannot accommodate" (p. 98). Paradoxically, in Simmel's view, Schopenhauer's hedonic pessimism leads him to the extravagantly optimistic conclusion that "it is sufficient not to be unhappy in order to be happy," and to the realistic conclusion that art is the negation of reality, a denunciation of it rather than a gateway to an experience in which "the question of being and non-being" is not posed. Simmel claims that were Schopenhauer consistent in calling aesthetic experience salvation from the will, he would have placed it beyond pleasure and pain. Instead, he declared that "the content and purely imaginative side of the world are such as to provide absolute peace and happiness" (p. 98). This inconsistency, Simmel believes, meant that Schopenhauer used the positive happiness of aesthetic appreciation, which he deeply felt, to counterbalance his pessimism, contradiction indicating here the effort to become adequate to totality while retaining a one-sided system.

Simmel's own view of the aesthetic experience is that whereas it "reveals a structure of the world that is absolutely bent on giving happiness," the happiness in art should not be confused with "the specific aesthetic reaction." That reaction is a special intentionality guided by the dual character of the art object as a particular arrangement of material or content that displays meaning. It is a paradoxical form which both derealizes experience through its self-enclosure and yet indicates the inner meanings of flowing life. The basis of art is the contradiction that it is "expected to show us what life is by letting life dissolve before our very eyes" (p. 104). The attraction and joy of art lie in this contradiction, which cannot be resolved intellectually, but which offers the possibility that "art is one of the structures that allows us to have insight into the problems that they pose in such a way that we grasp those problems in their purity and see that they are insoluble" (p. 104). The paradoxical character of art and aesthetic experience guarantee for Simmel that they are not adequate to the task of redemption from the will: "Real and irrevocable redemption has to wrestle with will," but "art just turns away from it" (p. 104). Simmel's discussion of art is more marked than any other by a distinct position that he affirms and defends. Perhaps that is because he has removed art from personal and cultural crisis; it is, indeed, a temporary relief from crisis, which shows his underlying bond with Schopenhauer.

When, in Chapter 6, Simmel turns to the problems of morality and the ascetic denial of the will, he seems far less sure of his footing than he was in his discussion of art and even of pessimism. In contrast to the systematic development of themes in an intelligible order of critique that informed the preceding chapters, in this chapter Simmel makes successive approaches to various points, weaving in and out of arguments and reaching no decisive conclusion. Here, where Simmel culminates his criticism of Schopenhauer, he wrestles most intensely with the polarity of holism and individualism. Schopenhauer's ethic of altruism, though distorted by metaphysical interpretation, contains a fundamental insight into moral experience, that the bases for moral judgments outrun the self-conscious choices of the ego. Yet to adhere to that insight would lead ultimately to banishing duty from the moral life and, along with it, its foundation in the separate and self-responsible individual. Here Simmel returns to the problematic of his earliest work. He still insists on the primacy of the form of duty in moral experience, but he does not explicitly base it on a theory of objectification. He remains relativistic, allowing for an indifference of form to content, but he insists on the sense of objectivity in the experience of obligation, that a duty is felt to be both mine and external to me. And he adds an appreciation of the holistic account of morals, which is based on identification of I and Thou.

According to Simmel, the moral dimension of life is the least accessible to adequate interpretation by Schopenhauer's metaphysics because it is inherently practical, that is, it presupposes a division between ego and alter which is incapable of being fused into the kind of unity that marks aesthetic experience. There can be no evil, no "pain, guilt, and inner contradiction," according to Simmel, until "will becomes singular existence, that is, where it assumes the form of imagination" (p. 105). The moral life is inherently reformatory, measuring itself against the demands of an ideal which the self finds itself obliged to achieve, whether or not it is capable of doing so. Schopenhauer must attempt to elude this central feature of moral experience because he seeks to make morality an instrument of liberation from the will. Yet his effort is doomed to failure, because the principle of morality he offers, the altruistic relief of suffering, presupposes the distinction between ego and alter that it seeks to dissolve. Identification with the other through compassion is not fusion with the other, and such identification through participation in the unity of will makes it a matter of indifference, whether one reduces the suffering of another or one's own, thereby nullifying the moral viewpoint altogether. For Simmel, Schopenhauer has given an aesthetic interpretation of morals, which follows from his basic temperamental leanings. Yet though he has failed to acknowledge the autonomy of the ought, a duty which must be "fulfilled simply as a duty without regard for the results defined by its content," he has illuminated the moral significance of identification. The speculative possibility that Simmel offers here as an alternative to Schopenhauer's is the Kantian perspective. For Schopenhauer, "our action is the expression of a fundamental and unchangeable being," whereas for Kant, "we possess, as bearers of practical values, an unlimited plasticity of response to ethical demands that is not prefigured by a pre-existing being" (p. 121). Simmel, though he leans in the Kantian direction, does not take sides in the debate, because either position is at its limits self-destructive. The Kantian viewpoint, when relieved of its rationalism, must posit the self anew in each moral situation, destroying the continuity of moral life. Conversely, Schopenhauer's perspective achieves continuity by abolishing momentary decision and subsuming it under the notion of an invariant character. Both positions make contact, however, with psychological fact and, therefore, cannot be renounced. We experience guilt in the Kantian way when we acknowledge our failure to honor an imperative. But we also feel guilty, as Schopenhauer has it, when we refer a seemingly trivial act to the total pattern of our character, when we identify our momentary self with our wider self. Indeed, the greatest moral agonies and self-inquisitions arise not when we fall short of an ideal, but when we acknowledge the relation of a single deed to a mode of life which is revealed to be corrupt.

In concluding Chapter 6, Simmel attempts to take some of the sting out of Schopenhauer's insight by posing an alternative speculative possibility to the doctrine of the invariant character. He argues that "Schopenhauer naively identifies the statement that character is given by birth with the assertion that it is immutable" (pp. 128–29). Allowing that a change in character could not, for Schopenhauer, occur in time, "because time is merely a form of perception that organizes and orders phenomena," Simmel states that "it is a speculative possibility that this fundamental being-as-such, which shapes phenomena necessarily in its image (any new metaphysical character would be represented in a new empirical phenomenon), contains a quality which reveals itself as a total change in our essence at certain temporal moments" (p. 129). Simmel admits that "we cannot describe such a structure," but holds that it is no less mysterious than metaphysical unity and immutability. The speculative possibility that there is a "transcendental change in and evolution of our being" does not, however, remediate "the most tragic ethical situation," which is revealed by Schopenhauer, "that we are fully responsible for a basic being which cannot be annulled, but the 'freedom' of which, while providing the ground for responsibility, is also immutable" (p. 128). We would still be responsible for what we had not self-consciously willed if fundamental being were mutable, so, in this case, Simmel has offered a possibility that has no apparent consequences for the problem it seems to address. He cannot reconcile here the division between Kant and Schopenhauer.

Simmel uses his speculative possibility that basic being is mutable to provide a ground for his discussion of Nietzsche's ethics, with which he concludes the work. The notion of a changing being is compatible with an evolutionary interpretation of morals, which "holds that to become different is the ultimate and inherent meaning of our essence and is the form of our metaphysical substance" (p. 129). The great confrontation turns out not to be between duty and altruism, but between holism and individualism. Here there is a different set of speculative possibilities. For Schopenhauer, our essence "becomes definitive and final only when it reveals itself as identical with the essence of all other beings and testifies in truth to the structure of the metaphysical unity of the cosmos." For the opposing position, which is Nietzsche's, "our actions must express the structures of an unmistakable individuality, because only individuality and not any supra- or sub-personal all-unity is the final element of being" (p. 112). Behind Kant, then, lies the individual who must accede to, repudiate, or even generate the imperative. Perhaps this is why Simmel is not eager to criticize too thoroughly Schopenhauer's moral theory. The individual, liberated from the illusion of a rational norm of duty, tends toward extreme differentiation. The indifference of the form of duty to content can eventuate in the dissolution of the bonds of solidarity among human beings, as each pursues a special demand. The threat of vital solipsism is as great as that of the annihilation of the self in its identification with unitary will. With no rational or religious imperative to bring against extreme individualism, Simmel's only recourse is to an ethic of identification.

In the concluding two chapters of *Schopenhauer und Nietzsche*, Simmel turns to individualism, the position that had up to now served as the major speculative possibility he offered to oppose Schopenhauer's thought. Here he must reverse field and bring to bear what he can salvage from his critique of Schopenhauer on the radical pluralism of Nietzsche's view of life. The root difficulty of Schopenhauer's interpretation of being was its subsumption of all diversity—most important, the separate human personality—into the monistic unity of purposeless will. Without individuality or its corollary, positive value, Schopenhauer had to end his reflections by appealing to the ascetic renunciation of life, his salvation from, or perhaps retribution against, a reality devoid of meaning. However, the affirmation of individuality, value, and, with them, life carries its own danger. In his discussion of Nietzsche, Simmel reintroduces his notion of the personal and cultural crisis of modernity. He observes that "the modern differentiation of personalities and the individualization of doing and being that has been created by the social division of labor have by now entered into reciprocal relation with increased sensitivity to the pictures of the human world that envelop us" (p. 152). When this sensitivity to the explosion of diversity becomes extreme, the personality becomes "fragile" and may experience an "absolute isolation and being-for-oneself in which the individual no longer even understands the other person's speech" (p. 152). It is just this vital solipsism which is fixed as the crisis of modernity in the late essay, "The Conflict in Modern Culture," but here it is introduced as the basis for Nietzsche's radical individualist philosophy and as the conclusion it must seek to elude. Simmel's tendency is to defend the individuated self, yet in Nietzsche he confronts the possibility of an individuality that is not relative to objectified form, but to the dynamic of the life process. Each individual is here the *a priori*, creating, perhaps, a unique form that cannot be shared with others. From today's vantage point one might say that Simmel glimpses the insight that the essence of modernity is schizophrenia. To allay the crisis, Simmel turns to the past for any principle of unification it might offer.

Most of chapters 7 and 8 present a running dialogue between individualism and various holistic concepts that might be opposed to it as speculative possibilities. The protagonist is Nietzsche who, for Simmel, took the bold step of grounding the meaning of life in the process of life rather than in a form opposed to or transcending it. Schopenhauer made form an appearance, but Nietzsche interprets it as a manifestation of evolutionary dynamics, realized in and by the individual. Nietzsche's individualism is neither hedonistic nor egoistic, but is grounded in the thesis that the evolutionary process is both consummated in and carried by the individual. It is a world picture drawn by a moral, not an aesthetic, temperament, which demands but cannot find an ideal outside its vital being. Thus, Nietzsche regards the increase of life, the ascension of its level in the evolutionary scale, as the goal of life. This goal, however, is final only in a strictly formal sense, because evolution is open-ended, and any of its levels is but a way station to the the next one. Yet, inasmuch as evolution is only consummated in the individual, the perfection of the highest individuals becomes for Nietzsche the sole purpose of life. This view leads to his aristocratic ethic of distance and differentiation which denounces any democratic or altruistic view as an inversion of values, a consequence of the triumph of the weak multitude over the strong few.

Simmel's primary critical move against Nietzsche is to show that his ethical ideal of qualitative evolution is not a logically necessary consequence of an evolutionary individualism. Although evolutionary theory had promised to bridge the gulf between "ought" and "is" through a purpose immanent to life, it could not fulfill that promise, because the experienced variety of life includes evil as well as good, adversity as well as beneficence, the negation of value as well as its affirmation. In this light, any evolutionary ethic must be based on a criterion external to the life process, which, in Simmel's view, is grounded in personal temperament. Having separated Nietzsche's ethic from his interpretation of life, Simmel is free to counterpose against that ethic alternatives that are genuine expressions of the democratic-altruistic sentiment and are no less affirmations of the individual life than the aristocratic position. He argues most cogently that an altruistic morality, such as Schopenhauer's, might be cast in the terms of an imperative for life. From there he brings a series of alternative moral viewpoints against Nietzsche's. For example, in its concern for the individual soul, Christianity might be understood to have offered as radical an individualism as did Nietzsche, though with a different content. Democracy, too, need not be based on *ressentiment*, but might express the metaphysical depth of joy in the ordinary given it by Nietzsche's antagonist, Maurice Maeterlinck. Similarly, socialism might have a basis in a genuine concern for quantitative evolution, for increase in the values of life for each one. However, none of these alternatives, which remediate the distance opened up by Nietzsche's aristocratic vision, resolves the root problem of individualism, which is not moral but metaphysical or ontological—that is, the collapse of individuality into life, which threatens equally aristocratic and democratic ethics, in that both depend upon adherence to objectified form. It is here, in his encounter with Nietzsche, that Simmel witnesses, perhaps, the failure of the possibility of moral unity that had been latent in his earliest work.

The curse of modernity, which is expressed most clearly in Nietzsche's thought, is the immersion of the individual in the life process. In discussing the doctrine of eternal recurrence, Simmel notes that although "Nietzsche replaces a final goal with an evolutionary process that contains diverse goals and values," thereby making each goal and value a stage, he still must face the "disquiet of boundlessness," which "fosters an insecurity which is based on the impossibility of any overview of the whole" (p. 178). This boundlessness of life, its lack of any overall and unifying form, is the other side of extreme individuation, indeed, is its ground, because it is the flowing matrix of individuality. For Simmel, the deepest motivation for the doctrine of eternal recurrence is Nietzsche's desire to give some form or boundary to life. He argues that through eternal recurrence, "Nietzsche retains any perspective and any conclusion that being can still exhibit after an absolute goal has been eliminated, because, although each cosmic period is limited, there is still a regulative idea demanding the growth of values towards the limitless" (p. 178). Thus, Nietzsche puts a "ring" around the boundless, and places within limits "the infinite drifting that results from the restlessness of his nature and the negation of a cosmic goal" (p. 178). Simmel, of course, does not grant to eternal recurrence any special metaphysical priority: it is Nietzsche's way of responding to the personal and cultural crisis of modernity, a compensation for the vision of boundless life revealed through his temperament. For Simmel, Nietzsche's legacy is to have shown that modernity condemns the individual to immanence in a goal-less life while, paradoxically, remaining separate within it and ever more qualitatively differentiated. The critique of rationalism has resulted in the collapse of mediations between the self and wider life.

As a work of critical philosophy, *Schopenhauer und Nietzsche* ends in a stalemate between the opposing metaphysical perspectives of holism and individualism, and their respective ethical correlates, altruism and aristocratic individualism (the ethic of nobility). But Simmel's inquest into the meaning of life is also a germinal philosophy which provides both the bases for his late metaphysical vitalism and for a dynamic individualism, which is not precisely defined, but which determines the bias of his critical efforts. Having cut himself off from rationalism in metaphysics and morals, Simmel strove to vindicate the objectivity of cultural form, but had lost the ground from which to do so. Kant had been surpassed by a thought which had discovered the comprehensiveness of life. But life was an equivocal concept, holding within it the possibility of impersonality (Schopenhauer's will) and extreme personality (Nietzsche's individual). These possibilities were the two candidates for the real *a priori*, for which Simmel quested after he had deconstructed Kant's critical philosophy. In *Schopenhauer und Nietzsche*, Simmel acknowledges that both the impersonal and personal interpretations of life have support in psychological fact, the former in our sense of a totality that englobes the self, and the latter in "the feeling of freedom and being-for-itself of a single soul," but he does not explicitly accord preference to either one of them. His very method of criticism, however, is biased in favor of individualism, because it contains the substantive premise that metaphysics is a temperament expressed in a world picture. There is no access for him, through philosophy, to anything fundamental but the individual, who provides the interpretation of the multiplicity that is other than himself. Thus, one may say that in *Schopenhauer und Nietzsche*, individualism is the effective ground of Simmel's own thought, because he does not provide his own metaphysical view of life. This individualism is, of course, primarily methodological, following from his philosophy of philosophy, but it has a substantial basis in the experience of individuality, which provides him with his ultimate point of reference for his criticism, and with his response to the personal and cultural crisis of modernity.

The foundation of Simmel's individualism appears at the beginning of Chapter 2, where he presents his most general description of the human condition. He had argued in Chapter 1 that man is the "indirect animal," who expands the primal triad desire-means-end by adding ever more ramified chains of means. Now he presents a complementary view focusing on the multiplicity of human essence. Unlike other animals who have only "unilateral activity and life-potential," man "is a manifold being, which means that his relation to things is presented in the multiplicity of modes of perception in each individual, in the entanglement of each individual in more than just a single series of interests and concepts, of images and meanings" (p. 15). The diversity of human essence is fundamental for Simmel, and insures that there can be no genuine unification of variety from outside the self. Indeed, philosophy, which attempts to coordinate multiplicity around a single theme, even if that theme is pluralism, is grounded in the negation of its goal: "The basis of all philosophy is the fact that things overflow any single determination" (p. 15). Here Simmel's own critical method might be turned against him. The "fact" of multiplicity seems here to be more axiomatic than empirical. One might offer the speculative possibility that the acknowledgment of diversity presupposes a relation among the various dimensions; otherwise they would not be perceived as different from one another. This might be a Kantian response to Simmel's position, allowing for a return to rationalism. But Simmel does not entertain it and, so, must refer diversity to the self, which, though it is manifold, is somehow also a moving point of unification. He argues that the polar tensions, such as mechanism and meaning, and nature and spirit, are not reconciled in man, but "meet" in him: "He extends from one world into the other, his own dual nature providing the assurance that the opposing worlds do not fall apart. The symbol of the specifically human sense of life is to be this boundary, feeling that one stands between polar opposites in a decisive way, whether they refer to life in general or to its particulars" (p. 21). The human self in its full extension is here the real *a priori*, though one whose unity is definable only negatively as the dynamic juncture of opposites. Vital self-contradiction, as Santayana called it, is the root out of which all one-sided metaphysical interpretations grow.

But what is this self, ego, individual, soul, or person, who experiences contradiction as its essence? Simmel offers no precise response to this question, but one may pose some alternatives. One alternative, which would seem inappropriate here, is that the experienced self is indicative of metaphysical individuality. Simmel poses metaphysical individualism as a speculative possibility against metaphysical holism, but he clearly does not embrace it himself. At the opposite pole, one might interpret the self in the Kantian fashion as a form. Mamelet notes that Simmel gave this interpretation in his early work: "As for the concept of 'me,' it is, finally, purely formal, so alien to any determined psychological content, that the most opposing tendencies can be equally incorporated in it: it defines only the circle by which we demarcate the frontiers of all of our representations; it is only a frame, not an apprehensible or representable reality."[23] But as Simmel explains the self in *Schopenhauer und Nietzsche*, it is more than a mere frame, though less than the essence of being: it is the vital process of unification which

23 Ibid., p. 44.

is known through its capacity to withstand tension. This third possibility—that the self is a dynamic totalization of forms and contents which is never fully achieved—seems to be the closest approximation to the ground of Simmel's germinal philosophy. Had he been fully aware of its significance, he might have expanded it into a theory of life as narration, such as that offered by his admirer, Ortega.

The dynamic self appears explicitly at the very end of *Schopenhauer und Nietzsche*, when Simmel makes his final judgment on the two philosophies he has considered. He notes that the views that life is valueless and that life is value are "not theoretical knowledge, but the expressions of fundamental states of the soul," which "cannot be reconciled in a 'higher unity'" (p. 181). Barring any unification based on "objective content," the only achievable unity is one made "by a subject who can regard both positions." Simmel concludes optimistically that "by sensing the reverberations of spiritual existence in the distance opened up by these opposites, the soul grows, despite, indeed, because of, the fact that it does not decide in favor of one of the parties. It finally embraces both the desperation and jubilation of life as the poles of its own expansion, its own power, its own plenitude of forms, and it enjoys that embrace" (p. 181). The expansive self is the high point of Simmel's individualism, a position from which he falls in his late work, which is tragic, if not pessimistic. Its counterpart is the fragile self which sinks into vital solipsism because it cannot withstand the tensions of multiplicity. Here, perhaps, lies the reason for Simmel's turn toward tragedy: self-expansion is not an inherent dynamic of the self, but the defining characteristic of a strong self. Just as Nietzsche did, Simmel must admit gradations among individuals. Strength here is tolerance, what William James called the "inner tolerance of life." This is an aristocratic virtue, because in modernity strength is rare and fragility pervasive.

There is a terrible sadness to being condemned to a self-enclosed and differentiated life that has no exit from its own inherent limitation but still must acknowledge an otherness to itself, a wider life, that engulfs it, first creating it, then preserving it, and all the while and, finally, at last destroying it. Under this awful judgment of modern insight, the fragile self implodes into schizophrenia, vital solipsism; or explodes into collectivism, still solipsism. The strong self does not flee from its condemnation, but strives to tolerate the primal tensions of its existence, to expand, to conquer the spirit of gravity that pulls toward contraction, but to resist the temptation to burst through its real bound-aries in an act of faith or flight of fancy. This is the ethic inherent in *Schopenhauer und Nietzsche*, the response to life turned upon itself and deprived of any fixity of form, that is, of meaning, sense, purpose. It is a vital ethic that shapes the critical philosophy of the work, but it is also an essentially intellectual ethic that opposes reason to dogmatism, including the rationalist dogma. Tolerance of the diversity and disunity which characterize the vital and intellectual experience of the self be-comes the reason to affirm life, and enjoyment in expansion, what Freud termed Eros, crowns its transitory successes. The absence of for-mative meaning for life, the absurd, is here made into a test for the self, which is presumably able, at times, to pass it; an absurd life with a joyful cast. Simmel's ethic is a product of pre-World War I European culture, which grappled with crisis, but still saw a way to transcend it; that is, pessimism could still be a counterpoint to the dominant theme of optimism.

After World War I the balance for Simmel's generation shifted to the primacy of cultural, if not always personal, pessimism. Weber's "iron cage" and Freud's discontented civilization are vivid symbols of this new mood, and Heidegger's being-toward-death is its legacy. Simmel, too, changed in his late work, published in the wake of World War I and completed as he struggled against liver cancer. That work may best be considered here as a return to the problem of the meaning of life, conceived still in terms of the lines laid out by Schopenhauer and Nietzsche. In the major production of his late period, *Lebensanschauung*, Simmel returns to the duality posed by nineteenth-century philosophy of life. But now he has his own idea of what he calls "absolute life," which has a "unified character" and is metaphysically prior to personal existence, to the individual. From this vantage point Simmel is able to accomplish what he could not do in *Schopenhauer und Nietzsche*, that is, to synthesize the opposing positions. Simmel argues that "Scho-penhauer's will to life and Nietzsche's will to power doubtless lie in the direction of concrete fulfillment" of his own idea of life, though "Schopenhauer feels boundless continuity to be more decisive," and "Nietzsche stresses more individuality encased in form." [24] Thus, Simmel makes the distinction between holism and individualism—a distinc-

24 Georg Simmel, "The Transcendent Character of Life," in Levine, *Georg Simmel*,
   p. 368.

tion he had held to be irreconcilable in his middle period—relative to a comprehending unity: "What is decisive, however, what constitutes life, is the absolute unity of both."[25] One may question, however, whether both sides are included on equal terms. Just as the tension in *Schopenhauer und Nietzsche* is held by the self, shifting Simmel's bias toward Nietzsche and optimism, so a unitary conception of life would seem to dispose toward Schopenhauer and pessimism. Simmel attempts to achieve a genuine synthesis through a notion of absolute life, which includes the relative contrast between life in the narrower sense and content independent of life.[26] Life in the narrower sense is the dynamic flux that surrounds and moves through the mutating individual, whereas content independent of life is that which stands out as defined and formed for experience against that flux, including the self-referential ego. Absolute life is able to comprehend and unify the opposites of flux and fixed, continuity and individuality, because it is defined as a self-transcendent process, in the two senses that it perpetually generates more of itself (it is "more life") and objectifies itself into crystallized forms or individuals (it is "more than life"). Life, then, is a broken unity, but somehow still a unity. It is clear that this view, which Simmel admits is paradoxical, is also dogmatic in the sense of his analytical critique in *Schopenhauer und Nietzsche*. A nonpersonal absolute life cannot be experienced by a relative individual, for whom the irreducible tension between narrowly defined life and content independent of life must subsist. The gap between them can only be bridged by the intellect, which is able to offer only a speculative possibility, to which another, in this case the dynamic individualism of the middle period, can be posed. What Simmel has done is to use the speculative procedure of Fichte—who overcame the opposition between the empirical subject and its object through positing an Absolute Ego—on the category of life. But whereas Fichte, concentrating on the self, produced a moral picture of the world, Simmel, focusing on life, evokes a tragedy. His purely speculative unity, though psychologically well grounded in the inward grasp of individual lived experience, is an absurd absolute, for it continually precipitates meanings and then destroys them without even the remediation of an evolutionary development. Yet, to transform the self-transcendence of personal existence into a symbol of being

25 Ibid.   26 Ibid., p. 372.

itself is not merely dogmatic, but ethically gratuitous. It gives us nothing more than ourselves, though on a grand scale.

Simmel's synthesis does not give equal weight to the respective parties. It is difficult to discern any significant difference between absolute life and Schopenhauer's metaphysical will, both of which objectify themselves into individuals but also ceaselessly move beyond them. The pessimism latent in an absurd absolute also shows forth in Simmel's late work. In his description of the modern crisis, "The Conflict in Modern Culture," he observes that life wishes "to obtain something which it cannot reach: It desires to transcend all forms and to appear in its naked immediacy."[27] Culturally the rebellion against form leads to the attenuation of the mediations necessary to organize social life and to fortify the fragile self. But Simmel has nothing to offer against that rebellion. Indeed, he must claim that it is an inevitable outcome of modern self-discovery. Where Simmel departs from Schopenhauer is in his response to the failure of meaning. He does not opt for renunciation of life, but for the embrace of its struggle. Prefiguring Heidegger's interpretation of modernity as interregnum, he observes that "the bridge between the past and the future of cultural forms seems to be demolished; we gaze into an abyss of unformed life beneath our feet." But, he adds, "perhaps this formlessness is itself the appropriate form for contemporary life." Identification with the formless form of absolute life does not provide the peace that metaphysics traditionally sought or even the challenge of Nietzsche's evolutionism or the affirmation of the expansive self: "Life is a struggle in the absolute sense of the term which encompasses the relative contrast between war and peace: that absolute peace which might encompass this contrast remains an eternal (*gottlich*) secret to us."[28] Simmel here closes down the discourse on philosophy of life, occupying a position between the optimistic holism of Bergson's creative evolutionism and the optimistic individualism of James's pluralistic universe. Bergsonian life is present in his vision, but it lacks an upward dynamic. The Jamesian individual is there, but without the compensation of the will to believe. As one of the three great closures of vitalism, Simmel's is the closest to the psychological facts of personal existence. Its tragic vision, which grew out of Simmel's

27 Simmel, "The Conflict in Modern Culture," in Levine, *Georg Simmel*, p. 393.
28 Ibid.

uncompromising quest for a real *a priori*, not only reflects his own life-long struggle, but is far more pertinent to the cultural and personal life of the twentieth century than are those of his more optimistic counter-parts. Simmel's strain of thought was continued in the succeeding generation as a reflection on personal life in existentialism. His own turn into metaphysics produced one of the last great monuments of that art, a monument to deconstruction, a life that deconstructs philosophy and a philosophy that deconstructs life.

AUTHOR'S PREFACE

THE PRESENTATION OF SCHOPENHAUER AND NIETZSCHE involves opposing problems of interpretation. Schopenhauer is a thoroughly explicit writer. In view of the specificity of his thinking and its expression, it is not possible to attempt the kind of "creative" interpretation of his doctrines that would change the prevailing opinion and that is still feasible with Plato and Spinoza, or even with Kant and Hegel. A presentation that intends to transcend pure reporting, in Schopenhauer's case, has to project the doctrinal content critically against the wider network of cultural facts and psychological origins, and of epistemological norms and ethical values. It is, thus, unnecessary to provide a merely logical interpretation of Schopenhauer. In Nietzsche's case, however, a logical interpretation is impossible. Were I to attempt to deflate the poetic and emotional ecstasies of his diction into the language of sober and cool sciences, I would not only work a transmutation of form, but I would also push his words to a level of abstraction that they were not intended to occupy, and would thereby leave them necessarily open to competing interpretations. Whereas Schopenhauer is already too precise to allow for a simple presentation of the content of his philosophy, Nietzsche is not precise enough for such an approach. These opposing considerations result in the same consequences in both cases: the real task at hand is not a simple presentation of the philosophy of a particular thinker, but the exposition of a philosophy about him.

The object and intention that structure the character of the following discussion aim at a contribution to a general cultural history of the spirit and at the transhistorical importance of the thought of the two philosophers in question. The essential requirements of the task at hand coincide with the essential nuclei of the two personalities addressed here. These nuclei could not be presupposed generally and prove to be quite surprising. Both Schopenhauer and Nietzsche very often discussed problems that were not necessarily connected to the central cores of their respective thought and were even quite distant from them. One could not exclude *a priori* the possibility that one might find at the peripheries things of the greatest importance for philosophy or for history, just as the subjective by-products of the lives of many people have turned out to be objectively their most profound and significant contributions. The possibility and justification of the following pages rest on the presumption that the above possibility is not pertinent here. I presuppose that the very few *leitmotivs* at the innermost cores of the doctrines of Schopenhauer and Nietzsche are the most objectively valuable parts of these doctrines and the parts that will endure. By presenting only the ultimate core of a web of thoughts, the sensational paradoxes that characterize both philosophers (even if time and acquiescence integrate them in the case of the older one) disappear. Things that are logically or ethically revolting and everything that is eccentric turn out, therefore, really to be accidental and of no importance. The art of mental fencing, a surprising antithesis or a paradox, must be seen as ornamental or as the attack or defense of relations of thought, and not as aspects that touch the real essence growing from the inner depth as the expression of a certain type of human soul.

The positive core can be found where the nucleus of a doctrine, its subjective center, coincides with the center of its objective importance, as occurs in the case of every original philosopher who answers questions about "things out there" "from his own inner depth, from the inner depth of mankind," as Goethe once remarked concerning Schopenhauer. Thus, the program of our presentation can be further defined: the depiction of a person through a cultural-historical interest can never be an exact copy of the whole life as lived. Depending on the interest, much will be excluded and much else will be placed in focus. Whatever is retained, the essential, will be composed into a single coherent picture which has no immediate counterpart in reality but which is comparable to an artistic portrait providing, instead of the real totality of the object, an ideal interpretation and a meaning derived from the method and the goal of presentation. One must select from the totality of the philosopher's utterances those that form a coherent, uniform, and meaningful context of thought—and it does not matter if the totality also includes contradictions, weaknesses, and ambivalence. In the evolution of cultural history such selection occurs constantly through extraction from and addition to a complex of thoughts that are coherent in themselves. We see philosophers that way: neither psychological fluctuations nor the vacillations of actual thought, surrounding or contradicting coherent thinking, are visible. This process occurs in the historical reality of the philosopher and must be anticipated methodically in the presenter's consciousness. Once biographical interests have been replaced by strictly philosophical and cultural-historical concerns, the process of selection, derived from the discipline of history, gains the specific import in the history of philosophy that the contradictions and utterances of a thinker that are at variance with the essential direction of his thought need not be considered. That a philosopher meanders between mutually exclusive ideas or brings such ideas together in a single thought process may speak against his psychological make-up or against his capacity for self-criticism, but it does not exclude the possibility that one of the contradictory lines of thought is correct or, at least, important. It is possible to select quotations from Nietzsche's writings that uncompromisingly contradict my interpretation of him, but it is sufficient that this interpretation be coherently argued from the texts and that its objective importance justifies the assumption that it constitutes the original core of Nietzsche's doctrines, which are so essential to the intellectual climate.

SCHOPENHAUER AND NIETZSCHE

1

Schopenhauer and Nietzsche

THEIR POSITION IN CULTURAL HISTORY

T IS A PARADOX THAT ALL HIGHER CULTURES OF our type are structured so that the more they evolve the more we are forced, in order to reach our goals, to proceed along increasingly long and difficult paths, filled with stops and curves. Man is the indirect being and becomes more so the higher his cultural development. The will of animals and of un-cultured humans reaches its goal, if that will is successful, in, so to speak, a straight line, that is, by simply reaching out or by using a small number of simple devices: the order of means and ends is easily observable. This simple triad of desire-means-end is excluded by the increasing multiplicity and complexity of higher life. Now the complex of means is itself turned into a multiplicity in which the most impor-tant means are constituted by other means and these again by others. So, in the practical life of our mature cultures our pursuits take on the character of chains, the coils of which cannot be grasped in a single vision. It is sufficient to think of how food is procured. Primitive cul-tures have simple mechanisms to secure food, which are sometimes sufficient and sometimes not, whereas modern man finds bread on his table through an entanglement of apparatus, innumerable actions, and traffic patterns. The long strands of means and ends, which transform life into a technical problem, make it completely impossible to remain clearly aware at every instant of the terminus of each strand. On one hand it is impossible to keep track of the entire sequence, and on the other, each step before the last one requires the whole concentration of one's spiritual energies. Thus, our consciousness is bound up with the means, whereas the final goals which import sense and meaning into

3

the intermediate steps are pushed toward our inner horizon and finally beyond it. Technology, which is the sum total of the means of a civilized existence, becomes the essential object of struggle and evaluation. Thus, people are eventually surrounded everywhere by a criss-crossing jungle of enterprises and institutions in which the final and definitely valuable goals are missing altogether. Only in this state of culture does the need for a final goal and meaning for life appear. Life, as long as it consists of short means-ends relations, each of which is sufficient and comforting in itself, knows nothing of the restless questioning which is a product of reflection about a being that is captured in a network of means, detours, and improvisations. Only when all of these activities and interests—with which we have concerned ourselves as though they were absolute values—become transparent in their character of being just means, does the anxious question about the sense and meaning of the whole arise. Beyond individual means, which now become transparent as being not the end but only a stage, the problem looms of forming a truly perfect union in which the soul is redeemed from the confusion of peremptory existence and in which unfulfilled desires ripen and are stilled.

In the world history with which we are conversant it appears that humans first found themselves in this condition of disquietude in the Greco-Roman culture, specifically at the outset of the Christian era. At that time the systems of living had become so complicated, the units of acting and thinking so complex, and the interests and movements of life so manifold and dependent on so many conditions, that in unconscious mass tendencies as well as in the self-reflection of philosophical consciousness a disquieted search for the goals and the meaning of life was ignited. The carpe diem of hedonism seemed to preempt this question, but in fact it was just an argument for its existence: the sensual enjoyment of the moment has its end in itself; by dissecting it into individual accentuated moments hedonism forcibly took life away from the need for absolute unity. The mysticism of imported Oriental cults, as well as the widespread inclination toward anything occult and the offensive against polytheism, show quite clearly that people could no longer make sense out of the width and breadth of a complex and complicated life.

Christianity brought redemption and fulfillment into this situation, which was, perhaps, the most essentially exigent one in which historical mankind found itself. It gave the absolute meaning to life, which was needed after life itself had been lost through its multiplicities and formalities in a labyrinth of means and relativities. The salvation of the soul and the kingdom of God now became an offer of absolute value for the masses, a definitive goal beyond the meaninglessness of an individuated and fragmentary life. The masses, indeed, lived by this final meaning until, in recent centuries, Christianity lost its appeal to and power over innumerable people. The need, however, for a final goal in life has not been lost; on the contrary, every need develops deep roots if it is satisfied for long periods of time. Thus, life has retained a deep desire for an absolute goal, especially now that the content has been excluded which allowed habituation to this form of inner existence. This desire is the heritage of Christianity. It has left a need for a definitivum of life's movement, which has continued as an empty urge for a goal which has become inaccessible.

Schopenhauer's philosophy is the absolute philosophical expression for this inner condition of modern man. The center of his doctrine is that the essential metaphysical essence of the world and of ourselves has its total and only decisive expression in our will. The will is the substance of our subjective life because and insofar as the absolute of Being as such is precisely an urge that never rests, a constant movement beyond. Thus, as the exhaustive reason of all things, it condemns to eternal dissatisfaction. Inasmuch as the will can no longer find anything outside itself for its satisfaction, and because it can only grasp itself in a thousand disguises, it is pushed forward from every point of rest on an endless path. Thus, the tendency of existence toward a final goal and the simultaneous denial of this goal are projected into a total interpretation of reality (*Gensamtweltanschauung*). It is precisely the absoluteness of will, which is identical with life, that does not permit an external resting place: there is nothing outside of the will. Contemporary culture is also aptly described through its desire for a final goal in life, a goal which is felt to have disappeared and is gone forever.

It is just this world, which is moved by goal orientation and yet is deprived of a goal, that is Nietzsche's starting point. But between Schopenhauer and Nietzsche lies Darwin. Whereas Schopenhauer stops at the negation of a final goal and, therefore, as a practical consequence can only hold to the negation of life-will, Nietzsche finds in the fact of mankind's evolution the possibility for saying "yes" to life. For Schopenhauer, inasmuch as life itself is will, it is ultimately sentenced to being valueless and devoid of meaning: it is what plainly should not be. Schopenhauer sees in the abhorrence of life the tip of the iceberg of horror which fills some natures in the face of brute existence, as opposed to others who are filled with the happiness of sensual or religious ecstasy, by Being as such taken as a form independent of content. He misses out completely on the feeling for life as celebration, which is all-pervasive in Nietzsche. Nietzsche takes a totally new concept of life, which is very much opposed to that of Schopenhauer, from the idea of evolution: life is in itself, in its intimate and innermost essence, an increase, maximization, and growing concentration of the surrounding power of the universe in the subject. Through this innate urge and the essential affirmation of increase, enrichment, and value perfection, life can become the goal of life. Thus, the question of a final goal beyond life's own natural process becomes moot. This image of life as a poetical-philosophical absolutization of the Darwinian idea of evolution (Nietzsche in his late period probably misjudges the influence of Darwin on him) seems to me to be the expression of a sense of life which is ultimately decisive for every philosophy. The deep and necessary parting of the ways for Nietzsche and Schopenhauer lies here.

Life in its primary sense, beyond the opposition of corporeal and spiritual existence, is seen here as an immeasurable sum of powers and potentials which, in themselves, are aimed at the augmentation, intensification, and increased effectiveness of the life process. It is impossible to describe this process through an analysis, however, because its unity constitutes the ultimate and basic phenomenon of ourselves. Real life is evolved to the degree that innate elements have developed which are geared to strengthening the specific being. Thus, whether or not a real occurrence should be called evolution or development in a historico-psychological or in a metaphysical sense does not depend on an externally posited final goal which would provide by itself a certain measure of meaning for means or transitions. Nietzsche's attempt is to remove the meaning-giving goal of life from its illusory position outside of life and to put that goal back into life itself. There was no more radical way to do this than through a vision of life in which self-directed augmentation is but the realization of what life provides as potential, including means and values. Every stage of human existence now finds its meaning not in something absolute and definitive, but in something higher that succeeds it in which everything antecedent, having been only potential and germinal, wakes up to greater efficiency and expansion. Life as such has become fuller and richer: there is an increase in life. Nietzsche's "overman" is nothing but a level of development which is one step higher than the level reached at a specific time by a specific mankind. He is not a fixed goal which gives meaning to evolution, but only expresses the fact that there is no need for such a goal, that life in itself, in the process of replacing one level with a fuller and more developed one, has its own value. Life becomes its own ultimate term in a process in which contents are only sides or phenomena of a mysterious process of unity. Because life is development and continuous flux, every constitution of life finds its higher and meaning-giving norm in its next stage, to which its dormant and shackled power awakens.

That is the point at which the interpretation of Nietzsche has to begin in order to understand how he addressed the problem of the historico-psychological situation by determining the consequences of Schopenhauer's doctrine of the will. But Nietzsche does not posit the decisive question in an abstract and logical form, nor does he solve it that way. Question and solution have to be distilled from his statements which mainly are geared to individual questioning. The resolution of the interpretative task depends on the possibility of defining, through the mediation of Nietzsche's concept of life, a kind of evolution not dominated by its final goal. At first glance it seems that only by virtue of a final goal can a string of events be turned into genuine evolution and a mere succession of equivalent stages become an ascending hierarchy of these stages. How could the later stage be posited as more evolved than the earlier one if its greater worth were not legitimated by a greater proximity to a definitively valuable final term in a series and by a richer participation in an ultimately expected fulfillment? The mere change from one thing to another, which shows only the causal connection of things, becomes evolution in the evaluative sense of that term only through a goal that has somehow been presupposed. Thus, the concept of evolution, considered by itself, would smuggle an absolute final goal through the back door, though its purpose should be to redeem life from such a goal. It is possible that this problem can only be avoided by a very clear formulation: evolution should be understood only as the unravelling of latent energies inherent in a given phenomenon or as the realization of what is latent as potential. But then, someone might say, every event has to be understood as evolution, because everything is the actualization of an existing potential. That is correct, but, remaining merely in the area of psychological and social evolution which is so important to us, not all potential is actualized! Untold potentials remain in their fetters, are shackled by strings of events occurring haphazardly, and are pushed—by lack or by excess of development—off the courses that they would no doubt have taken on the basis of their own leanings. Thus, we can speak of natural evolution in its proper sense if latent energies with definite directions exist in a being or in a complex of beings, and if a substantial or decisive portion of these energies reach the realization for which they are objectively geared.

Here an unlimited optimism makes itself felt. The presupposed quality of the potential inherent in humans is such that the value of realization is already guaranteed or, better, is established through the realization of a substantial part of the potential. Some could object that the kind of evolution which is basic to the value of life can include only the valuable and not the adverse potentials of our essence. Thus, the theory would be based on a circular argument which finds the value of life in the evolution of life, whereas evolution already presupposes a selection according to a criterion of value. We will discuss this argument in detail later. It will suffice for now to note the breadth of our interpretation of evolution. The change from quantity to quality, so typical for all human spirituality, gains its deepest metaphysical exemplification just here: those divisions of life which are called bad and worthless are precisely those which immediately or through their consequences subdue a relatively substantial quantum of tendencies in our essence, whereas those cohorts which are called good and valuable are the ones which basically succeed by freeing a maximum of bound energies in us and in mankind. For the pessimism of Schopenhauer, however, every "more life" is in itself bad. The meaninglessness of life's factuality is understood simply in terms of a quantitative reality, such as the transfer of dormant life potential into actuality.

For Schopenhauer the inner rhythm of human life appears as an unremitting monotony. Thus, his idea of the teleology of life is decisively distinguished from that of Nietzsche. When I inspect Schopenhauer's depictions and evaluations of human life, I sometimes get the impression that the deepest substance of his pessimism is not drawn from positive pain so much as it is derived from ennui, the dulling monotony of

days and years. It is the absence of the idea of evolution which condemns the world and mankind to being always the same, without solace. As long as life still had an absolute purpose, varying relations to
this purpose provided for a rich play of light and shadow. After this
purpose had disappeared the pain of ennui, and anger about the slack
dreariness of the course of life, became the only adequate reaction of
feeling to life, though the desire for purpose lived on and refused to
accept dully a uniform givenness. The fact of ennui is proof to Schopenhauer of the meaninglessness of life: if we are occupied by nothing, if
we are not filled by any individual content, then we feel, solely and
purely, life itself—and exactly this experience causes an unbearable situation. The turning from Schopenhauer to Nietzsche reveals itself here
more radically and profoundly than at any other point. The deepest depreciation of life and the highest triumph of its process depend equally
on the negation of an absolute purpose or value outside of life: on the
one hand, life seems to turn around on itself, empty and meaningless,
like a rat in a drum; on the other hand, evolving life takes back into its
innermost and intimate essence the purposive character which had been
taken away from it by external forces.

The different pictures that Schopenhauer and Nietzsche draw of different human meanings stem from the same root. The haughty attitude
of spiritual aristocracy which sometimes shows up in Schopenhauer's
thought is inconsistent with his fundamental convictions. If life does
not have a scale within itself for measuring differences in value, the en-
suing monotony must be continued into relations between people. If
existence does not have positive value or, from the viewpoint of his idea
of perfection, if existence only gains value by approaching annihilation,
then a gray always-the-sameness, an absence of rank and distinction,
should be as typical for individual moments of existence as it is for the
totality of moments. At least when Schopenhauer formulates moral duties he draws these consequences: genuinely moral individuals do not
make a distinction between themselves and others; they recognize, if
not theoretically then practically, the deep metaphysical unity of all
being. Individualized separation is only a deceptive appearance, the consequence of our subjective forms of apperception. It seems as though the
absolute unity at the root of our essence is not the cause of our ultimate
homogeneity, but is the expression or reflection of that homogeneity
which results from the lack of a definitive and difference-producing

purpose for life. The new creation of such a purpose, as undertaken by Nietzsche, will institute sharp differences among ranks and will put a new aristocracy into existence in place of a metaphysical democracy. The evolution of the totality of life is not based on an equal development of all of its exemplars: the formula is that our genus consists at any given moment of a chain of more or less developed existences, among whom only the most highly developed display the fullness of life's evolution. This means that evolution tends toward the infinite, though the differences within the chain of evolution indicate definite differences in value among individuals. The principle of evolution turns Nietzsche into an aristocrat because it refers the meaning of every lower level of existence to the next higher one. "Higher" is only possible if there is or has been a "lower," as opposed to a concept such as "equality before God" or "the absolute value of every individual soul." Schopenhauer merely negated concepts of equality, whereas Nietzsche could not accept any value if there were not something below it. No level could have absolute value in itself, but would have to be the result of a lower level, which had its meaning in this potentiality, opening up fully and becoming the condition for fresh transcendence of its own existence. If life is evolution, then aristocratic inequality of its forms is logically cemented into its structure. Similarly, if purpose is switched out of life its forms undergo a pervasive levelling.

The negation of an absolute purpose for being, which is the common starting point leading to the differences in attitude between the two philosophers, ultimately has bearing on the value involved in Schopenhauer's devaluation of the world. If there is no absolute goal, such as Christianity provides, and no relative one, such as Nietzsche's theory of evolution offers, then it follows that the accent of value has to rest on emotions, on pleasure and pain, which are closed into the moment. Whoever rejects a meaning for life has to become a eudaemonist, because pain and pleasure are the only accents in a life composed solely of moments having no import beyond themselves. For Schopenhauer, the empirical and by itself decisive argument for a world without meaning, given *a priori* by its structure as will, is that no amount of happiness can equal the sum total of pain and that no instance of pain can be redeemed by any experience of happiness. The negation of the will to life, his offer of a practical solution to the mystery of the cosmos, is, if successful, nothing but redemption from the experience of pain in life. Nietzsche saves himself from making momentary values absolute by defining the essence of evolutionary values in terms of the transcendence of individual moments. On this basis it must seem to be pure perversity to him either to have the value of life depend on pain and pleasure, or to place all being on the same moral level—perversity, indeed, to limit experience of values to the occasions of existence when existence is destined to transcend itself in an overtowering way. Pleasure and pain lead life only toward a dead end. To take the moment for what is definitive would be the same as coming to a full stop in the middle of a sentence. Working within his concept of evolution, Nietzsche correctly prefers to speak about "accidental occurrences." These are only reflexes, falling back into the subject of an ongoing life and having no consequence for its goal, which is the necessary improvement in the quality of our kind. Even pleasure and pain can be subsumed under these final values of life: "The discipline of great pain," as he says somewhere, "causes the exaltation of mankind." The entire difference between the worlds of Schopenhauer and Nietzsche lies in their opposing judgments of the importance of eudaemonistic considerations. For Schopenhauer, happiness and pain are definitive of life's value, because they are all that is left in the structure of the soul which eludes ennui after the disappearance of a final purpose for life. For Nietzsche, happiness and pain are the embodiment of ennui, stations of life not worth stopping at because they are just stations. If they nevertheless catch a ray of sunshine it is not because life evolves into them, but because they evolve toward life and become a means to its enhancement.

Even the apotheosis of happiness at the conclusion of Zarathustra is not contradictory:

> 'Joy—deeper than heart's agony:
> 'Woe says: Fade! Go!
> 'But all joy wants eternity,
> 'Wants deep, deep, deep eternity!' [1]

He only takes one characteristic of happiness here and that is the one transcending the moment. Further, he understands that characteristic not in its psychological reality, but in an ideal sense which stretches out toward reality. Every joy contains the desire for its duration, and its fleeting reality is intertwined with a will to and even a moral require-

1 Friedrich Nietzsche, *Thus Spoke Zarathustra*, trans. R. J. Hollingdale (Baltimore: Penguin Books, 1961), p. 333.

ment of duration. Such an ought is just like a legal contract which is not rendered void by an inability to enforce it. From this special category some of eternity's splendor is infused into happiness. Thus, happiness partakes in the importance that Nietzsche accords to the concept of eternity, which at first appears to be mystical, but is actually only a logical consequence of his basic vision of life. For Schopenhauer, the eternity of all being must be the most terrible of thoughts because it means for him the absolute opposite of redemption, the absence of any chance to put an end to the process of the cosmos in which every single moment is simply utter pain without meaning. Inasmuch as there is no redemption within existence, eternity is the precise logical opposite of spiritual and metaphysical negation, which is the only concept in which Schopenhauer can find solace and a sense of existence. Nietzsche escapes from the pessimism of a life without meaning through the single concept, which is only thinkable on the grounds of eternity, of the triumph of a life continuing upwards ad infinitum and leaving behind any imperfections of the present. Eternity has to be available—at least as an ideal and as a symbolic expression of the rational forms of existence—to function as a frame in which the processes of redemption and meaning in this world can be contained. This is the bridge leading Nietzsche from a pessimistic point of departure to optimism. Thus, he grasps the possibility, transcending itself toward the absolute, of combining the NO toward everything given and presently real, with the YES toward existence as such, and the chance for this imperfect presence to move into the unlimited space of evolution toward perfection. The concept of eternity is the continental divide revealing the different currents and directions in the thinking of Schopenhauer and Nietzsche, which all flow from the same original spring.

The sympathy of modern man will tend to favor Nietzsche in an encounter with the general ideas of the two thinkers. Someone might be opposed to the Darwinian concept of evolution, yet there is great solace and something inseparable from modern thinking in the idea that life in its innermost meaning and latent energies has the possibility, tendency, and promise to continue toward more perfect forms and toward a more of itself by transcending itself beyond the now. Thus, Nietzsche becomes a light illuminating the totality of the human landscape. This leitmotif is so dominant when Nietzsche strikes it that despite his antisocial escapades, he seems to be far and away more adequate in expressing the feeling of life in our time than does Schopenhauer. An aspect of the tragedy in Schopenhauer is that he defends the weaker cause with more impact. He is without a doubt a greater philosopher than Nietzsche. He has a mysterious relation to the absolute of all things that is shared alike by the great philosopher and the great artist. Listening to the depth of his own soul, he awakens the murmurs of the deep reasons of being in himself. Even if these sounds were subjectively colored and would resonate only in similarly attuned souls, the important consideration here is the depth of resonance and the passion for the totality of the cosmos. People who are not metaphysical get caught up in particulars. Thus, the extension of the subjective life into the abyss of existence is missing in Nietzsche. He is not challenged by metaphysical questions but by moral ones, and he is not looking for the essence of being but for the innate imperatives and for the being of the human soul. He evinces the psychological genius for representing in his own soul the spiritual life of the most heterogeneous types of people, and he displays an ethical compassion for the value of man as idea. But his aristocratic will and brilliant mind are not complemented by the great style of Schopenhauer, which evolves from his having been attuned not only to the sounds of men and their values, but also to the primeval music of being. Strangely enough, this style seems to be lacking, particularly in people of extreme psychological sensitivity and refinement.

This inequality of level is all the more interesting in view of the fact that both thinkers start from the same answer, which then turns into a question, that is, from their evaluation of culture. But to pursue the parallelism of presentation in these two thinkers to the point of describing a confrontation of their teachings would be to fall into the wrong perspective on the problem. Such a comparison would eliminate the personal flavor, which can be discussed only in terms of the total interrelation of intertwined thoughts. This flavor is essential to the full taste. Each factual statement gains its philosophical importance, its organic character, only as part of a specific and structured spiritual unity, as a personal but typical aspect of the totality of life. The more "personal" a refined individual is, the more jealously he will defend the proper meaning of every expression as but a part of the whole structure of the specific being which is himself. Certainly the essence is not automatically the sum total of all single manifestations. But to compare single manifestations always distorts, whether the result of the comparison is sameness or difference. Even comparing total personalities seems to be flawed in a similar way, though it is more difficult to show why that is so. Personality is simply incomparable to the degree that it is personality. The problem is intrinsic to the concept and is not merely a consequence of the complications or the difficulties of the task. Every comparison has to reach for the shared denominator. Thus, a singularity which takes its measure only from its own idea of being or from norms transcending the personality is necessarily violated by comparison. But the cunning depreciation and transformation of great personalities which is accomplished by drawing parallels and correlations seems to give the epigones greater and closer access to them. Perhaps, if we use this form of leveling, it is the only way to approach them while respecting their dignity.

Personality in the sense used here is a goal of evolution which is always imperfectly realized: human qualities remain almost always on the level of comparability because they have not been integrated into total individuation. Every great philosophy, however, is the anticipation of a unity of form which is unattainable in actual life. Art is the vision of the cosmos through the eyes of a temperament, whereas philosophy is the temperament seen through a world vision. Philosophy is both structure-giving and explanatory of the elements of the cosmos, and hence is one of the great attitudes of mankind with regard to being. This vision excludes all themes which do not belong to the unity of the one and all inclusive harmony, and is something that life is unable to accomplish. This vision of life has the unity of the ideal personality and, therefore, every philosophy, with the exception of eclectic ones, is basically incomparable.

I was able, however, to compare Schopenhauer and Nietzsche in the preceding pages, because I was not aiming at the pure individuality of their thinking, but at their specific place in a framework of culture. Up to now I have cited them only as representatives of a cultural period who have shared in developing its fundamental potentials. Thus the figure of one can be painted against the figure of the other. A depiction of them starting from their own centers, which is a task I will now undertake, would deny, however, the use of this measure. Yet the right to present these two thinkers together derives from their distinctively developed personalities. The correlation between them is not within themselves but in the mind of the observer. Both of them have transformed the contrasting themes typical of empirical life into pure and total representations of life.

2
Man and His Will

F THE REAL DIFFERENCE BETWEEN THE HUMAN being and the animal lies in the multiple aspects of man's essence and powers in contrast to the unilateral activity and life-potential that cages in the animal, then the subject's multiplicity is reflected in the variety and range of pictures obtained from objects. The image of an object obtained by an animal, probably after many trials and experiences, is the exclusive expression of a uniform nature, of typical needs and apperceptions, and, therefore, of a typical relation to given things. Man, however, is a manifold being, which means that his relation to things is presented in the multiplicity of modes of perception in each individual, in the entanglement of each individual in more than just a single series of interests and concepts, of images and meanings. Thus, for man, the object is not only a desired one, but is one of theoretical understanding, of aesthetic evaluation, and of religious meaning. The soul's disposition to reflect its own multiplicity in the richness of meanings transcending greatly the simple meaning of things has been brought by philosophy from a sheer occurrence to a principle and an inner necessity. The basis of all philosophy is the fact that things overflow any single determination: a manifold thing is also uniform, a simple thing is complex, the earthly is divine, the spiritual is material, the material is spiritual, the still is in motion, and whatever is moving is simultaneously at rest.

As a result, the irregular multiplicity of our interpretations and apperceptions of things eventually results in a single theme, just as the essential form of a philosophy is sublimated into one formula: Kant defined everything knowable as phenomenon, as something delineated by our powers of cognition, leaving things as they are beyond these powers and, therefore, in eternal darkness for us. By starting every process of cognition with the transformation of things-themselves into images, he expressed most generally and fundamentally the situation in which a thing is not just one thing. The object is rendered not only part of a certain order, and beyond that of another specified order, but regardless of which definable and knowable order is identified, there is at least one order which is fundamentally beyond definition and beyond knowledge. The plurality of existence is here made logically part of the essence of an object: no matter how many forms may describe an object, these forms are relations to us and there always remains an untouchable aspect of the object. That the multiplicity of the object is a reflection of our manifold subjectivity culminates in the fact that the subject must leave everything that is not itself outside itself. The basic condition is reflected in the object: regardless of what it is for us, the object is additionally something for itself, which is essentially unknowable.

Kant's negation of problems, however, results in a new problem, despite his basic delineation of the boundaries of knowledge. A philosophical desire arises for the thing-itself, for being beyond imagination. A quest is joined to establish a relation with this being, whether it be in a "knowledge" that is quite different from any given conception and that is liberated from the limits of subjective forms, or in an immediate relation that would not be knowledge but more than knowledge. The total philosophy of Schopenhauer is a way to the thing-in-itself. For Schopenhauer, it was certainly not the case that the concept of thing-in-itself had created a problem by offering an empty schema which had to be given flesh. Such would be the approach of an epigone or of someone who had merely flung the toga of philosophy around himself. Schopenhauer was a philosopher at heart, who from the first had a characteristic world-sentiment shaped by its direction toward absolute being, toward the simple totality of the manifold of things. Put more precisely, whereas in most human beings inner life and the mobility of the soul are expressed sufficiently in the spiritual formation of a piece or a part of the world, philosophical depth requires an image of the totality of existence: the philosophical temperament lives by uniting the roots and branches of being into a single composite picture. The categories of phenomena and things-in-themselves, which allow one to grasp the multiplicity of phenomena in a unity, gave Schopenhauer the most perfect technical possibility for changing his basic vital sentiment into a world-view.

The forms of our intellectual activity, which in Schopenhauer's interpretation shape the knowable world of phenomena, are constituted so as to lead directly to the other side or mode of existence of phenomena, that which is correctly called the thing-in-itself. The intellect follows the principle of causality as it forms the world out of the material provided by the senses, which means that whatever object may appear before our eyes (the object of our recognition), it appears only through the power of another object, which in turn is an element of the world only because of yet another object. Any configuration of space depends upon interrelated boundaries, any happening upon a cause that it develops into a cause for the next event, and any action on an interior causality which might be called motivation. Objects of experienced and of experienceable reality must be delineated, finite, and relative. The form of referring back to something else, being for something else, or being determined by something else is the way in which our intelligence creates the world as imagination or, more precisely, we create the exterior and psychological complex, which we call nature in the most comprehensive meaning of this term, through the human intellect's correlations of given contents, the position and quality of which are determined by other contents. The basic essence of the intellect is to oppose subject and object as cosmic elements so that contents are isolated and subject to a relativity they are destined to transcend. Along with the perceiving subject the object is posited, and with the perceived object the subject is posited: each conditions the other; where one ends the other begins; and if either disappears so does the other.

Thus, not only does the phenomenal character of the world as such lead to a transcendent basis for phenomena, to a being-in-itself that is not merely for us, but the special mode in which the human intellect creates the phenomenal world demands an absolute basis for its existence: the insurmountable relativity of the phenomenal world presupposes that this world exists as an absolute when viewed from another side. Relativity is a reciprocal formation, a definition of a mode of being by both sides of a relation, which needs a substance, a generic being, to lead it into existence. Something must first exist in order to become dependent, whether as something on another thing, an object on a subject, or as a subject (which would be logically impossible without an object). In retracing the chain of causality there is no resting place in any empirical phenomenon, but a movement into the infinite. Yet such a connection of relations could not occur were it not supported in its totality by an absolute being. Thus, each phenomenon, each combination of forces, and each of the soul's decisions can be queried for its origin, but why there are things, forces, or decisions cannot be determined from the series of relativities. The latter question can only be answered by an appeal to original being, which is to reveal itself as beyond the two basic essences of the perceiveable-natural world—that is, beyond phenomenality, which needs something nonphenomenal to be the root of its appearance, and beyond relativity, which logically demands an absolute to be its material.

Schopenhauer, however, was suspicious of the concept of something absolute because of his animus against the philosophy of his contemporaries. Schelling and Hegel had tried to impart a new fixity to existence in their reactions against Kant's apparent subjectivism that transformed everything observable into phenomena. They perceived the contents of existence as immediate revelations or as the pulse of a metaphysical life. They distanced themselves from dependence on subjectivity by positing the real as the objective as such, interpreting the empirical phenomenon as a metaphysical one. They did not accept the epistemological rupture between a world as imagination and a thing-in-itself, in which the world succumbs to relativity and each part of existence becomes absolute. Schopenhauer, however, had to reject an absolute that was perceived in such a transsubjective and levelling way, because, for him, the immediately given reality is a deceptive glimmer, a dream of lost souls, and a veil that obscures true reality and is destined to be torn away. Here is the great dividing line between the two main human types. For one, the substance and definite meaning of existence fills every point appearing in a pantheistic unity. The divinity of being is resplendent in every content, either without any gradation of intensity or through understanding the absolute essence of the world as appearing in an evolutionary sequence in which every phenomenon is an irreplaceable and an incomparable step. For the other, a harsh dividing line is drawn through the cosmos making space for the absolute, for being-as-such. He separates from the total world a world of nonessence, in which the roots of things do not express themselves as such and in which there is space for everything relative and transient, subjective and insubstantial. But on the other side, out of touching distance, is the reality that rests in itself, the core of being which is sensed by the first temperament in every phenomenon but which is now placed outside the mere singular appearance of anything phenomenal. These temperamental oppositions are not rooted in philosophical speculation, but in the total breadth of the soul's life. They appear everywhere in fits and starts, in velleities and partial realizations. They are the alternatives whenever something essential or basic is sought in the realm of particulars, either practically or theoretically: either the discovery and realization of unifying value is or should be based on the totality of phenomena, or unity is achieved more purely and comprehensively by a division which leaves certain levels of existence at the outset unreceptive to and beyond the absolute. Thus, our sensitivity to differentiation grounds our initial desire for unity and the picture that corresponds to it. Philosophy picks up this opposition and follows it from rudimentary through mixed forms to its final consequence, though there are occasional efforts to pacify both tendencies equally. And here we have the form of Schopenhauer's enterprise. The world of singularities as a world of phenomena obeys the norms of our intellect and, thus, is not related to the basic essence of existence in itself. There is the greatest difference thinkable between the two realms of being and, as we will have to explain, the basis of things in its purity and unity can only be perceived by sharply prescinding from all the demarcations of the world of singularities. Absolute reality, however, is the essence of all of the singular splinters and embraces in unity the totality of the cosmos from the vantage point of true reality. In prying away metaphysical reality from phenomena on one side and making them interpenetrate on the other, the needs for difference and for unity are made equally to subserve the formation of a world-image. Although the phenomenon expresses existence completely in its own language, and everything empirical has an exclusively relative character, Schopenhauer's world-view is oriented toward the absolute, from which he nevertheless firmly seeks to dissociate himself. But he could do so in only two ways. First, the thirst for reality can be quenched by phenomena and their relations and laws. This is, so far as I can determine, the ultimate meaning of Kant's philosophy, which Schopenhauer thoroughly misunderstood. Kant's conclusion is that the world is phenomenal and is, therefore, fully objective, real, and perfectly understandable, because everything beyond phenomenality would be as the proverbial dove on the roof, an empty phantasm. Schopenhauer's conclusion, which he deduced from Kant's axiom of the phenomenality of the world, comes to the opposing result that the world is unreal and that true reality must be sought beyond it. Kant senses reality as a category which produces experience, whereas Schopenhauer, who thirsts for the metaphysical absolute, senses reality in opposition to experience. For Kant, the phenomenality of existence is the point of arrival, of rest for thinking, until thinking amalgamates its own limits, adding thereby an inconsequential transcendence. For Schopenhauer, phenomenality becomes a mere tool that inscribes a locus for the absoluteness of an ulterior existence. He used the Kantian possibility of rejecting the absolute specifically to legitimize the absolute.

The other way of building a world-view without the cornerstone of the absolute leads beyond the distinction of phenomenon and thing-in-itself. In this case all being is interrelated, regardless of categorial classification. Truth and value, existence and rights, and freedom and laws are here not determinants of an independently perceptible object-in-itself, but belong to singular objects only in relation to other things, the qualifications and fortunes of which depend on correlations to the given object or to others. Just as a body is heavy in itself, yet also is only so in relation to another body, no sentence is true, no thing is precious, and no existence is objective but in the array of world-contents in relation to each other. Thus, as knowledge progresses the parts of the physical world are more and more made into functions, into relations that provide determination for the totality of interconnected things. From this viewpoint Schopenhauer poses the wrong question in his effort to transcend the relativity he acknowledges in the empirical world: Where are the substances which are subject to relation, which enter into interrelation as subjects?

This question naively presupposes just what relativism denies, that relativity must be carried by an absolute. Here we merely have a transfer of a category that is valid only for the practical and the nonfinite to a basic category of existence, though the practical dimension is but a secondary layer of existence. However, there is no question of right or wrong about the effort to dissolve the being-for-itself of things into a being-for-each-other. We must only point out that this general metaphysical view is just the opposite of Schopenhauer's vision, which searches for the being-for-itself behind any being-for-each-other and for the absolute that carries and justifies every relativity.

Inasmuch as Schopenhauer closes off the two ways of constructing a world-view without the absolute, he must search for something unconditioned to add to the conditioned data, for a permanent essence to what is fleeting, and for an in-itself to phenomena. The aim is to find the connecting point where the two worlds meet for the seeker, that is, where the immediately given world provides access to the other one. This bridge and connection, which is at least one of those that are possible, always appears at the same spot in the human soul, in our own subjectivity, when philosophy reduces and splits the multiplicity of existence, which it is given at the outset, into a duality of worlds. However one draws the line that divides everything thinkable into opposing units, the human being will always contain both of them. Whether it is the realm of ideas and the realm of spatiotemporal events, the divine order and the arena of the anti-Christ, the alienating mechanism of things and their meaning and value which we need in order to live, or the natural-corporeal structure of existence and the cosmos of soul and history, duality is not reconciled in man, but meets in him. He extends from one world into the other, his own dual nature providing the assurance that the opposing worlds do not fall apart. The symbol of the specifically human sense of life is to be this boundary, feeling that one stands between polar opposites in a decisive way, whether they refer to life in general or to its particulars. The coherent duality that determines the form of a world-view may be the root or the effect of what is called man's personality, the form of his freedom, which is never to be absolutely and in his total essence bound to any single potentiality of existence. This is why, in the contrary view of Spinoza's pantheism, which opposes dualism, there is no use for the concept of a free personality. The categories of phenomenon and thing-in-itself, which provide the most perfect and basic foundations for the division of world-views, also provide the purest possibility for the ego to reunite the two worlds. Because the ego bears the world of phenomena, the boundaries of this world must coincide with those of the human intellect: the sum total of the ego's imagination, which is the world of phenomena, must have a being with the function of perceiving. Even if the contents of perceiving were dreams and insubstantial glimmerings, the being in which they occurred would have to exist in reality, independently of the reference to reality of any perception. Whereas the subject projects his images, including his self-image, that very process may be grasped as absolute reality when seen from the other side. In perceiving himself the subject makes himself a part of his world of experience, but as the being who appears to himself he is carried and carrier, object and absolute subject, and content and action producing content. At this single point we have the phenomenon and the dimension behind the phenomenon, its in-itself: we have it because we are.

Schopenhauer's metaphysics are rooted in the idea of the subject as possessor of phenomenon and thing-in-itself, as citizen of two worlds. This determines his way toward the absoluteness of existence. Humans find themselves as corporeal phenomena, as bodies among bodies. Their matter and their movements are subsumed under natural laws, just as are those of all other objects, and their actions follow the strict causality of incentive, stimulus, and motive. Thus, from the objective standpoint, our visible life is as understandable and as mysterious in relation to its inner dimension as is any other phenomenon. However, the motions of our body are given as deeds of our will, in a different mode from that in which the motions of external bodies are given. Whatever becomes visible as motion is inner action of the will and vice versa: every true act of our will is immediately and without exception also a physical activation of nerves. Only the confusion of mere wishes with the real, decisions aimed toward the future, obscures this correlation. As Schopenhauer says, only execution validates the decision, which before execution was but a mobile intention. To "like to do everything" is only the faint sound of the will, but not its reality. On the other hand, any influence on the body is immediately an influence on the will. Such an influence is pleasure, if it conforms to the will, and pain, if it opposes the will. But, following Schopenhauer, there is no pain that we abhor in itself and no pleasure that we embrace as such. All such response is a phenomenon that comes later: in reality pain is but the rape of our will. The experience of pain as an impression is not the cause of my rejection, but my aversion itself is the real and primary event that we call pain, and the same argumentation applies in the case of pleasure. Similarly, will and phenomenal action are not two things that follow one another serially according to causality, but are, respectively, the inside and outside of the same reality. The will as radical interiority and as the bearer of phenomenal action cannot become a phenomenon itself, in that our phenomenal action is intertwined with the surrounding spatiotemporal world of phenomena and, therefore, cannot utilize the final instance of fundamental will for any scientific explanation. It will only become clear later how this position squares with the fact that we nonetheless find will as a causal and a temporal link in our consciousness. Thus, our practical existence is given in two completely different modes: on the one side, we regard ourselves as objects and as parts of the phenomenal world, but on the other side we sense the inner shaping of these phenomena, the will expressing itself in them as the true reality behind them and, therefore, never able to incarnate itself in phenomenal form. At this single point the realm of mere contents of imagining is transcended, or, better, it is not transcended, but the realm beyond it is opened up ahead of, not so much as behind, it. Whereas we only know the singularities of our active life by looking at it and making it an object, the will is action, or, more precisely, the will is the being which is reflected afterwards, as the individual phenomena of our life, through the conscious intellect and its forms. In these two modes alone we exist for ourselves, as productive beings who give birth to our practical lives in each moment and as reflexes of consciousness of this original and creative being, that is as simulacra or images of it. And, in that we find nothing else but these two dimensions within us, following the Kantian formula for understanding the world, what is not phenomenal—that is, the will as the precondition for our phenomena—must be denominated as our metaphysical being, our being-in-itself. Thus, Schopenhauer has declared that the decisive trait of modern existence— the turn to the subject and the centering of all world-categories in the ego—is the primary bearer of the Kantian distinction, both sides of which are given in ourselves, in the only existents that we do not know merely from the outside. This deep experience follows us through life: in every moment we are both spectators and actors, phenomenon and radical cause of phenomenon, and created and creator. For Schopenhauer, this becomes the founding promise of a philosophical interpretation of existence.

In order to understand the meaning of this will, which is reputed to be our metaphysical reality, one should not seek it in singular psychological facts of volition oriented to certain goals, but in what remains after we have separated volition from all the contents, images, and motives that make up its raiment, its phenomenal form. All the volitions bound to a particular goal belong to the soul's empirical world and follow the laws of causation, for they are only reflexes of deeper events in us, of which we are not conscious as they shape the parts of our spatio-temporal life history. It is of greatest importance to exclude from consideration the so-called motivations, which all too often seem to exhaust the act of will, but which really belong to the network of an inner world of experience coordinated by laws to the external world. What remains as the ultimate and undifferentiated ground of our drives and intentions cannot be described in words because it is the radical principle of all conscious life. The impossibility of describing the will is obviously connected to the fact that every human being must have a confused sense of a moving will beyond the breadth of singular existence. This will is what we all are, beyond all distinctions, and, thus, philosophy can do nothing but pour into the forms of conceptual knowledge what reverberates in every human being as the subterranean fundament. Metaphysical as it may be, this, too, is knowledge. Thus, even here the will is transposed from the realm beyond—in which it is thing-in-itself—to the region of our imagining. And this leads to the final distinction and purification of the status of the will in Schopenhauer's world system. If we call the absolute within us "will"—and we may perceive this concept in as trans-singular and as unmixed a way as possible—that term must remain the name of a phenomenon within the soul, which merely hints at something that in itself cannot be named. As a phenomenon of the soul, however, will can indicate better and more clearly than any other part of our world what can never be phenomenon. In perceiving ourselves as strictly exercising will, beyond any of its singular and worldly contents, we do not touch the untouchable, but we approach it as closely as possible, stopping at a point which still is not the thing-in-itself but is only its clearest and most intimate revelation. In modern phraseology, the absolute itself becomes a symbol of itself, not a representation of itself in allegory. We remain restricted to the level of phenomena, even when we are conscious of the will and speak of it. At this level, there is not a firm grasp of being, though the veil that covers the in-itself of our essence is drawn tighter around the absolute, reducing the extent of its drapings while never lifting its veil. We must keep the above in mind lest Schopenhauer's metaphysic become a myth, a fantastic anthropomorphism. He has encouraged such mystification by claiming without qualification: "The will is the thing-in-itself." Without keeping in mind the qualifications we have adumbrated, this statement would be illogical because it would transfer the empirical to the transcendent, as is the case in primitive religions where the gods are created in man's image. Actually, however, Schopenhauer's interpretation of the will is intended to give more precise direction to thinking about the absolute within the confines of the relative. If, following Schopenhauer's intention, we speak about absolute being beyond phenomena, we are in what could be called a metaphysical state intermediate between being and perceiving, which is not a mixture of the two but is quite special and incomparable, and is coincident with Schelling's intellectual interpretation. It is this state that appears in all speculations which claim that God or the foundation of the world is coming into consciousness within us. It is the feeling that consciousness does not at this point have an opposing object, that the contents of consciousness are not split off from being in a heterogeneous world, but that being bears consciousness of itself in itself.

There is no question here of factual accuracy. Whether one senses beneath or, better, within all singular volition the unity of will in separation from its contents, or whether the will remains merely abstract—as does the concept of blueness which we abstract from blue things, or the concept of a tune which we develop out of particular tunes—will be the decision of uncontrollable feeling. For Schopenhauer the will is like a fuel that energizes the most different kinds of machines. Will lives only in singular acts, but the causes producing singular acts do not explain what makes them acts of will. Schopenhauer's whole approach seems to express a very deep and general, though dark, feeling—the same feeling that confers infinity to us and allows us to experience our ego as something infinite, despite the fact that life reveals itself only in finite and singular contents. No matter how inclusive the imagining, how energetic the act of will, and how passionate the emotion, we generally feel that we cannot express completely and permit to live all of the tensions, forces, and events that push upwards from the depth of our soul, however strong may be their relation to a single present act of the soul. The reservoir of energy that facilitates the moments of the soul's life and the contents of that life are superior to any culmination in a single act of will: the creative totality of the soul is not exhausted in such an act, though it obviously desires such completion. Thus we experience ourselves always as more than we are, as something transcending given reality and its continuous repetition of form through changing content. There crystallizes in consciousness the judgment that as finite we are more than finite, that in every motion that is singular by virtue of its specific content, something infinite in itself gives voice to itself just by failing to give voice. It is as an aspect of this directive mood that Schopenhauer finds a general act of will in every act of will that is singular on account of its separate content. This general will unquestionably transcends every possible individualization, none of which can posit a particular goal as its final end or be pacified by singular gratification. Schopenhauer expresses his viewpoint by assuming that through recourse to singular motivations and other causal connections, it is possible to explain psychologically why I now desire this or that definite object, whereas it is impossible to explain why I desire at all or why my total will is coincident with the direction of my total character and constitutes that direction. Every act of the will as finite can be pacified, but the will as such can never be slaked. It lives both in the singular act and beyond it, because the act is never great enough for will as such. Will is infinity within us, because we sense that every finite act leaves part of the equation unsolved.

The doctrine of will as the absolute is significant in two respects, though when isolated as a metaphysical dogma it might elude both of them. One important consequence of this doctrine is that our total being is not exhausted by the sequence and sum of our singular acts: there is a "more-than-that" which can be sensed alongside and beyond any particular "that." Surely this structure of our radical being seems to be nowhere more clearly revealed and never more explicitly symbolized than in will, the spiritual essence of which is to transcend anything given and in which the soul reveals its own inner essence of boundlessness through its immeasurable realm of objects. However, one must ask if an interpretation which is ultimately only a plausible analogy drawn from the realm of immediate consciousness is adequate to the final bases of life. What we feel as the inexhaustibility of our essence—as something "beyond," that is the source of all our singular phenomena—could lie just as well in other possibilities. Among these would be the infinity of logical connections, the unity of the soul which realizes itself only approximately and never absolutely in the experienced interrelation of its particular phenomena, or the soul's relations to external existence conceived of as prestructured infinite potentiality, such that whatever occurs in the soul is incited by an infinity of forms latent in us. Schopenhauer sensed with new and unsurpassed depth the problem that was formulated first by Fichte as the opposition of the pure and the empirical egos, that is, that we feel in every singular act of our soul an energy which bears this act but also surpasses it, and which renews itself without external causation while each of its special exteriorizations is strictly caused: it is an infinite and absolute energy which bears our finitude and our relativities. In Schopenhauer's metaphysics of the will this feeling of existence—which can only be expressed imperfectly—has found an interpretation that is, perhaps, more impressive than any other. But this impressive visual image, in which the will is symbolized as encompassing all particulars in its vital depth, does not really solve the problem any more satisfactorily than do the alternatives.

A second significant feature of Schopenhauer's doctrine of the will is that despite its possible overvaluation of metaphysics, it represents one of the few very great steps taken in philosophy with respect to the problems of human life. With some few exceptions, which amount really to a *quantité négligeable*, all philosophers prior to Schopenhauer conceived of man as a rational being. Even though all philosophers must agree to some measure of irrationality in human nature, they tend to interpret it as a deviation from man's real nature, from what he ought to be because that is what he already is, not only in an ideal and ethical sense but in his most radical essence and true reality. Thinking has always employed this double meaning of being: inasmuch as what is made other to and necessary for the victory over our real phenomenal being is also a being, this latter being is said to be our most fundamental and our most real being. As we will see more fully later, all metaphysical or generally radical foundations for ethics follow this formula: Become what you are. Not even a religious fanaticism which claims that man is but a child of Satan, who can achieve value only through a heavenly grace he cannot conceive, is exempt from this formulation. Even here there is the presupposition of a child's relation to God that has been lost, but that somehow is still mystically retained and thus provides the cause for grace. Thus, the concept of being is used first in a wider and then in a more narrow sense, creating the illogical predicament that we are what we are not yet and that we are not what we really are. This is the expression of a fundamental and typical need, or, perhaps, of human cowardice which does not believe that it can sustain a demand and an obligation that are not already fulfilled in some mysterious form and depth of being. This category of nonphenomenal being transformed man into a rational being despite the protestations to the contrary of phenomenal being. Thus, rationality appeared to be the human essence and the most basic human function which included all other values in its structure. Even morality was proclaimed to be under reason's domination, perhaps because philosophers of a rationalist bent must make reason the vehicle of all insight. The old and naively mystical idea that we recognize the same through the same is used here in a specific way: the object must be of the same character as the subjective ability to perceive it, because otherwise there would be no guarantee of a perfect interpenetration of subject and object. The Kantian thesis that the conditions of knowing are simultaneously the conditions for the objects of knowledge (knowing shapes its object) here engulfs the total character of subject and object, whereas for Kant the assertion covers only the predicaments of the object.

Schopenhauer destroyed the dogma that rationality is the deep-seated and basic essence of man that lies beneath the other ripples of life. It does not matter whether or not one accepts what he puts in reason's place; he must in any case be added to the company of great philosophical creators who have discovered new potentialities for the explication of existence. The energy that is most adequately expressed in thinking and in logic had been regarded as the ultimate basis of man, but Schopenhauer tore reason from the soil in which it had been rooted and turned it forcibly into an accident, a consequence or tool of the will, which now occupies the place reason formerly held. By forming the world of objects our perceiving allows the will to separate itself into diverse acts. But Schopenhauer had the profound insight that, in their status as activities of the soul, the contents of an idea and the logical connection of ideas presuppose a moving force existing beyond the mere ideal or logical relations to contents. When we deduce a conclusion from certain propositions we sense that we are following a necessary conceptual relation, that we are fulfilling a requirement already ideally inherent. But the conclusion itself, the fact that we realize a material relation in our thinking, is not identical or given with the impotent contents and correlations of concepts. In order to become mental reality, even the most logical statement needs a bearer, who has nothing whatever to do with logic. This process by which we produce ourselves is able to receive logical and factually necessary contents, and is, therefore, rational. But with regard to its own essence, the process of self-production is beyond the oppositions of reason and insanity, logic and

contradiction: it is nonrational in a strictly negative sense. Schopenhauer's will is not posited against, but outside, rationality and, therefore, outside its contradiction.

Schopenhauer has shifted the axis of our perspective on man. Rationality no longer constitutes the veiled but basic reality. Instead, it becomes a content or, if one wishes, a form that is accepted or rejected in a
merely derivative sense by the real life of our process of self-production.
This change in the human perspective is, therefore, a symptom of and a
factor in a radical shift in epistemology. The nineteenth century fostered
a widely held idea that our being, the decisive point and substance of
our life, only gains accidental, imperfect, and often mendacious expression in our ideas and in our consciousness. This conviction stems from
Kant, who placed our total empirical ego—that is, the sum of the ideas
that live in our consciousness—as the phenomenon of the thing-in-
itself, which, though defined by the forms of consciousness, is the transcendent and unknowable substratum of our mental world. Kant, however, was not led by this idea to oppose being and consciousness. First,
the world of empirical consciousness is, for him, the real and solid
being; the thing-in-itself behind this world is merely an idea. Second,
in his search for a positive content for the thing-in-itself, Kant constitutes reason as our final and essential substrate. Marx, however, acutely
perceives the contradiction of being and consciousness. He asks, Does
consciousness determine the being of man, or does being determine
consciousness? But he poses this question in a narrow sense and for a
special purpose, concluding that the societal being of man determines
consciousness. Rejecting eighteenth-century rationalism and its esteem
for consciousness, the nineteenth century values being as our immediate reality and considers consciousness one of its accidental and sporadic
powers, a flickering light that does not even symbolize a continuity
with being that would make being accountable to it. This shift in accent is as pronounced in some of the romantic and mystical tendencies
of the century as it is in the materialistic and historicizing trends. In
Schopenhauer's metaphysics of the will, there is an irrepressible feeling
that we are assured of being in a manner diverse from conscious recognition. Thus, rationalism—which was dethroned by Kant in the special area of epistemology and was replaced by experience as the sole
bearer of the possibility of cognizing reality—loses with Schopenhauer
its hold on a total view of man. We might be dependent on a life of

rationality and consciousness, but in being so we only become the locus for a flux of representations. And we are not coincident with the contents of imagination, even if they are related to the soul or to the external world. Schopenhauer has the courage to proclaim a radicalism which he creates to evade the concept of man as a rational being: the images of consciousness which limit our empirical life do not enclose the reality of our being and, indeed, cannot even touch it because this being is not of the same essence as rational consciousness. But this negative otherness, the formal difference between being and consciousness, is not sufficient. By characterizing being as a metaphysical movement, as the dark concupiscence of our essence which appears as the restlessness of volition, he opens wide the depth and breadth of the abyss between our reality and the limp and reflective pictures of consciousness. If there is, however, a unity of being and consciousness it is such that the rationalistic view of man must be pushed even further aside, because it sharpens division: all consciousness and intellect are mere products of the will, tools employed for its own purposes and subservient to its specific destiny, even if the will is unfaithful to that destiny here and there. Thus, the demotion of the rational character of life in favor of its character as being or power is based on will. If man is a rational being, then he experiences values and goals, which he desires to achieve just because they are sensed as ends: a final goal that has been posited and evaluated unchains desire, so the normal interpretation goes. But for Schopenhauer the purpose we esteem and to which we consciously aspire grows out of the primordial fact of will. I do not will by virtue of values and goals that are posited by reason, but I have goals because I will continuously and ceaselessly from the depth of my essence. Purpose is but the expression or the logical organization of willed events. So long as desiring is understood to be the primary way of achieving values posited by reason, the concept of purpose is the ultimate support for the rationality of existence. But Schopenhauer removes that support and leaves the intellect as the illumination of the willing process. Intellect here emanates from the depths of will, and specific purposes are formed by the categories of reason for will's own purpose; they are but sparks of reflected light, accents that structure a surface. And in terms of the above, a statement made previously becomes perfectly cogent: we always know why we are desirous as such. It is Schopenhauer's division and rearrangement of our being and consciousness that allows our existence to be composed comprehensively of singular acts, but not to consist in these acts. Thus, the whole of life, which is made other than the sum total of its singularities, becomes the factual unity we sense as the substance of the singular and as what lies behind it as the dark fate of life, a fate which is not added to life but which is life itself.

3
Metaphysics of the Will

N TURNING HIS BACK ON THE SINGULAR ROOT OF his being, man, for Schopenhauer, becomes the object of his own imagination and, therefore, of his observation and rec- ognition. He transcends his being, which is enclosed in itself, and through symbolization becomes part of a vast system of different potentialities, which as symbols have a uniform character and follow the same law. These chains of things, characterized by space, time, and causality, reach out, through the imagination, beyond our ego, even if in themselves they do not exist in us except imaginatively. Through the coordination of the ego with innumerable other elements, which is a defining and formative process, the image of ourselves is formed as it is present in our consciousness. As will be noted later, Schopenhauer holds that the circulation of matter and en- ergy applies as much to our own existence as to the motions of the stars and the blooming of flowers. Identity with respect to the law of nature binds us as corporeal and spiritual phenomena in the same chain, link- ing us into a unity with the lowest and most distant things of nature. Therefore, Schopenhauer concludes that we must attribute the same innermost, absolute, and intrinsic essence to all existences that are identical to us as phenomena. He proceeds to make his cosmic principle not only (as we have previously explained) a way of elucidating man's position, but the condition of being in general. If knowable phenomena are of an identical mode, it can be presupposed that their unknowable basis also has an identical mode. The whole of nature, including our- selves as experienceable existences, forms the surface of a compact sphere. Every segment relates to another one, but to nothing imme- diately above or beneath. There is only one point from which a different and transcending line begins, the point of our own existence, which provides not only phenomena but the experience of being itself: this is the only point connected to the center of the sphere.

If we follow Schopenhauer closely we realize that even will in ourselves is not regarded as being-in-itself (*Ding an sich*), because the latter is the unknowable. Thus, conscious will itself is a phenomenon, though the one in which the impenetrable veil covering our absolute being is the thinnest. Consequently, if we only adjust our eyes, we lucidly see the vestiges of the same basic being in the rest of nature. The urge of the waters toward the depth, the urgent power pushing electrical poles toward unification (a power increased by obstacles in the same way as are human desires), the desire pushing the iron toward a magnet, and the incessant pull of gravity drawing earthly bodies closer to the center of the earth are all only phenomena of the same order, though more mute and more distant, as those that come to light in our consciousness.

One could easily call such a mode of explanation merely a humanization of nature or a realistic abuse of poetical-mythological analogies involving relapse into the primitive animism of an early mankind that had to explain the commotion of the waves as the wrath of a god of the ocean and the flow of the wind as the blowing of Aeolus. To my mind this critique seems shallow and beside the point. Certainly anyone is free to reject a metaphysical interpretation of life. It is possible to restrict oneself to the phenomena of flowing water, magnetized iron, and falling bodies as they appear, and to build a spiritual relation to the world on description, especially on a mathematical formulation of underlying repetitions. It is as hopeless to force a need to go beyond appearance on those people who do not feel one, as it is to explain the need for redemption to those who are not religious, or to explain happiness to those who lack a sense for art by recurring to the examples of the Mona Lisa and the B-Minor Mass. But excluding metaphysical needs from discussion should not be used as an excuse to protect stupid fantasies. This must be made clear in order to show that a critique of Schopenhauer's metaphysics has to be based on the legitimacy of metaphysics. Thus, Schopenhauer's interpretation of all natural existence as the appearance of will could only be called an infantile and superstitious humanization if he had merely transplanted into nature the will as we consciously experience it. But he is far from having committed such a methodological error. He aims at the basis of the immediate expressions of will in ourselves. He does not transfer a fact of psychological experience to a transcendent realm separated by definition from all experience. The above error, indeed, is committed so often in religion and metaphysics that it is used generally as a basis for the critique of any metaphysics, and is assumed to be valid *a priori*. But in Schopenhauer the concept of metaphysics is based on human-spiritual phenomena as well as on physical events. There is only a gradation of difference between these kinds of phenomena. Psychological will, because it is conscious, offers its transpsychological being to scrutiny more easily than do the purely material phenomena that for us constitute nature. Our metaphysical intimations and explanations have to descend beneath the surface of existence to its deeper levels in order to reach the shared basis of existence, because life is stratified into different levels. The experience of ourselves provides a clearer, stronger, and more readily described inkling of the nonempirical center than do nonspiritual phenomena. Thus, if we presuppose that the center of being is the same for spiritual and exterior phenomena, we may then assume that the former phenomena can be used to explain the latter. This is one of the few points on which Schopenhauer is often so remarkably misunderstood. His separation of metaphysical will from a conscious phenomenon also called will has not been clearly enough understood. This tangible spiritual fact of experience, which gives such a satisfying interpretation of the absolute, approaches but never touches that intangible absolute. There is a metaphysical basis of things—which is not included within empirical-human forms but that founds the human as well as everything else—beyond our phenomena and all others. Although objectively all phenomena are at the same distance from the center, subjectively the distance differs. The totality of the world is reduced to the human factor if, as Empedocles believed, the world takes shape through the love and hatred of the elements, if teleological metaphysics makes the good of man into the creative purpose of all existence, or if the god who forges and moves the world is guided in his work by motives and affections identical to ours. In contrast, Schopenhauer has reduced man to the denominator shared by the totality of the world. In man, for whom the levels of denominator and phenomena coincide, he finds the possibility for such a reduction of thinking.

Thus, the accusation that would reduce Schopenhauer to the methodological level of a primitive-poetical animist is not justified. Certainly, however, his metaphysics contains presuppositions growing out of a personal faith. Leaving aside the special content of an explanation of existence, there is the overriding presupposition that the absolute and the phenomena as such (*das An-Sich der Erscheinungen*) are identical in every case. For Schopenhauer the above seems to be a self-evident consequence of his idealistic starting point. The disjunction of things into multiplicities is made possible by space and time: our imagination contains the more-than-one only as a one-beside-another or as a one-after-another. Insofar as space and time are forms of the imagination, "being" must be free of them when it is not imagined. Being cannot contain multiplicities, but is One, though not in the sense of "one" or "individual," which would presuppose another individual. The difference made by a second or third is inapplicable here. Metaphysical unity is not an abstraction from multiplicity, but is absolute, being divided only in a multiplicity of different pictures of imagination in the forms of our intellect, just as a ray of light might be divided into the colors of the rainbow. Thus, if being, inasmuch as it is not imagination, can be touched at one point, then it must be at that point in which all the figures of imagination have their essence, a point which is not itself imagination. Each radius running between the phenomena and the singular unity must meet on the level of that one unity. There is a profound connection here between a metaphysics of being, which starts from the subject and is based on the ego, and the monistic or, if one prefers, pantheistic idea of the metaphysical unity of this being. The ego, for which existence is consciousness, could never have been used as the interpreter of the totality of being and as a bridge leading to it if the presupposition had not been made that the essence of ego and that of being is identical. The above presupposition characterizes even Fichte's idealism, in which the ego is the only thing that exists absolutely, producing the world through its imagination. Fichte's thesis could not be true if the imagining and creating ego did not find itself simultaneously as an imagined and created one, an empirical personality, existing on the same level, under the same law, and in the same mode of essence as the falling stone or the fish swimming in the depths of the ocean. All existence has to be a perfect unity unto itself (however that perfection be defined) and a perfect unity with respect to the ego, if this ego is to be able to find in itself and its content the point from which thought is in a position to explain the totality of things. Opposites need each other: they provide the basis and foundation for even the most radical one-sidedness. Nowhere is the above truth more clear than in the unavoidable intermingling of the idea of total unity with doctrines finding the reason and radical basis (*Realgrund*) of every being in the ego.

THE THESIS OF THE METAPHYSICAL UNITY OF ALL THINGS is a cornerstone of Schopenhauer's approach to fitting the world into a system. In order to see things in the proper perspective, however, one must understand that Schopenhauer is not correct to assume any logical necessity. He argues: Multiplicity exists only in space and time; space and time are exclusively forms of apperception of our intellect; therefore, what cannot be in our intellect (the absolute) can never be multiplicity but must be absolute unity. This conclusion, however, is not strictly implied. First, it is not correct to say that the multiplicity of reality could only exist in the forms of one-alongside-the-other and one-after-the-other. The assumption that our consciousness exists only as a temporal sequence of its elements is merely a traditional error. If I think a sentence such as, "Life is pain" the content of consciousness, "Life" precedes the content of the consciousness "pain." But even if there is a temporal sequence of the two contents, there is also a contemporaneity and a togetherness which constitute the sentence and are its unity of meaning. If the two concepts strictly followed each other, that is, if one concept had disappeared by the time the other entered into consciousness, then the two could never constitute a sentence. Our soul has a mysterious potency, readily observed, to combine into one unified idea a plurality of elements that come to mind, one after the other. The process of conceiving the sentence, "Life is pain," depends neither on space nor time nor any of the applications of a principle of causality, but is rather a process of the soul by which different elements are brought into a form containing no before and no after. But even if the constituent elements are transformed, the result is not merely an absolute and transcendental unity: a strangely composed multiplicity remains as an irreducible residue. The incomparable construct of the human sentence combines multiplicity and unity in such a miraculous way that the multiplicity of its elements survives the termination of their space-time configuration; and the unity, which is palpably alive, is independent of all opposition and all relativity, the latter condition which Schopenhauer finds only in the realm of the transcendent. And there is an additional fault in the logic by which Schopenhauer reaches his conclusion. According to his argument, insofar as the character of the thing-in-itself must be different from that of phenomena, and the character of phenomena is multiplicity, therefore, the character of the thing-in-itself must be unity. The above dogmatics are not unassailable. It is not an indisputably necessary conclusion that all existence be subject to the categories of phenomenon and thing-in-itself (*Ding-an-sich*), though all philosophy following Kant's, including Schopenhauer's, presupposes that proposition. The hypothesis that the real, that which exists, is constituted by consciousness assumes that immediate reality is spiritual, an assumption that could only be self-evident for modern subjectivism. Schopenhauer's declaration that the world is my imagination is not at all certain absolutely and *a priori*, but only follows from the presupposition that the category of subject and object, valid *within* the empirical-real world, is also valid for what surrounds this world and for the inclusive totality. But even if the above presupposition is conceded, and everything that is typical for the phenomenon has to be excluded from the essence, the result is not that the basic essence must be unity, but only that the multiplicity and difference of experienced phenomena are not applicable to the basic essence. The negation of a concept does not immediately and self-evidently create a different positive concept. The same error occurs in statements such as "whatever is not finite has to be infinite," "whoever is not altruistic has to be egoistic," and "whatever cannot be dissolved into parts must be indestructible." The above kind of reasoning leads to a theory and practice that follows a norm such as "whoever is not for me is against me." But the recognition is growing that things cannot be incarcerated into a dualism of purposes in which the negation of one is without exception identical to the affirmation of the other. As long as we have two positive determinations, the human intellect cannot have absolute certainty in the use of the principle of *tertium non datur*. There is always the possibility of a third way that might stay as open as the second one, which up to now was regarded as the only remaining option after the first way was excluded. The above consideration contradicts Schopenhauer's conclusion that whatever is not phenomenon must be unity. Let us agree that experienced multiplicity, individuality, and diversity are only caused by the phenomenon, which is an idea produced by our forms of consciousness and cognition, and that, therefore, what is beyond the imagination, the in-itself (*An-Sich*), cannot be the carrier of these predications. In the above case the absolute could, indeed, be unity, but it could just as well possess a measure and mode of individuality and of separate being-for-itself that was as distant from the characteristics of phenomena, as impossible to detect empirically, as much an absolute, and as impervious to experiencing consciousness as Schopenhauer's postulated unity.

Here we have two opposed metaphysical possibilities, both of which are rooted in the depth of "world-feeling" (*Weltfuhlen*) and are brought to full clarity only by their complementarity. As Schopenhauer continually points out, the multiplicity and diversity of phenomena relativize them with respect to one another. Every part of the world of phenomena is limited in space, time, and causality by other parts, and it is only such limitation that gives each part a special character. Things create their individual forms mutually: they are waves in the flow of becoming, each one different from all of the others, yet under the same law as the others, dependent on the rhythm of their close and distant neighbors, and influencing the form of all the waves to come. Metaphysical individuality, however, is totally different from and even opposed in its essence to phenomenal individuality. In contrast to the world of experience, in which each unit is an expression of its complementary relation with other existences, metaphysical individuality, which is beyond empirical imagination, must be conceived of in terms of absolute units. The life and life-forms of each unit express its innermost essence, and the elements of each unit are internally related to the whole. Whereas in the world of experience everything is or is such as it is only because of the other things, in absolute individuality there is an ultimate element of being that is, perhaps, comparable to the feeling of freedom and being-for-itself of a single soul. Absolute individuality is under no external or relational necessity. It need not be characterized by concepts such as "unique" or "similar to others," because its essence is not based on other things but only on its innermost and radically independent facticity. One of the characteristic experiences of life—which is at the roots of such divergent philosophies as those of Leibniz, Schleiermacher, Herbart, and Nietzsche—is to find units rather than unity at the foundation of things. However, wherever the philosophical interpretation of the world is influenced and formed by the opposite desire, the formula of Spinoza applies: *Omnis determinatio est negatio*. Thus, individuality or determination is placed into the network of interrelated things and takes on its special form; that is, each being is not at all what the others are and only by its difference can it be what it is. A unity of being is presupposed in which the formation of the individual is a consequence of separation, which means in this context partial non-being. The truly absolute being cannot attain nonbeing, so it cannot have any individually determined form: in a very deep and radical way each thing is identical with everything else. The fact of individual presentation might be understood to result from an inexplicable evolution that pushed individuals out of the original unity; or it might be explained as an artefact of imperfect subjective understanding; or such individual being-for-itself might be traced to some kind of mystical original sin of separation. In any case, such individuality is always considered to be something superficial on a secondary level of the world that results from a late dissection and does not reach into the depths which are accessible to our thinking and which contain an absolutely uniform being. In contrast, the essence of metaphysical individualism is the claim that special forms of being are rooted in the innermost depths of being, despite their superficial empirical presentation. Thus, individuality is not a form of being special that is based on interrelated determination and influence, but something existing in its own right that is founded on an inner principle. Metaphysical individuality is presented as endowed with being-for-itself and being-by-itself, which are predicates distinguishing the comprehensive metaphysical unity from the relativity and interrelatedness that constitute the form of phenomena.

Thus, it becomes clear that Schopenhauer's argument, from the diversity of phenomena to a transphenomenal unity of being, is not logically necessary. There is room for a third way. The empirical and relative multiplicity or plurality of being can as well be conceived of as a negation of a metaphysical absolute multiplicity of being as it can be understood as a negation of the kind of metaphysical unity Schopenhauer propounds. The decision in favor of one or the other of these possibilities is not a matter for thought itself, but is rather an outgrowth of a fundamental leaning of the whole personality. It is a question of emotional fulfillment, which comes either from seeing the world radically united through its basis, or from seeing the world resplendent in the richness of an infinite number of independent units.

It is important to note that Schopenhauer's metaphysics leaves no room for the concept of personality, which is simply lost between the ego as imagination and the ego as will. The world of imagination is the realm of individuation, of the separation of existence into distinct individual beings, but such separation does not constitute individuals in a true and absolute sense. Separate existence in the realm of phenomena is only constituted by separation and not by a radical being-for-itself. The form of phenomenal individuality comes into existence in a network of neighboring things ranged into the relations of before and after, left and right, and higher and lower, not through an inherent necessity independent of everything external. Or, looking at the matter from the other side, in nature, defined as the complex of recognizable phenomena, there is a circular flow of energy and matter that draws everything into its continuum. There is no delimitation here of one thing against the other in any real sense. An eternal necessity, which flows along without interruption, leads one phenomenon into the other. Thus, it is only our secondary imagination making distinctions which allows us to speak of "one" or the "other." The marks of division made by secondary imagination are not pregiven in the objective structure of things, which structure itself is also of the imagination, but in a primary sense. By analysis and synthesis of phenomenal elements we create individual beings as we need them for practical or theoretical purposes. Thus, every phenomenon that is declared to be one and individual is only such in an ideal sense and because it has been marked off in the flow of natural existence, which itself is not separated for subjective purposes. In Schopenhauer's interpretation there is no ego in the metaphysical foundation of things and no ego with the inner independence to oppose the world and other egos: personality is devoured everywhere by a unity that does not allow for limitation. Within the unity upheld by Schopenhauer, personality would be a logical contradiction, because it is just personality, in the sense of its perfect conception, that can stand up against the whole world. Personality has the self-enclosure, self-sufficiency, insistence on its own right, and perseverance in form to allow for an infinite number of contents to pass through it. Only a work of art has a similar unity and wholeness that permits imperturbable self-reference. The form of a work of art, which makes it a "world for itself" and which symbolizes being as such, is given to it by a personal soul transforming its own mode of being into its work. Schopenhauer's negation of personality in order to preserve the absolute unity of being points, however, to a significant relation: the quality or function of things, understood as their specific and absolutely real essence, is also a requirement yet to be fulfilled in these things. The basic form of our essence is a radical dualism that will ever be objectified in two worlds, one of which is built on the other, but also opposes the other: there is a world of the surface and a world of the depths, a world of here and a world of the beyond, a world of phenomena (*des Scheinens*) and a world of truth, and a world of experiences and a world of the thing-in-itself. Whatever is real in one of the worlds is the true reality, but the other world is also in some way and in some degree real. Even if the elements of a world are fleeting and illusionary, they still have form, shape, and action that coincide or contrast with reality. That the demand for the realization of something that is already realized in its most radical reality seems illogical is a consequence of not keeping the dignities of the two worlds strictly separated: one being, man, is experienced as living in both worlds and, in particular, man experiences himself as the unification of those worlds. The structure of absolute being is defined by Schopenhauer so that there is no room left for individual personality. Personality does not exist for him. Therefore, he finds eradication of personality to be the task of our actions and of our existential formation. I will have to explain later how Schopenhauer has provided the final formulation of the salvations we might find in our existence, such as aesthetic salvation, in which the subject is totally subsumed in the idea of the thing and, thus, in the content of an imagination; ethical salvation, in which the "I" eradicates any difference between itself and the "you"; and ascetic-metaphysical salvation, in which the soul exchanges her individual form, here being-for-herself, for the pure formlessness of nothing. Schopenhauer's antipathy toward personality is made apparent not only because he ignores or negates the concept of personality, but because he postulates the negation of personality as the content of any "ought" whatever. He is intent on cutting the root that in other world-views (*Weltanschauungen*) anchors distinctiveness and belonging-to-itself, which are the marks of the sovereignty of individuality, to the depths of existence.

For Schopenhauer, the real character of all existence is shown in the fact that the will, which is the clearest exteriorization of the radical essence of the world, is absolutely unified, or, to put it differently, that the unity of existence is will. The above fact determines for him the entire harmony and order of phenomena. Uniformity of being through time and space is exemplified for him in the facts that plant and soil, animal and food, and eye and light are congruent with one another, and that the parts of an organism and its phases of evolution are conceptually correlated. For Schopenhauer, the above uniformity indicates will, which in living beings must take the form of a will to life. The will displays its fundamental unity in the required togetherness of all phenomena, which only, however, exist by virtue of the apperception of the intellect. One would be unjust to this metaphysical interpretation, which is typical of and basic to the entire work of Schopenhauer, if one saw in it only an illegitimate competition of speculation with a scientific-causal interpretation of things. The area in which only science is legitimate is not touched on here. The question of why there is a possibility of answering the questions of science in a satisfactory way is not addressed by explaining the mechanics of the lawful harmony of all events, by appealing in Darwinian fashion to the adaptation of organisms to their circumstances, or by utilizing any other mode of connecting phenomena to phenomena. Science explains the laws of individual correlations, but not the fact that the elements of this world form a unity and follow laws. It is possible to dispense with the question of the unity of nature or to declare it to be unanswerable, but someone who attempts an answer cannot be refuted by appealing to considerations to which that answer does not refer. There would be reason to protest only if an answer to the question of unity claimed to be on the same level as scientific explanations or to infringe upon or replace them. Indeed, not every metaphysics has avoided making the above claims, but there is no necessity for metaphysicians to commit this error. Why the Austrians were victorious over Frederick II at Hochkirch and why they were defeated by him at Liegnitz are not correlated to the problem of why humans wage war. As Schopenhauer himself stresses, it is as unwarranted to explain physical facts by appealing to something as general as the will that permeates the whole of nature as it is to explain them by resorting to the creative power of God. Physics looks for causes, but the will is never a cause. The relation of will to phenomena is never similar to that of cause to what is caused. What in one respect is will, is in another respect a phenomenon that needs another phenomenon to be its cause. The chain of science should never be broken by the metaphysical potency of the will. Even the existence of a chain of phenomena and a world that is tangible in the forms of apperception are not caused by will as a thing-in-itself, but are themselves phenomena that follow along once there is will. The relation between will and phenomena is not to be understood in terms of the causal nexus that ties phenomenon to phenomenon, but on the basis of the inner essence of will. We may appeal to the analogy of the way we understand the spiritual expressions of a human being, one through another, psychologically. None of the special contents of the spiritual expressions is explained by the fact that the human being has a soul. But the concept of a soul, though its object is invisible and cannot be demonstrated to exist—in that for immediate experience each human being is only the sum of visual, auditory, and other sensory impressions—is the basis permitting appeal to a chain of psychological concepts.

The unity of metaphysical will also is responsible for the decisive implication of Schopenhauer's methodological principle, that is, that the will which moves the world from its interior, or better, which constitutes the world in its basic respect, cannot have a definitive goal and cannot reach real satisfaction at any point. Schopenhauer is completely opposed to a harmonistic interpretation of being in that will, because it is the absolute One, does not have anything outside itself to quench its thirst and to put an end to its ceaseless quest. Metaphysical will can only live off itself, which means that each being needs another being in order to take from the latter the possibility of life and then to move on to new depredations. In its thousand different disguises, which provide the momentary illusion of satisfaction, will finds only itself, because there is nothing outside itself. Thus, the will to live is its own nourishment. Humanity, which is the locus of the highest consciousness, is the arena for the maximum increase of a self-devouring will whose unity excludes the possibility that it could ever achieve satisfaction. Humans view nature as an array of products to be used and consumed, and there rages among them a constant struggle of all against all, which is barely hidden and is hardly interrupted by moments of truce. The fact that mankind is a metaphysical unity of will means that the phenomena that develop out of it necessarily exercise will over one another: one phenomenon has to live at the expense of the other and has a desire to do so. Schopenhauer evinces fundamental understanding of the tragedy of yearning life when he states that will as the absolute reality of being can only satisfy its absolute longing as a whole and never through a part alone. And the infinite character of the will means that it can never be satisfied in any given moment. Will is essentially split within itself, because it always posits itself outside itself and moves from here and now to there and then. But the unity of the will is the reason why its inward split can never be healed. One being cannot find quietude within another: the moment at which desire and object meet can only be the beginning of new willing, because the object in its fundamental essence is nothing but the same being that is manifest in desire. Every single act of will, which is bound by the singularity of its content to the world of phenomena, has a goal and an end; every man knows the reason for his specific action at any given moment. However, the question of why one wills at all can be regarded by a person who is acting only as a pointless and unanswerable query, which in fact indicates that will is self-evident. We have arrived at the absolute finality which we make finite only when we question whether it makes sense to search for reasons any longer. We know how to find reasons for every single physical movement, but we cannot provide any reasons for movement and causality as such. Schopenhauer understands the infinity and incompleteness of will, which are consequences of its being the metaphysical one beyond which there is no being. In the inorganic realm the character of will is expressed paradigmatically by gravity, which is a symbol for a continuing urge without an attainable end. Even if all matter had congealed in one mass, the struggle between gravity and impenetrability would still go on and would exemplify the urge of will—halted but not stilled—as the fundamental tendency of matter. And with regard to the other side of reality, human desire similarly is not fulfilled by the fulfillment of a wish. The desire can never be satisfied, and only the objects given in consciousness can change. Thus, it only seems to be the case that achieving a momentary goal appeases a wish in a definite way. The attainment of a goal always leads sooner or later, and in a manifest or hidden way, to disappointment and new desire. The essence of the moment of will in our desires is never to find peace. Only individual contents and motives can find an end and peace, but they are parts of a different layer of being. Their change and even their satisfaction do not touch will itself, although will is expressed by them. Our multifarious desires seem to promise anything we could wish for, yet they deliver nothing. They are nothing but phenomena based on a will that is without finality and without rationality. All being is sentenced by the oneness of will to finding always only itself and never satisfaction.

A life without hope and consolation, which is more deeply rooted than in any other pessimistic philosophy, is therefore presented in Schopenhauer's metaphysical proposition. At first finding the basis of a multiply divided reality in absolute unity takes on an optimistic tone. The chaos and adversity of the elements of being, their strangeness and indifference, is often even more difficult to bear than a frontal attack. Thus, the idea that diversity is only phenomenal and illusory appears to carry salvation with it by rendering the forms of multiplicity and opposition superficial in relation to an ulterior existence with a single essence and root. Is it not a telling symbol that the term for "being split in two" (*Entzweinung*) is one of the strongest ways of describing animosity? Thus, it becomes obvious that the unity of the world cannot help but be interpreted as a principle of peace and reconciliation. If one follows Leibniz and Herbart in proposing a metaphysical design in which the foundation of being is composed of a multiplicity of independent elements, then struggle and division can be eliminated from one's formula for the world only by declaring that these elements are devoid of relation to each other: only if there is no interrelation whatever and if every element is a world unto itself can the whole be exempt from the alternatives of war and peace. But to have Spinoza's harmony and peace in life, or Schelling's reconciled aesthetic harmony, it is necessary to forge the resplendent diversity of phenomena into a transcendental unity. The tragic note in Schopenhauer's philosophy is that the oneness and essential identity of all being, which is formally a guarantee of a peaceful experience of the world, is turned by its characterization as will into the harbinger of division, of existence without peace, and of desire never to be satisfied. Thus, the hunt and flight of existence, purposeless drifting, and the unbridgeable gap between the present and our real intentions and dreams are now precisely rooted in the center of life, which by virtue of its oneness would otherwise guarantee the peace of being and its reflexes. Schopenhauer turns the form of monism—which provides for peace and solidity of world-views, and for their coexistence, by plentitude of content—into an agency of disquiet, deracination, and inner contradiction. The incongruity between formal science and an evaluation of the whole of the world that is based on sentiment becomes obvious in Schopenhauer's thought. The above discrepancy was covered over by most philosophers because they postulated as a medium or content a rationality that was also the vehicle of science. As men of science they could resort to mystical or speculative longing, to sentiment, or to the urge of an intelligence determined to survive, in order to harmonize with a world that seemed to them to be a realization of rationality. As long as the absolute essence of the world was understood to be intelligent, it seemed correct for intelligence to understand the world in logico-systematic forms, for example, divine intelligence, a personified logic (the Platonic ideas), Leibniz's intelligence that embodied all the elements of the world, or Fichte's ego that intelligently creates the world. Until Schopenhauer's time, the formal definition of a satisfying philosophy was understanding the world conceptually in terms of scientific rationality. The deep metaphysical need, which was concealed under the form of science, did not, therefore, become conscious of its diversely mediated and even immediate relation to existence, and of its profound alienation from all logical and rational knowledge. As long as rationality is the content of the image of being, it is a veiled fact that scientific intelligence cannot provide us with a depiction of the ultimate roots of existence. Only the doctrine of existence as will, that is, as absolute nonrationality, can reveal the full dimension of the dualism between scientific and metaphysical man, which, though it may be reconciled in individuals, is given as a split in spiritual life.

I think that it is possible to show a fundamental relation between a metaphysic of the will and the mere negation of the rationality of existence, if that rationality is understood as the positive fulfillment of a negative definition. First, we must distinguish between the contents of being—which are amenable to causal inference and are interrelated conceptually—and the form or facts of being that constitute reality. The individual facts of existence that can be verbally designated are basically understandable in terms of their qualitative denotation. Hence, Hegel was able to call everything that exists rational as well: in principle, rationality can make any content of existence part of an ordered system and can logically integrate anything defined by qualities. The same rationality presented in ourselves as thinking determines and orders things in a general way. Only so is our thinking, moving strictly within itself, able to reach the truth of things. The process of conceiving, which operates by rational inference and correlation, is, however, totally inadequate to address being as such. There are things that we define in their relation to one another and through the logical necessity by which one follows the other. They are, and that is a brute fact which taxes the limits of our intelligence, only to be accepted and are not capable of being further elucidated. The necessity that governs contents that depend on other given contents does not exist in respect to the fact that these contents are real. It would not be self-contradictory if there were no being at all. Indeed, neither the fact that there is being nor the condition of no being at all is rationally intelligible. Therefore, Hegel, who aims only at the spiritual structure of the world's content, equates pure being and pure nothing, though he concedes that there is a difference between them which cannot be expressed or put into words. The logical inaccessibility of the concept of being offers an opportunity for quite opposite emotional sentiments (*Stimmung*) to experience the world in their own ways. Thus, in Spinoza's thought we feel ecstasy in reference to the marvels of being, which are captured in realistic forms: everything individual or singular is devoured by the abyss of being, because the individual is a qualitative designation and, therefore, as singular, it is not being. Spinoza's passion for being cannot tolerate anything other than pure and unlimited being, and so he reduces God to a mere expression of it. The irrationality of being, however, escapes Spinoza, because he overlays the fundamental difference between the content of things and their being with the distinction between the general and the special features of things. His enthusiasm for the mystical depth of being is both cause and effect of his acceptance of that depth as something logically manageable: in order to make the depth of being rationally acceptable he calls it *causa sui*, by which he means that the causality that makes things intelligible resides within it and that it is intelligible through itself alone and not in terms of anything else, because there is nothing else. Schopenhauer, in contrast, is profoundly shattered by the dark fate of being. Being immediately is its dark fate and only brings that fate with it in a derivative sense. Schopenhauer discerns clearly that being cannot be elucidated and cannot be made accessible to our rationality, and, therefore, is unspeakably frightening to the point of being unbearable to a metaphysical sentiment, unless one decides, as Spinoza did, to embrace it in mystical love.

Thus, the interpretation of being as will bespeaks an eruption of the dark and unintelligible compulsion underlying the interpretation of being as rationality. If being is willed, it somehow becomes more intelligible, as though a motive were unveiled that could be reenacted in ourselves. Herbart offers the insight that change is so contradictory and unacceptable to us that we use the concept of causality to make it perceptible and meaningful. Causality is a crystallization of the imperative not to rest with a change that immediately presents itself as the last step of a process, but that as such is problematical for our reason. The unintelligibility of change is shattering and is only mitigated by making it manageable through introducing the concept of causality. The same sort of motive identified by Herbart might lie behind a metaphysics of the will. By characterizing being as will, a simplifying and explanatory quality is introduced into a dark mystery. Although the problem of uncaused being is merely pushed back one step to the level of will, the absolute will of the world provides, through its form as will, a quality that redeems the rigidity of the concept of being as such—an element of productivity, and an interrelation of isolated moments—even if one grants that will is ultimately beyond intelligibility and is alien to sense and purpose. The appeal to will is similar to responding to an inexplicable expression of human essence by saying, That is just the way they want to do it. That which is inexplicable is not merely attributed to the will, but will is interpreted as the inexplicable per se. Nevertheless, by recurring to the will we simply feel better and feel that a certain elucidation has been achieved, because there is no longer merely mechanical fact or eventuality devoid of any influence of the will. Unlike Hegel's statement that everything real is rational, Schopenhauer's opinion would be that everything real is nonrational. The former thinker looks at the content of reality, whereas the latter views the reality of content, the fact of a being impenetrable to rationality. The nonrationality of being interpreted as will expresses the twofold metaphysical urge to find the element of our essence and of the world at large, which gives a positive content to a negative definition. This element is will, insofar as it is simply willing without regard to any determining content. As intellectual beings we are only carriers or vessels for imagined contents. Strictly speaking, it is even the case that we *are not*, insofar as we merely imagine: the only thing remaining of us is a will in terms of which we are real, but by virtue of which we are absolutely removed from the rationality of our being. As an expression of the irrationality of being in concrete terms, will adds a redeeming touch or at least facilitates understanding, because the will puts every moment outside itself in order to bind that moment to each preceding one. The appeal to will, then, does not provide a causal explanation of being (will is not subsumed under causality), but by a process of quasi-identification it reinterprets an unbearable and rigid closure in terms of a more accessible life situation. Thus, the metaphysics of will achieves a general form of understanding, even if our intelligence cannot use this form truly to penetrate the ultimate and, perhaps in principle, the only mystery, insofar as everything else is a matter of content and, therefore, is intelligible in principle.

I return now to the metaphysical unity of the will, in which a pessimistic double-motif is hidden. Every goal or end of the will that actually is achieved can only be a point of transition and never a final destination, because will is self-identical in all things and in all moments of life: when one reaches a goal one is received by oneself. We may grant that actual achievements are relative satisfactions and that phenomena are restless and always moving on because their insatiable hunger has deeper roots. However, the absolute metaphysical will, which is ourselves, is not only characterized by unsatisfactory and disappointing ends, but also has no end at all that is intrinsic to it. The end is always something outside willing, yet there is nothing external to willing and, therefore, no end can be outside it. For the will within the world of phenomena every end is an illusion, but for the absolute will there is not even an illusion, because a division of absolute will into different levels is possible only in space and time. And there is a strange logical twist to the discussion of metaphysical will. Thinking derives the concept of will, which is something alive in individual acts of will, by abstracting from them, that is, by excluding whatever makes them different from each other and by retaining only what they all share. But aside from differences in intensity, which obviously do not play a role here, the only difference in acts of will is among their goals and ends. What makes one act of will different from another one is precisely a diverse goal. The concept of will, therefore, can only be reached by abstracting totally from the ends which in their diversity constitute individual will. The nuisance of dealing with a "pure will" is the result of a logically necessary abstraction which is required to make will a uniform and general concept. This is the same problem one would face if one undertook Spinoza's attempt to reduce all realities to an absolute oneness of being by eradicating the forms that separated them, and then complained about the lack of beauty in existence, which after all resulted from a logical procedure for producing a concept of existence that eliminated form, the only thing to which beauty attaches itself. Thus, the problem at hand is not very serious. The end of an act of will and the particular definition of that act are equivalent concepts. If one eliminates the particularity of will in order to achieve a concept of the generality of willing, then one must eliminate all ends. And there is no use in lodging pessimistic complaints about the fact that the general, undifferentiated, and uniform will lacks any end. A complaint in such a case would merely be a tautology that repeated the definition of the concept. Such a statement does not permit any conclusions about the importance or the value of the will, just as the sentence, "A defoliated tree has no leaves," provides no information about the tree.

Thus, the cornerstone of metaphysical pessimism—the unavoidable futility of a world-will which seems to take away any sense or meaning from existence, must be absolutely and uniformly general, and dissolves all specific forms in its oneness—cannot be a basis for value judgments, because it is an *idem per idem* that predicates the uselessness of the will by eliminating use and end in the process of construing the concept of will. Schopenhauer's basic thesis, then, may be logically attacked, but there are still more pointed questions to raise. Our critique is based on the assumption that will is an abstract construct (*abstraktes Denkgebilde*) that is derived from concrete individual acts of will by eliminating the differences between them. But is it possible that abstraction is a way of thinking that leads to something which exists in reality? Could it be that a general concept is matched by something that really exists? Might there really be a "pure will" devoid of any special ends? The empirical approach only finds individual acts of will, each of which always has an end. A pessimistic metaphysics of the will depends upon resolving the question of whether reality is exhausted by the empirical approach—rendering a uniform will an abstract concept—or whether a uniform will is reality proper and the empirical realities are its individuations and broken rays. The above problematic allows us to understand how an idealistic theory of knowledge that separates phenomenon and pure thing (*Ding an sich*) becomes an unavoidable presupposition of Schopenhauer's pessimism. The idea of a will that in its essence has no goal or end and is, therefore, at the deepest core of the world depends exclusively on the possibility of thinking of individual acts of will, which are always characterized by goals, in terms of a unity that is not divided by ends. Only idealistic categories can provide the orientation and perspective required to show that everything given empirically is only a shadow, a glimmer, or a reflection, indicating the division that true being undergoes in consciousness. Empirically, an undifferentiated and uniformly absolute will is a construct without any significance, but idealistically it can be understood as a basis for and a truth of being that is untainted by the veil of multiformity through which it is turned into experienced phenomena. Here we obviously confront a matter of life or death for metaphysics: Do abstractions from particulars that are carried out by thinking lead to constructs containing only what has been put into them? Or is abstractive thinking, which is a process that is clearly closed in upon itself, able to grasp a real being with real predicates that lies beyond thinking? If one agrees with the latter position and is aware that it can no more be proven than its contrary, then one is left with the metaphysical elaboration of a psychological exegesis of man discussed above: rationalism, which previously shaped philosophy almost exclusively, takes it for granted that goals and values, through their attraction, influence the development of the impulses of will in humans; Schopenhauer, in contrast, accords primacy to will, which then is individuated into ends and into specific points within the endless stream of a deep abyss, and is shaped into individual singularities by the superficial forms of our consciousness. Just as the will of man is related to its ends, so metaphysics discerns a uniform basis and essence of existence which is divided into phenomena only by the perception of reason. Therefore, through a purely logical process of abstraction from phenomenal multiplicity and a retention of the shared elements, it is deemed possible to reach the sole completely real substance. If multiplicity is projected onto the phenomenon, then the parts are interrelated in the unity of the pure thing (*Ding an sich*), of which they are appearances. Thus, the most general concept of a unity of existence lies beyond the mere kingdom of ideas. Thinking returns to its point of origin, moving from absolute oneness toward the division of consciousness into bits and pieces, on the opposite path from the way of the world.

Through his process of thought Schopenhauer has a special metaphysical impact: his special right to think that there is unity in the existence of the world does not only produce a formula or a theoretical design of the world, but also contains immediately a value judgment. If will is the essence and the specific quality of being, and it is uniform in all singular phenomena, then its concept must exclude any end, salvation, and satisfaction. Thus, the world is a stage for a radical opposition: metaphysical will is not only distant from its goals, but it is devoid of any end at all, despite the fact that it constitutes the will to seek an end; desire is not only deprived of winning an object, but it has no object at all. The above logical contradiction becomes possible on a metaphysical level when the reality of the world-will is declared to be absolutely one, and to have no object that lies either beyond itself or within divisions of itself. The radical inner contradiction in the substance of the world, which is not regulated by any logic because it is the radical basis of logical structure and the final court of appeal for logical relations, can be expressed within reflective consciousness only as a logical contradiction and, thus, only in a concept, the use of which is self-contradictory. Within the world of phenomena, primordial will, which is divided into specific acts of will, expresses itself in the dissatisfaction associated with every momentary satisfaction and in scurrying from one mirage promising fulfillment to the next. Similarly, the continual struggle of individuals and of species against one another—the dog-eat-dog mentality and the reciprocal destruction of living objects—is only a symbol of a deep root within the mirage-world of objects. And finally, the pain and suffering of the world, the preponderance of pain over pleasure, the debit on the balance-sheet of happiness, and the preference for the negation of life over its acceptance, because acceptance is worse than valueless, are merely reflections of a quality of the world-being in the sphere of the sentiments.

4
Pessimism

URING THE PAST SEVERAL DOZEN YEARS, THE AB-solute preponderance of suffering over happiness in life is the definitive portrait of life's value that gave Schopenhauer's philosophy its general significance and signature, with respect to the culture of emotion (*Stimmungskultur*). Schopenhauer made suffering into the absolute substance of emotionally experienced existence and did so against a manifold of pessimistic interpretations which declared the world to be a vale of tears, life not to be worth living, and happiness a passing dream: he made suffering into an *a priori* definition that grows out of the central roots of our existence, and made sure that none of its fruits could be of a different essence. Here for the first time life is not an accident of being, even an overgrowth of it, but life itself is directly reflected in feeling. If, in addition, one admits that all happiness is pacified will, and all suffering is the negation of will's fulfillment, then the metaphysics of volition demands the primacy of suffering. Factuality is decisive in this case, because it would not be sufficient if in reaching its goal the will would be simply the cause of happiness (*Lust*). Inasmuch as every effect generally can be derived from different causes, the fundamental impossibility of our quenching our desire could not exempt Schopenhauer's pessimism from the following argument: even if the will's fulfillment as the source of happiness could be stanched forever, happiness could trickle forth from somewhere else. Therefore, one has to turn the empirical sentence, "Pacified will is happiness," into the metaphysical expression, "Happiness is pacified will." And inasmuch as it follows from the unitary nature of will that it never can really be pacified, the negative balance of suffering over happiness in life is established.

One can interpret Schopenhauer's intention as presenting the ultimate and deepest essence of the world in the sphere of feelings, just as visible phenomena place the world into the sphere of recognition. His comprehensive notion of happiness and suffering touches the ultimate problem of the meaning of life and proves to be a veritably irrefutable counterpoint to the usual argument of some scholars of ethics that happiness and suffering are exclusively subjective conditions that do not touch the most basic structures of life. The aimlessness of life in itself accentuates happiness and suffering in a special way, giving them a specific value in themselves that neither is drawn from a higher goal nor transcends the moment of awareness. This is a philosophical theory of absolute and final goals similar to Kant's, which splits off sense data into a secondary realm of relative unimportance, or to Nietzsche's theory of the relativity of goals in the light of evolution. But once there is a place for happiness and suffering in the supreme sphere of life, as there is for Schopenhauer, they can gain such importance that they color the meaning of life in a new way. They are the cornerstone of Schopenhauer's world-view, because no transcending goals could diminish them.

Schopenhauer draws a decisive consequence from the volitional character of happiness when he states that all happiness is "essentially always negative": "Desire, which means death, is the antecedent condition of every fruition. Thus, being made happy is never more than being liberated from some suffering, some pain, some necessity. . . . After everything is finally conquered and reached, no more is won than being freed from some suffering or some desire, and thus one returns to the initial situation." These simple and quite logical sentences throw more light into the darker shadows than ever could any enumeration of positive suffering or unobtainable happiness. Thus, though the measure of what we call happiness might be as great as anything imaginable, it would be shot through with negativity from its very beginning. Life does not provide for real gains, but only for compensations, for payments on a mortgage to will. The supreme performance imaginable, though it would be obviously beyond realistic expectation, would be the pacification of every desire, the replacement of every desire by the happiness conditioned by it. Such a happiness would have to be more than the mere cessation of death or of the pain of desire and would, thus, clearly be a hallucination, a logical impossibility. Pessimism normally arises from the quantitative comparison of pleasure and pain, thereby remaining somewhat relative and remediable; but for Schopenhauer the concept of lust is basic. As an *a priori* of life this concept is beyond every empirical correction. Any experience of happiness, whether large or small, is made possible by the pain of nonpossession, that happiness being the equalization of pressure. If anything could be called the basic error of life, its absolute and all-encompassing formulation would be the negativity of happiness.

The logic of the above formulation rests on a psychological fact. If we did not know from experience that the fruition of desire is accompanied by a specific sensation that we call pleasure, then Schopenhauer's theory could not exist. The grounds for the theory can be tested against psychological facts. It seems that the most important fact upon which to base a critique is that the will which is connected to the absence of something valued or which expresses a privation positively is, in almost all cases and especially in those which are decisive for a specific temper of life, not merely a flash of lightning illuminating the question of attainment or repulsion on the spur of the moment. The will, on the contrary, is usually persistent, at least for a time, and is realized through a sequence of practical acts, each of which is a step toward the will's final goal. If I am not completely mistaken, the stepwise development of the will is not always accompanied by a sensation of pain and privation, but this sensation appears when there are obstacles in the will's path. Depending on the nature of the goal and on such special circumstances as personality and taste, innumerable experiences indicate the will's progress. Their essence is the expectation of each of our volitions: there is an expectation of appropriate time and method, of conditions to be met, and of energy to be spent in order to reach the goal. If an action develops according to expectation, then there is no concurrent experience of pain attached to it, except for some possible special circumstances, though one is yearning for a goal as yet unachieved so long as one is still on the way to it. The will's progress is attended more by a pleasurable sensation than by a painful one. Pain enters only at the moment when we experience obstacles, when the goal is obscured, and when our power dissipates. It is simply psychologically false to claim that all volition is painful because its basis is in deprivation and because deprivation accompanies willing until it disappears in fruition. Even if one interprets metaphysically every deprivation as volition, the psychological picture remains different: volition is a movement to end deprivation, and deprivation normally does not become painful if it is carried smoothly by volition toward its goal. Conceptually, volition means not-having, but factually it is on the way from not-having to having, and is, thus, in-between. Just as love—which Plato calls the intermediate phase between having and not-having—is not in itself experienced necessarily as unhappiness, so the hedonistic reflexes of volition mix the suffering of a point of departure with the happiness of approaching the destination.

It is of overriding psychological importance to recognize that we experience the happiness of the goal not only and exclusively in the touch-down, but also, through anticipation, in the approach. The happiness of anticipation is not an illusion in which we pretend to contain the uncontained and are stimulated by phantasy rather than reality; instead, quite legitimately and undeceivingly, the hope for happiness turns into the happiness of hope. Indeed, we live hedonistically on credit, but expected happiness is truly experienced. Juridical definitions of property do not provide a third position between possession and the intent to possess, in that law only knows a yes or a no. But the clarity of legal alternatives does not apply to sentiments: the pleasure of future possession is not only a future pleasure but is already present on the way to possession, so long as attainment is not beyond hope and there is progress toward it. How significant is the thought that happiness is logically justified only if the goal is attained, if psychological fact decides to the contrary? Though Schopenhauer cannot get away from this thought, psychological fact is and must be all-important for him when he entertains the question of the value of happiness in life. The pain of deprivation, which is the starting point of the process of will, does not cease, even when it is modified by deviations and personal nuances, only after the achievement of the desired goal, but is already ceding to the genuine happiness of anticipating fulfillment on the stations of the road already travelled, in the measure that one closes in on achievement.

The above argument can even be improved, and thereby used to challenge the logical merits of the arguments employed up to now to support pessimism. Why is it that through all the genuine mediating moments between the poles of not having and having, there is a slow and steady process in which the pleasure of goal-attainment is accrued, on credit, step by step? The ultimate value and decisive importance of the stages of having attained and possessing rest, for us, on nothing but an emotional state. Whatever we call possession, attainment, or victory has an importance that radiates in different directions such as the juridical, the physical, and the conceptual. But none of these reflections of achievement would interest us were it not for the emotional dimension, the feeling of pleasure and the sense of value, which are not only the effect of possession on us, but are its inner essence, its subjective reality for us. This conclusion is but the consequence of an idealistic theory of knowledge: the object *is*, theoretically, my imagining of it and, inasmuch as all of its objective determinations are included in the process of imagining, that object is practically my sentiment, and its relation to me is completely subsumed under my reaction to it. We can now explain why the feeling of happiness connected to the attainment of the will's goal, whether it is real or delusive, is already reached while one is still on the way to achievement. Even granting that juridically or conceptually there is no partial possession, total possession itself is nothing but feeling, and the continuous growth of feeling through a sequence of phases is intelligible immediately. This situation is made perfectly transparent through the example of love. We should be out of our heads if we cared to describe love's progress in the terms of Schopenhauer's theory of the will, as if love's goal were the interior and exterior possession of the loved one, and the happiness experienced by the lover were the liberation from a pain produced throughout the time of not yet being perfectly in possession. Even if the initial phase is also the final one, reality and experience prove beyond discussion that in many instances love is experienced as happiness, though it is destined not to succeed: the happiness of an "unhappy love" is often witnessed. And if a love is free to develop toward fulfillment, then the earliest steps of this development are already joyful: courting the beloved while almost not daring to hope, seeing the increasing signs of being accepted, hearing the first expressions of a love that is still far away from full possession. There is an ample scale of increasingly rich joy, which is destined, perhaps, to reach a definitive possession and a final climax. But achievement will come through an uninterrupted increase, not in a big leap from pure misery to pure happiness. The gradual growth of happiness is possible because even a realized attainment and possession that was adequate to its own concept would be irrelevant did it not contain the one trait that is essential for us, the feeling of happiness. Thus, there is no difficulty in proceeding through a continuum, through stages of feeling the same quality, on the way to the summit, and one need not be bound to the end of material possession or even to its imitation. This is also the reason for the right to accuse someone of adultery, "who looks at his brother's wife with lust": there is a sliding scale from the first steps in an erotic sequence to the ultimate ones. The only ones ignorant of the gradual character of such transformations are those who observe the external discontinuity of physiological having and not having, and who, therefore, miss the inner development, which for morals and happiness is the only important factor.

In general, one must be extremely careful to avoid speaking simply about errors when one addresses decisions based on ultimate sentiments about world and value, for these are beyond the alternatives of true and false. Such decisions are the expressions of a specific being, of a specific attitude of a soul toward the world: their "truth" consists in an adequate and honest expression of the reality such that it can be imitated from within. Truth in the above sense is not conditioned by the measurement of material statements against their objects as realizations of affirmations. Thus, even if the real content of statements about world and value is nonlogical (not real and subject to contradiction), these statements might sometimes express the essence of a metaphysically taut soul opposing given reality even better than objective propositions, in spite of or even because of their special form. But even if the metaphysical or ideological value of a statement is not necessarily impaired by incorrect content, these two dimensions should be kept separate, all the more because incorrect content can reveal the meaning and power of metaphysical value. Now we can grasp Schopenhauer's obvious error when, for the sake of pessimism, he denounces as suffering the entire phase of not-yet-possessing in every process of willing: it is the partitioning, with what appear to be logical concepts, of life into having or not having the desired object. Such partitioning is appropriate to the exterior, physical, and juridical dimension of existence, but it is definitely inapplicable to the dimension that is significant for the question of eudaemonistic pessimism. There is no logical basis for Schopenhauer's conclusion, in light of the happiness attending the stages of willing and the marked independence of the process of willing from real and definitive possession. Real happiness is merely an accompaniment of strife, quest, and endeavor, such that achievement of the goal does not only fail to provide added happiness but is as irrelevant as is a beacon after one has put into port. Pessimism would be justified if the following conclusion were valid: As long as we exercise will, we do not possess, therefore we are miserable and suffer as long as we exercise will, because life is basically constituted by acts of will, and goal attainment lacks temporal extension and is momentary. But Schopenhauer falls short of the logical conclusiveness of this position because he mistakenly translates the conditions of external possession and nonpossession into the decisive dimension of emotional response.

The above is in my opinion the ultimate reason for Schopenhauer's misuse of the concept of will. The essence and originality of Schopenhauer is related to two important shifts of accent within the philosophical interpretation of the world. First, the will and not "reason" (either the "world reason" of Stoicism or Kant's "practical reason," which was regarded as the subjective and objective support of existence) is viewed as the radical root of the soul and world. Second, in the wake of all of the typically optimistic transfigurations of reality, the deep and irrevocable suffering of the world has finally found its first real and basic expression. Schopenhauer's error can be traced back to his attempt to create a systematic unity between these two essentially independent and great results of thinking. He had to extend and transform the concepts of will and feeling so that the external alternative of having and not having would be able to embrace the total contradiction of happiness and suffering. Thus, he could deduce the preponderance of not having (suffering) from the weight and extensity of the moment of will in our life, and render happiness the simple cessation of suffering and frustration, something definitively negative. He did not bestow spiritual and conceptual independence on happiness and suffering, as he did quite freely on imagination, but rather defined their essence, and not merely their causation, as pacification or nonpacification of the will. Thus, he obviously evades the specific and elementary qualitative dimensions of feeling which cannot be subsumed under the will or the imagination. Only the will and the imagination could be retained in a world in which the metaphysics of will was used as the justification for pessimism. As a consequence of Schopenhauer's concept of will, our inner fate had to be torn into having and not having, and only "imagination" could be allowed in as an additional concept, in that its ideality and objectivity could not in any way influence the decision for pessimism.

It is, indeed, an interesting spectacle to see Schopenhauer, who is one of the truly free and intellectually honest spirits of our time, over-powered by his need for system, emotionally necessitous for a unity not implied by the object that concerned him. If he had allowed feelings to retain their own rhythms, which do not, indeed, follow the logic of the will, then his metaphysics of the will could not easily have been brought to eudaemonistic pessimism. Eliminating the specificities of feeling and retaining as elementary factors of the human soul only will and imagination, it seems to him, as a consequence of his need for a system, that he must logically deduce one of the two great discoveries from the other.

His metaphysical foundation for pessimism allows Schopenhauer to leave what for him is an unimportant empirical basis to followers who, in a naively empirical way, avidly enumerate individual areas of life in their search for the preponderance of sure suffering over attainable happiness. They add and subtract activity and passivity in our balance of life in order to reach the final result of negativity. Schopenhauer is too great a thinker to expect basic decisions about the totality of life to follow from adding reflections on single instances, but he would be pleased at the results of such a procedure. If we assume that an average human being pursuing happiness were offered the sum total of life's happiness at the cost of the sum total of its sufferings, Schopenhauer would advise against the bargain: the average person would lose out because the quantum of happiness would have to be increased substantially to break even—the joys offered are overpriced in relation to the sufferings that would go along with them. The result of such a calculation is not decisive for pessimism; though it cannot be verified by an enumeration of single cases, it also cannot be refuted by this means. The metaphysical way to pessimism is also determined by ultimate convictions that are beyond proof. Thus, proof must come from beyond empiricism and beyond metaphysics.

Pessimism holds that the world's existence is a greater evil than its nonexistence would be, because suffering, the negative value, out-weighs happiness, the positive value. This assertion presupposes either an empirical or an *a priori* measure that would make suffering and happiness comparable. But far from being self-evident, the possibility of such a comparison is even contradictory, though that appears to be para-doxical in view of the fact that our practical life continually depends on comparing negative and positive values. Every exchange, expenditure of labor, or contract includes a comparison of the gains in happiness with the dedication, effort, and things to be sacrificed, that is, with the quantum of unhappiness that must be accepted in the bargain. If negative value prevails in the calculation, then we feel constrained to reject engagement or enterprise. But I believe that I can show that this fact of experience does not allow for any conclusion about a basic and existential weighing of happiness and suffering.

The continual empirical comparison of positive and negative values is not based on their superposition and, thus, does not allow for a common quantitative measure. If we compare two quantities of the same quality, for example, two joys of the same kind or two similar passions, then we know almost immediately which one is greater: their similarity allows them to be measured against one another, just as two sums of the same kind of money can be compared. But whenever the price of a commodity is in question, a third factor must be introduced in order to establish equivalence, that is, the general market condition of the specific article, which allows one to define a certain amount of money in circulation as the average acceptable price. The price requested for a commodity will be deemed too high if that commodity can be purchased more cheaply elsewhere. The same seems to apply to the price we have to pay in suffering for our specific joys. Excluding cases of extreme suffering that are close to physical death, an inexperienced person could never be in a position to judge whether or not a certain quantity of suffering was worth a certain quantity of happiness. Only the experience of life allows us to overcome uncertainty about the proper price to pay in suffering for quantities of happiness. And this uncertainty never disappears altogether: the measure is constantly redefined by new experiences. But what could this measure be, which is reached only approximately in practice, but which has a presupposed objective meaning for the pessimist? It seems to me that such a measure could only be found if we could compare the totality of the world's experiences of suffering with the totality of the experiences of happiness, and if we could show mathematically how much of each reached the feeling individual. Only the individual whose hedonistic balance showed on an average less joy and more suffering would have paid too much. The average balance as an expression of the general hedonistic fate of the world would be neither negative nor positive, because it is the medium that allows us to measure the positivity or negativity of the individual's fate. If it were possible to measure the sums of happiness and suffering directly or through the use of a common denominator, then a different result would be possible. But inasmuch as we cannot do this, the measure for the individual case has to be derived from a factual totality. It would be as meaningless to call this measure large or small as it would be to call the average size of a human body big or little. The individual can be large or small, that is, greater or lesser than average, but the average itself is not subject to comparison because its very nature is to make possible the measurement of individual phenomena. Unless we know about other humans on other planets we cannot compare averages. Similarly, it is not possible to ascertain that the human being as such has more suffering than happiness, that he pays too high a price for happiness, or that there is no just proportion between positive and negative values. All such fundamental assertions of eudaemonistic pessimism presuppose the methodological error of trying to measure the measure and of applying a quantitative comparison to the general fate; such a comparison is justified only for the individual's hedonistic fate, insofar as in that case we have an empirical or instinctive representation of the general fate.

One must admit that the vast majority of human beings complain about an adverse balance between the measure of suffering and happiness, though this is obviously impossible to claim if the average provides the measure. And we have the feeling, not dampened by logical considerations, that the average man is cheated when he has to pay with the sufferings of life for the quantity of happiness in his life. But the measure used here does not meet rational criteria, because it represents an ideal and a wish, and not reality and the relation between totality and its constitutive elements. Even if a buyer has no right to demand more commodities for his money than permitted by the concrete market situation based on the average proportions of money and commodity quantities, he would, as a rule, be happier subjectively if he could make a cheaper purchase. If we do not run into tangible opposition, we are all inclined to extend our subjective desire for a favor into an objective demand for justice. The "general human being" has, in fact, more pains than joys, but this "more" is not revealed through a measure provided by the thing itself, but through the desire for more joy. The desire for human happiness transcends toward the infinite and, thus, no imaginable proportion between happiness and pain can be satisfying. Yet just such a proportion, transcending our actual portion of happiness, seems to be a realistic and justifiable demand, even if the quantity in question is still rather vague and problematic in our minds. The above exemplifies a typical psychological tendency. When suppressed classes cry out for general equality, they are only expressing the general human tendency to transcend a present level of having and being, and to reach a higher one. For those on a lower level of society, the next highest level is merely the first station on a journey leading toward the infinite; but as long as this station has not yet been reached and, thus, cannot serve as the vantage point for new vistas, it seems definitely to be a worthy destination and its attainment a requirement of objective justice. Once the next level has been achieved, it becomes a new base for the yearning of the individual to leave others behind: he awakens with the same power which led him to the previously unconquered level and to an equality with those who were once above him. The idealistic demand—that the human being has a right to have as much happiness as suffering and otherwise is cheated—is used by pessimism as a realistic argument. But this demand is really a consequence of the quest for equality, a crystallization of the desire for more happiness than is actually provided for people. In reality this desire cannot be satisfied, because the relation between happiness and suffering cannot be reasonably compromised. No quantity of suffering is acceptable to man and no quantity of happiness would satisfy him after a short period of adjustment. From the vantage point of desire, which led to the demand for balance, no balance would satisfy us; satisfaction would come only with the disappearance of both suffering and a life of absolute happiness.

The above critique shows that it is not logically tenable to draw a pessimistic conclusion from the position that happiness and suffering are unjustly distributed. Schopenhauer seems to have anticipated this problem and even to have responded to it by appealing to the previously mentioned psychological genesis of a hedonistic ideal of justice. Schopenhauer admits, when he is most radically pessimistic, that no proportion of happiness and suffering could be just and satisfying, because to achieve satisfaction, happiness would have to be absolute and not merely relative, and suffering would have to be altogether absent. He alludes to this problem in claiming that the fact of any suffering, rather than some quantity of negative value, makes the existence of the world contingent and gives an infinite advantage to nonbeing over being, because suffering as such has no compensation; no happiness of whatever intensity could make good any suffering. This sense of value, taken in its depth and absoluteness, can only be appreciated and not criticized, even though we realize that it is based on an absolute contradiction which produces a general perspective on life and world that is itself equally unassailable. The fact that there is something like happiness, that being has developed to this point, even if only as a flash of lightning in one consciousness, pushes the world up to a new level of values, the time-transcending importance of which could be lost and buried by any quantity of suffering. The mere possibility of happiness, even if its realization is sparse and fragmentary in actual life, englobes our existence in light. Schopenhauer believes that he can switch off that light by defining happiness as something purely negative, as the momentary ineffectiveness of suffering. This is the weakness in Schopenhauer's thinking, which bespeaks his inability to provide a firm basis for pessimism: he should not, despite his judgments and evaluations, have overlooked the positive moment of happiness which differentiates it as a psychological fact from sleep and death, the two other states that end suffering. His majestic justification of pessimism in terms of the fact of suffering, however, is not impaired by this discussion. There is nothing to mitigate a world in which there is suffering, regardless of any happiness that exists in this world or of its magnitude. It seems that certain souls have a degree of sensitivity to suffering that leaves the depth of value in their existence untouched by any appearance or measure of happiness, just as there are souls sensitive to achieving happiness so that stimuli of any other kind simply do not reach the deepest levels of their personalities. Great suffering can assail persons who are sensitive to positive value, but it is never the final moment of their destiny. Even if they are personally excluded from positive value, they experience serenity and happiness as the real meaning of life. Thus, life, for them, seems to be good, not just because of some mathematical balance between suffering and happiness, but because there is such a wonderful phenomenon as happiness, which is capable of awakening in them the resonance of the ultimate powers of life and grace. Schopenhauer's precise statement about the irrelevance of the quantity of suffering to the meaning of suffering might appear to be a paradox, but its insistent polarization reveals the real basis of pessimism, just as the same mode of evaluation can justify the purest form of optimism. Here we have in a certain sense a radicalization of the previous discussion. Happiness and suffering cannot directly be measured against each other, so the hedonistic value of life as a whole is beyond measurement: positive and negative value share no common denominator that could register their pluses and minuses. Only experienced life provides the measure for the hedonistic average of human existence and permits in an individual's fate a determination of "above" and "below," of "too much" or "not enough." Of course, happiness and suffering always remain foreign to each other and never close into unity. They become factors in a single balance of human existence only by virtue of being experienced by the same subject. Thus, the real distance between them is apparent. In the final analysis, then, the decision for optimism or pessimism seems to depend not on a quantitative comparison of positive and negative values, but on the pure fact that there is both happiness and suffering in the world. Certainly this decision is not based on a process of reflective experience in which impressions of two kinds are compared in terms of a real or an ideal measure. But even if Schopenhauer's idea may be considered crude and one-sided, it still reveals that beneath the surface, the stand for the value or for the lack of value of existence depends in resolute and principled natures on the specific reaction their innermost soul exhibits to happiness or suffering.

That the decision for optimism or pessimism is based, for some natures, on a specific reaction of the soul that transcends the empirical realm is shown by the peculiar fact that individuals who have been treated severely by fate often do not hesitate in taking an optimistic approach to life. One might speculate that if someone were inclined to be sensitive to happiness, he would react with bitterness and gloom to the sufferings that fate brought to him. But, in fact, natures that are disposed to happiness seem to experience their rare and humble joys as transcendent, and to discharge their potential for happiness so fully and with such brilliance that they see life illuminated and not in the shadows of everyday experience. Where a positive reaction to the causes of happiness is stronger than its contrary and where the soul is readily permeable to sensations of happiness, the more vivid and repeated stimulation of even distant provinces of consciousness by these causes creates in the soul a broad basis for optimism (or for pessimism in the opposite case) out of minimal opportunities that could not have been developed even by a plenitude of sensation in natures of a contrary type. It seems to me that repetition of stimulus, in this regard, is a secondary psychological factor disposing toward happiness or misfortune that is at least as important as the primary differences in stimulus perception. The preceding general discussion may be exemplified by specific contents and configurations. Often we experience the thoughts and destinies which make us suffer merely as incitements to the infinite potential for suffering that is, to some degree, innate in us. Thoughts and destinies could not elicit these pains were they not on call in some form within us. What is terribly frightening is that we sense on such occasions an immeasurable supply of pain that we carry within us as a closed container. It is dark and as yet unreal, but also somehow present already, and destiny gives us pieces of it, leaving a vast quantity in stock. Most of the time our container is at rest, but sometimes, when it is opened by a single pain or vibration, it begins to move imperceptibly and we sense the terrible treasure of potential suffering that is just as much ours as an organ, and is more horrible than any experience of real suffering we could undergo. And the security that our latent sufferings could never completely be actualized is of no solace, but, instead, is the most terrifying thing of all: even if we do not feel all of this pain we keep it in its entirety. And, perhaps, a single experience of happiness is also surrounded by a more general joy, a kind of astral body. Perhaps not only beauty, but every experience of happiness is truly a *promesse de bonheur*, the resonance of bells that have not yet been touched in our souls. Only from a distance and only with inadequate concepts can one indicate the background of happiness or suffering. But if there is a specific psychic form in which the complexity of emotional potential gains a mode of emotional reality while yet remaining potential, then it is evident how decisive is the individual predisposition toward either pole of the emotional scale—independent of the real occurrences in life—for the hedonistic resonance of life.

The very theme of the unity of the will of the world is as much the cope-stone in the edifice of pessimism as its metaphysical foundation. The same theme also establishes the connection between pessimism and the domination of will over life, for which Schopenhauer ceaselessly searches.

As long as the world is the way pessimism explains it and as long as that remains factually so, not only our needs for happiness and for a meaning to existence, but also our ethical feelings, must be in revolt. This becomes abundantly clear in view of the efforts of theology to explain God's mercy and wisdom in the face of evil in the world. Such attempts are always in vain, but are ever repeated. But as soon as existence is made completely and exclusively a phenomenon of will, it is fully justified as exactly the will's decision. Our sense of fair play and justice is satisfied in empirical circumstances if we can say that someone affirms his misfortunes, would not have wanted things otherwise. The same holds for the pains and absurdities of the world itself and, to state it in extreme form, even for the most horrible injustice: if the world is will, then this will is responsible for itself. The world is as it is because it wants things to be that way. There is a metaphysical will behind all phenomena, giving them their reality and comprising the motive force of all actions. This metaphysical will is absolutely free because it is dependent on and determined by nothing else. Just as in the domain of relativity the individual may be liberated from innumerable sufferings by ceasing to desire, so the absolute will could cease to desire the world and thereby abolish all of the pain and suffering that go along with it. Just as culpability is always willed, so willing is always culpable, not in a moralistic, but in an ultramoral sense: By its very existence willing is caught in the antithesis and unhappiness of its essence. Thus, the suffering of the world is an act of eternal justice, compared to which all empirical and singular retributions are only imperfect reflections strained through time. In the totality of the world, culpability and punishment are not temporally separate, because the will of the world has already posited all pain and suffering, all injustice, and all the tragedy of existence by the simple act of willing itself. Putting the matter paradoxically, it is not, in itself, meaningless and unjust that the world is meaningless and unjust, inasmuch as that is the logically inevitable expression of the will's nature. In this conceptual union all of the faults of the world and all of its sufferings balance each other, because they both express the same fact of the ultimate nature of the world as will. The freedom of this absolute will, in contrast to causally conditioned singular phenomena, renders existence culpable. The suffering of the world is the penitence for its existence. And that suffering can be neither greater nor smaller than its culpability, because suffering registers the unitary reality of the will in the language of the sentiments.

But the ethical sentiment cannot be content with this equation of culpability and suffering. Adding the aggregate of culpability and the aggregate of suffering into two sums is possible only through abstracting from the actual distribution of culpability and suffering, from the fact which indicates the most essential injustices of existence. Even if in the world as a whole or in its metaphysical meaning positive and negative values were equalized, it would still be possible that the culpable deed was done by one person and the consequent suffering was undergone by another, as in the case of the fraud and the defrauded, or of the egoist and his victim. Inasmuch as the possibility of such injustice is a consequence of the spatial separation of phenomena, it is necessarily grounded in the basic structure of the world as a totality and, thus, it cannot be neutralized by some abstract or metaphysical justice which, even if it gave meaning to the whole, could not confer it on the relations among its parts. As I showed above, Schopenhauer gains a meaning for the world by immensely accentuating the metaphysical unity of the will of the world; through its existence, the one who inflicts pain and the one who suffers it, the persecutor and the persecuted, are basically an undivided unity and are torn apart only by the spatial dissection of the world of phenomena. Separate individuals exist only in a realm of illusion constituted by our subjective forms of apperception, which are superimposed on the true nature of things. Thus, the question of the distribution of positive and negative values can only be raised for the world of representation; it is vacuous and meaningless in regard to what we really are, to the absolute unity of being. A cruel person who pursues his interests at the expense of others' sufferings, or who even takes delight in those sufferings, believes he can afford to do so because there is an absolute difference between himself and the others. But such individuation is deceptive and is known to be so in the most intimate spheres of human existence, though not in the concepts of reflection. The pain of conscience is the experience that gives us the fundamental knowledge that our being is not separated from the totality of being. Pangs of conscience are the inarticulate expressions made by insurmountably powerful inner forces that dominate the sentiments of one who does evil, making him feel that at the deepest root of his essence he is identical with those who suffer by his hand. Thus, anguish of conscience is the form in which the evildoer experiences the pain of his victim. As Schopenhauer said, then, the facial expression of evil people always seems to express inner pain.

Schopenhauer touched the core of the problem of a theory of the emotions when he introduced the metaphysical identity of torturer and tortured in a developmental view of the antagonism between individuals ranging from mere disregard of the other's pain to extremely cruel pleasure in it. But his assumption that a cruel person suffers from an indomitably strong will, the pain of which he tries to mitigate by making others suffer, is a grotesque utilization of the concept of "companionship in misfortune." This psychological deduction of cruelty seems to me to be a far-fetched banality. I think that the identity of a cruel person with one who suffers is immediate and is not merely the consequence of an act. The deepest mystery of the pleasure experienced through the pain of others lies in the fact that the cruel person must feel that pain himself in some way, because otherwise it could provoke no reaction in him. As an observer he can only take note of sounds and movements as clues to sensations, but he cannot feel the other person's pain. Is there any other way than through the intimations provided by our own emotional potential for interpreting the permanently inaccessible conscious events of other persons? Only our own feeling, even if it is deformed and inharmonious, can transform a distorted and crying automaton into a human being who feels pain and who, therefore, can be an object of pleasure for a cruel person. Psychology has not been very successful thus far in explaining the process by which a pain experienced by some subject is, through an external representation, transported into another person's consciousness and thereby transexperienced. But in whichever way and however plausibly psychology succeeded in explaining this affair, it would still not reach the metaphysical basis for its correlations and explanations, just as the descriptions and generalizations of chemical processes still leave open the questions of what the deep structure of matter really is and how it grounds factual phenomena and relations. The fact that it is possible to feel the feelings of another person and, thus, to feel them as belonging to oneself would point to the deep structure of the soul and the world even if psychology could analyze the operation of this process. Schopenhauer obviously felt the metaphysical mystery keenly when he advanced the idea that cruelty, the hallmark of divisive individuation, is bound to the identity of the world's basic structure. But he claimed that feeling the other's suffering is the just and instantaneous penitence for cruelty, when in reality it is already present in the cruel act itself and in the mysterious intermingling of the sentiments and emotions of two people. Though pleasure in the pain of others seems to constitute the distance between man and man in an extreme and unconditional way, it is actually only possible through abandoning that distance, thereby indicating the removal of the barrier between I and Thou, because such pleasure in the Other's pain is intimately connected to pleasure in our own pain. This paradox of the sentiments also has not yet been given adequate conceptualization by psychology. One could say that pleasure in pain resuscitates a polar tension of emotional potential and creates an unprecedented expansion of the "I," in that no other concurrence of emotions includes such oppositions. It is remarkable how much indecent arrogance is seduced by pain, both imagined and real. Few people hold with ease the opinion that nobody does as much as they do, but there are many who are arrogant enough to believe and to proclaim: "Nobody suffers as much as I do!" This sentiment of an overweening personality is able to transit to a pleasure in pain, the theme of which, in light of our remarks about its content and foundation is, in the first instance, pleasure in the power of making other persons one's property. Property allows our will to form itself without meeting resistance, and psychologically this formation of will is more effective the more it proceeds against the will or disposition of the possessed. Thus, pleasure in pain is a province of natures who are thirsty for power and self-expansion, but who cannot reach their goal by the positive exercise of power or by merit. The expansion of the ego would, therefore, seem to be the hidden goal of cruelty toward others and toward oneself, even though at first blush the two appear to be opposed to one another. In fact, pleasure in the pain of others and in one's own pain—sadism and masochism, as their pathological sexual extremes are respectively denominated—go hand in hand with each other in many people, though in innumerably different proportions. The theory that cruelty to oneself is a purely secondary phenomenon, an inward deflection of an errant misdirection of the original tendency of cruelty to others arising from legal or moral obstacles, seems erroneous to me. The case is, rather, just the opposite: pleasure in one's own pain is already a basic ingredient in cruelty to others, though in an obscure, latent, and unrecognizable form, because feeling the other's pain is the condition for its becoming the object of our con- sciousness and of our will. And even on an abstract level, the phenome- non of pessimism itself is constituted by these two intertwined drives. There is a sublime cruelty in the destruction of otherwise acknowledged values, in the passion that is the only means by which otherwise sub- liminal sufferings are made conscious, and in the valuation that our being does not deserve more and better than this life and world offer. But the general pessimistic attitude normally is not merely intertwined with subjective suffering, but is also accompanied by pleasure in it. The celebration of one's own pains, the lascivious fixation on every mis- ery, and the compulsion to exaggerate one's misfortunes, even to one- self, all appear in the form and against the backdrop of a pessimistic outlook on the world. The pleasure in one's own pain and in the pain of the other works here to create a uniform phenomenon. Thus, the ques- tion of metaphysical unity—in the depth of which the suffering of the "I" expresses solidarity with the suffering of the other, and which is unveiled by the reunification of phenomena that previously were di- ametrically opposed—can be legitimately raised again. Schopenhauer's doctrine of an eternal justice based on the identity of I and Thou is, therefore, of permanent importance because it is based on an unerring homing instinct.

But as an answer to the problem of the distribution of happiness and suffering, the concept of metaphysical unity—through which Schopenhauer makes the torturer a participant in the pains of his vic- tims—is wanting. The victim is also a participant in the culpability of the torturer, which is a paradox fraught with deep consequence. Not only are the mediations of practical and ethical shifts in balance be- tween suffering and happiness at stake, but so is the pessimistic posi- tion itself: Is the value of life, including the correlation happiness- misery, really dependent on the summation of positive and negative values, and, therefore, on the average hedonic fate of human beings? Schopenhauer has no trouble answering this question. His concept of metaphysical unity forestalls any demand for a distribution of hap- piness and suffering according to autonomous values, because it pre- cludes any individuation of the bearers of positive and negative values in the definitive realm of value. Schopenhauer's dogmatic limitations are evident here. The theme of unity is sufficient to make him fail to comprehend that there could be a specific and definitive value, independent of quanta and averages, regulating the greater or lesser realization of hedonic values among persons, or their distribution. He also cannot understand that, in a thoroughly objective sense indicative somehow of some ultimate, the existence of a plurality of people could be of greater or of lesser value, not only because the sum of their happiness might increase or decrease, but that it would do so according to a criterion governing the distribution of a fixed quantum. Such a criterion would not operate mechanically, but would be dependent on norms of justice, utility, and organization. Indeed, we are confronted here with two opposed convictions about value, which evince the complete incompatibility and impossibility of logical disproof that is characteristic of ultimate decisions. If happiness and suffering have a metaphysical importance beyond their phenomenal representations, then, logically, their form or mode of distribution among individuals can have just as much importance as can their quantities, over which optimism and pessimism contend. We presuppose here that individuality possesses absolute reality and significance, because if it did not the relations among the positions of individuals could not exemplify definitive values. Even when equality is made an ideal, the fundamental importance of individuals must be upheld, because if it is not, then the equality or inequality of their relative situations would become unimportant. Where a unity beyond all individuals is the bearer of all values and interests, only the hedonic summation into which all individuals are merged can be important. But where the differentiation of individuals is on the same fundamental plane as is their identity, the question of distribution supercedes that of quantity. Many followers of socialism are convinced that we cannot change the average quantities of happiness and misery, but they value the equal or just distribution of the hedonic totality. Fanatics who seek equality, justice, aristocratic order, or a hierarchical society would all accept even a reduction of the quantity of value in the whole of life if the distribution of the remainder would be regulated according to the system that each respectively deems to be solely able to bestow meaning on life. This paradox clearly shows how closely the accounting of human life, in terms of quantities of happiness and misery, is related to the metaphysical doctrine of unity. Once individuals are made definitive realities, the question of how much each one is happy or suffers as compared to the others gains supremacy over the question about the absolute quantity of values, because definitive individuals are not composed in a uniform subject, but exist as a whole only in the abstractive summation of an observer. Schopenhauer is not able to view individualities and their relations as initial and final factors, so he deems the phenomenal character of individuation to be more a consequent than a ground, thereby exhibiting a strange inflexibility in his thought that makes any idea of development or evolution foreign to him. I will undertake later to show how this intellectual sentiment impels him to define individual persons as living through absolutely immutable and given characters. The pessimism of the will rests on this inflexibility and this hypnotic obsession with the point of unity in all existence, because the absolute One cannot be redeemed by the progressive development of individuals. Here we also find the ground for the previously mentioned obscure fatalism governing the value of individual character, which does not permit change in the quality or direction of life, but only allows different reactions of the same hopelessly fixed unity of essence to variations in external circumstances. And, additionally, we find here the reason for valuing life according to the sum total of happiness and misery, which can only be the province of the metaphysical unity of being. Such a valuation must exclude those deep and autonomous values, which, regardless of their quantity, are exhibited in the distribution of the sum total and dependent upon the changing relations of the participating individuals rather than on the retention of a specific absolute quantity. The same element in Schopenhauer's spirituality that obscured the importance of the successive development of individuals, of which he had to be aware, also effaced the special significance of relations among individuals.

It seems paradoxical that inflexibility should be a characteristic trait of Schopenhauer's spirituality, in that he found the essence of the world to be continuous mobility. Mobility, for him, was not only an essential property of the world, but was the world's substance, and he went so far as to deny even an ideal point of rest for the world by negating any final goal for mobility, even in the infinite dimension. Perhaps his inflexibility was an inner compensation of his spiritual nature that protected him from his compassion for the unquenchable thirst and feverish movement of all being, a compassion for mobility without rest or aim that might have destroyed him. Certainly, it is the philosopher's nature to provide for but one of the multitude of the rivers of human nature, by turning its fragmentary, interrupted, and deflected course into a pure, straight, and unobstructed flow toward the infinite. He labors under a one-sided presupposition, which, however, transcends the rudimentary character of empirical life. It is one of the most difficult but necessary tasks of a psychological and object-oriented analysis to find where this philosophical one-sidedness, which presses the totality of the world into one form, does not live up to its promise and must be supplemented by the nearly subterranean efficacy of its opposite. The logical contradictions of the philosophers are often nothing but the intellectual phenomena that represent such deep-seated complications of the soul. Every one-sided and differentiated development and activity of the individual reaches the limits of its independence in the fact that the power supporting and generating it comes from the total organism. But a certain degree of one-sidedness eventually alters the normal functioning of the totality, which is based on an equilibrium of energies, to such an extent that the organism can no longer produce the power necessary to maintain the one-sidedness. Thus, every highly differentiated exteriorization of life needs, for its own sake, parsimony and mediation. Even when each thinker plays the symphony of the world radically and enthusiastically in the key of his characteristic emotion, some tunes from another quarter of the soul suddenly intrude. They give a hint of the typical basis of even the most differentiated intellectual character, which represents not only its carefully nourished special tendency, but also, at least to some degree and with some similitude, the oppositions and mediations of humanity.

5
The Metaphysics of Art

HE MODERN THEORY OF EVOLUTION TENDS TO IN-
corporate the different functions of the soul, each of which
seems to lead a life of its own, into the total process of life.
The contents or results of aesthetic or intellectual or practical or religious activities do, indeed, delimit separate
fields that are characterized by their own laws and are expressed in their
own languages. But the sovereignty of such a separate world only extends to a content that is independent of experience. The picture of life
in which each of the diverse streams runs separately from the others is a
consequence of thinking about contents independently and abstractly,
and of cutting them off from the real energies of the soul's life. Thus,
the subsumption of contents under a uniform hierarchical system such
as evolution provides is an indisputable improvement. The progress
made by evolutionary ideas is unfortunately blunted by orienting the
inclusive teleology exclusively toward the most primitive and superficial necessities of life, such as the struggle for physical survival, the
care of biological life, the procreation of the species, and economic opportunities, all of which have been accepted as goals established for us
by "nature itself," to which moral, spiritual, and aesthetic activities are
taken to be the means. But psychological fact reveals a different picture, in which unity is created by reciprocal causality. For example, the
intellectual and economic functions serve one another, and the erotic
and aesthetic desires exploit one another's potentials. The worlds of content are strangers to each other as long as they are understood only in
terms of their forms or ideas, but life experience shows that they are
interrelated as end and means to one another, and that they coalesce
into a unity of life. The functional unity of reciprocal relations can be

expressed in a crystallized and quasi-substantial concept similar to that of the "state," which expresses the political reciprocity of its elements, but which is also conceived as something beyond its component individuals that causes their relations. Nietzsche's concept of life reveals such a subsumption of inner processes under a single general purpose that coordinates every individual. Thus, Nietzsche regards life as an absolute value, the essentially important thing in the manifestation of existence. The pure and indissoluble concept of life includes all of our enumerable individual functions: will, as well as thinking and feeling, are only means to the increase of life. With regard to the structure of metaphysical thinking, it is noteworthy that Schopenhauer exalts the will to absolute importance and interprets life as a revelation of will and a means to its self-expression and identity, whereas Nietzsche views will as an organ and instrument of the life process. According to Nietzsche we will because we live, whereas for Schopenhauer we live because we will. For both thinkers, however, the intellectual functions are made subordinate to the positive predications. Our acceptance of truth is a consequence of the practical impulses of life and will, and is independent of the ideal value of truth as autonomous science. Thus the contents of intelligence are filled with blood and warmth. Indeed, in the process of their subjection to will these contents lose their independence and their proper value, and are made to prescribe specific objectives for the underlying will-form of our existence, which shapes itself into individual beings in a ceaseless circular process of task and urge, and of touch and letting go.

Schopenhauer, however, also teaches that the intellect has the potential to free itself, at least intermittently, from bondage to will. Intellect for him is not logical and constructive thinking alone, but the sphere of consciousness in which the real image of the world is formed. He takes for granted without elucidation that we are able to immerse ourselves in the observation, or even in the imagination of an object, sufficiently to still completely all of the movements that are specific to us and that express the hidden or open impulses of will. In such moments of absolute contemplation we are filled so totally by the image of a thing that our normal and painful condition of will, in which the "I" and its object are opposed and are divided from each other by unbridgeable chasms of space and time, is cancelled. If we deliver ourselves to the contemplation of a phenomenon, we do not feel an "I" separated from its content any longer, but are lost in the content of the phenomenon. Thus, in contemplation both egoism and the urge to possess disappear, the first because the "I" who is its bearer has disappeared, and the second because perfect contemplation provides all that we could want or wish of a thing. Happiness and unhappiness are attributes of the will remaining beyond the limits of pure contemplation, for which things exist only as imagination and not as stimuli of our desire.

The core of an aesthetic constitution is the total separation in ourselves of the world of imagination from the world of will which is ordinarily the medium, impulse, and lifeblood of imagination. In pure contemplation the existence of things in our intellect, which is otherwise subservient to the ends of life, cuts its link to will and becomes a pure picture in its own space, absorbing the "I" into the imagination and leaving it without any special existence. The radical conversion of the inner man through pure contemplation is an aesthetic salvation that occurs when we are filled by the pure and imaginative content of any object that has been freed from bondage to an interest of will. We call beautiful only those objects that make it easier for us to engage in a contemplation that has been freed from its roots in our will: a work of art is an object that necessitates contemplation, and an artistic genius is a man who is more perfectly and inclusively able to free himself from domination by the will than are others. The content of imagination, which abstracts from desire and practicality, and includes things and fancies, congeals into the new existence of art, which, as Schopenhauer wonderfully expresses it, finds its end everywhere. The importance of art for Schopenhauer's metaphysics is that in its existence between creative genius and individual receptivity, art is both effect and cause of the emancipation of pure intellect from will.

I have already indicated that the first change wrought by art within the subject is that individuality and the special situation of man within space and time becomes unimportant. The aesthetic dimension of a sunset, for example, is the same, regardless of whether it is seen from the window of a jail or of a palace. Thus, the eye that enjoys a picture and the ear that is attuned to the tones of music dwell in a kingdom in which it does not matter whether the eye or ear belongs to a monarch or to a beggar. Indeed, nothing whatever matters about the man who is seeing or hearing an aesthetic object; neither qualities nor those relations specifying a particular role within the chain of time, space, causality, and society need be taken into account. The contemplative man is removed from the network that makes him a part or a point of transition in a senseless and endless chain pushed forward by will. The relations that affect the individual because he lives in reciprocity with other individuals are all removed. Schopenhauer makes the beautiful observation that the same action which is regarded as sexual love— when it is carried out and instigated by will—becomes, when its imaginative aspect is stressed, separate from the will and a purely objective appreciation of the aesthetic value of the human figure. Will and contemplation are the two deeply interrelated destinies of man. Contemplation of a work of art, which is a specific imagination, is the fullest expression of the contemplative destiny, requiring sheer observation and deliverance to the image of the object. Aesthetic contemplation must abstract from one's destiny as a single and chance individual and must sever relations to the real world that are exterior to the momentary view, and become cause and effect simultaneously. The momentary character of aesthetic imagination does not prohibit it from being basically beyond time, because the temporal relation, which fixes each moment between preceding and succeeding moments, is alien to pure content. Aesthetic elevation is independent of a now or then, and of a here or a there.

All of the above discussion refers primarily to psychological events. It gains importance for a metaphysical world-view only through the specificity of the aesthetic object of subjective observation and through a response to the question of what aspect of an object is observed aesthetically and what differentiates aesthetic observation from observation within a normal, practical-empirical context. In regard to the above question the decisive motif of Schopenhauer's thought is revealed as the redemption from individuality and from the determination of the moving elements of life by spatial, temporal, and causal relations. The redemption won by aesthetic contemplation lifts the object from its entanglement with the environment, because the environment is excluded from aesthetic vision. The release of the object from its relativity simultaneously cancels individuality, because the latter can only be posited on the basis of elements external to itself. Schopenhauer, who follows Plato in this respect, calls that which is left over after the environment has been excluded the "idea of a thing." The precise object of art, to which we will limit our following discussion, and the ex-

emplification of this enhanced phenomenon constitute the central difficulty of Schopenhauer's theory.

All individual things, which exist within spatio-temporal reality,
have in addition to the causal and other relations that link them, a completely heterogeneous relation. We often experience innumerable individual phenomena only as examples of general ideas that are not affected by fluctuations in and frequency of their appearance and by their
position, and that hold fast to an ulterior reality which cannot be presented in its full and lucid purity by an individual reality. The general
idea is most evident in, though not restricted by, reference to organisms, which evince a potential for change and development that indicates in a special way that they tend toward actualizing a more perfect
form which is already prefigured ideally in them. The anticipation of
perfected form is not merely the "general concept" of a thing, which is
derived from a summation of individual phenomena and is perhaps
adorned by traits taken from the ideal or primary idea. The primary
idea of a thing is actualized in us in a very special vision that is
not exhausted by the singular, and the meaning of which is not even
touched by that singular. Indeed, the ideal shines through any of its
contingent realizations, regardless of when or how frequently they
occur, as an original totality or as a reflection. Any observed object is
not only an existent that is immediately accessible to our senses, but is
also an idea providing sense and meaning, even when the existent only
more-or-less approximates that idea. Thus, we see in the object not
merely individuality, but something transindividual that is shared by
an infinite number of individual things dispersed through space and
time, hidden in differentiated shapes as their self-identical and unitary
ideal form, and unlike a logical generality created by posterior abstraction, visible immediately to the eye that looks for it. These are, then,
objects of imagination that correspond formally to the subjects of
aesthetic imagination. When we view the object under its aspect of
"idea," which constitutes its innermost essence and its unattainable
ideal, we strip it of its individuation and remove it from its spatio-
temporal relativity and from its entanglement in physical being, just as
we are deindividuated from an aesthetic standpoint. The "idea," which
Schopenhauer concludes is the object of our "aesthetic vision," is something general that is vaguely visible behind the singular thing. We observe it in the singular thing, but its essence is completely indifferent

to specific configurations. On the aesthetic plane we see the general idea in an individual thing, whereas on the cognitive level we are able to think only in terms of logical generalities or concepts. In an object of art the ideal nucleus, which is identified in every object by aesthetic observation, is crystallized in an embodiment without any alien parts. The artistic genius entertains the object, which then reemerges displaying only its ideal value, and becomes more tangible and intelligible to all other subjects. According to Schopenhauer, the object of art is to the spirit as meat—which contains assimilated vegetables—is to the body. An aesthetic vision filled with content requires that the same determinants concur in both subject and object. Although these determinants in each case appear to be opposed to one another, their coincidence is decisive just because they seem to be mutually exclusive. Men and things are capable of varying from their pure and self-expressive essence, which is revealed in aesthetic vision and is free from natural and historical correlations. The pure individuality of both men and things, it seems, depends on isolation of the individual from the current of existence, which otherwise carries away both subject and object. In such isolation the pure individual can be unmistakably identified and has a destiny that depends solely on itself. Yet in his description of the shift from ordinary cognition to aesthetic vision, Schopenhauer destroys individuality by transmuting singular into general essence and creating something typical, generic, and representative of innumerable individual essences, each of which in reality can exist only now and never again. The aesthetic observer and his object are consumed simultaneously by the utmost degree of being-for-itself and by the absolute rejection of such being. The radical truth of the above antinomy can be experienced in any moment of perfect aesthetic delight.

Schopenhauer limits his discussion of the problem of singularity and generality to the object, eliminating the contradiction by creating a special metaphysical category. His vision of the world as explained up to now contains the two elements of the metaphysical unity of will, which are the absoluteness of being, and individual phenomena formed by our consciousness and ranged causally in space and time. Within his fundamental opposition there is no room for the fact that individual phenomena form groups with basically identical contents which allow them to be aggregated intellectually under concepts and lead to their individuality becoming deeply and almost necessarily an example of these "ideas." Nature provides the impression that there are a certain number of basic forms or ideas of creation that are the types for the innumerable phenomena which appear and disappear according to the laws of nature. The metaphysical will, which is the basis of existence, works with these seemingly pregiven schematic or principal potentialities when it forms the individual realities of things. If one grants that the world will is objectified, then the steps of this objectification are, to use Schopenhauer's expression, the typical ideal forms in which the individuals are brought together. Thus, the forms are provinces of a spiritual kingdom, each of which is characterized in its own way and is populated by innumerable individual essences that express the basic character of their type, more or less obviously and purely. The stages of the will's objectification form an ascending chain that reaches from materiality and gravity (the lowest mode of the will that can be expressed in a language appropriate to phenomena), through all the special classes of matter and form in nature, up to the human species. Schopenhauer's philosophy, however, lacks the idea of evolution and so his chain has no effect. In addition, the human species is so variegated that it is scarcely possible to subsume the totalities of more than one human being under a single idea: an idea that is destined to realize one individual personality can be fulfilled strictly only by this singular.

Thus, ideas are a medium between transcendental will and empirical objects, a third kingdom that Schopenhauer, whose strength unfortunately is not epistemological clarity, does not define in terms of its degree of reality. Perhaps in some degree the spiritual locus of the ideas can be determined by recurring to Plato. The Platonic doctrine of ideas began with Socrates' discovery that truth cannot be found in fleeting, untrustworthy, and sensual concepts of things which change from subject to subject, because truth must be permanent and objectively valid. Thus, truth must reside in rational concepts that are constant and that can always be recovered. Based on the above, Plato concludes that the truth of imagining requires that image and object be coincident. However, the object of a concept cannot be the sensually perceivable singular thing, because the properties of the singular are at variance with those of the concept (as was noted above) and thus are not fit to serve as a point of reference. In consequence, the object of a concept cannot be sensual and must be removed from the contingencies of individual existence so that it can supercede things by its changeless validity, just as a concept supercedes the mere apperception of things. Plato calls the superceding object the idea. Thus, an idea is originally not a metaphysical essence that becomes the object of our concepts, but is the result of the presupposition that a concept, because it is true, must have an object which bestows on it the dignity of truth by identity with it. The idea of a tree or of beauty is transformed into a metaphysical reality because the real recognition of the respective essence is made to depend on the general concept of tree or of beauty rather than on sensual imagination, and because that general concept requires a presupposed object to legitimate its truth. Just as Plato sought an object for the concept, Schopenhauer needs an object for aesthetic vision. Schopenhauer quite correctly felt that we behave differently when we approach an object aesthetically than when we approach it scientifically or practically. For him the incomparable essence of the aesthetic object is that it both retains an absolute being-for-itself—which is removed from all the entanglements, composition, and conditions that affect the specific life of things—and reaches beyond individuality and, in particular, beyond the importance of being typical for the individual. Through its dominant and norm-giving status, the idea includes a multitude of individuals within a special dimension in which there is no juxtaposition, succession, or causality. Schopenhauer's notion of the idea of a thing can be grasped by the process through which a vision presents itself as outwardly real in the aesthetic dimension and then gains its independence in a work of art. The idea is the type living as vision. It refers to the level of form on which reality, following the laws of spatio-temporal occurrences, casts the infinity of creatures. When considered formally, the object—which includes the content of aesthetic vision and the product of artistic creation—is, strictly speaking, unique and exists for itself alone, indifferent to anything alongside it or to anything that precedes or succeeds it in time. It is conceivable that in the hierarchy of ideas there are unlimited stages which provide infinite possibilities for artistic exposition, but each stage could exist only once and would be wholly original. Individual real things, however, exist as an infinite multiplicity in relations of spatial juxtaposition and temporal succession, even when they have been struck from the same mold. Thus, their essential form is on the level of will's objectification. The metaphysical construction of stages and levels on which will takes on visible forms is Schopenhauer's response to the need for an aesthetic construct combining

self-comprehending unity and uniqueness with superindividual validity and norm-giving power over a universe of singulars. Thus, the ideal
content and meaning of each level exists, in one respect, uniquely and
in perfect independence, but in another respect, in each one of the multitude of forms through which these levels are realized by nature. In the
domain of multiplicity, the creating or appreciating aesthetic vision sees
the original through its imperfectly realized representation.

If we consider the dimension of time in drama and the novel, and the
dimension of space in the visual arts, it might seem totally inconceiv-
able that the idea, the object of aesthetic vision, is neither temporal nor
spatial. With regard to the nonspatial character of the aesthetic dimension, Schopenhauer asserts: "The idea is not the form in space in front of
me, but the expression, the pure meaning, and the innermost essence of
that form. The idea, then, can be identical despite differences in a figure's spatial dimensions." Although Schopenhauer often anticipates a
modern interpretation of art (the understanding of art in a purely artistic way), his discussion of the idea places his thought at a distance from
that interpretation through both the influence of Goethe's classicism
and an intellectualist approach to the idea that lingers in his thought
despite his clarity concerning the opposition of concept and idea. A
purely artistic understanding of art would, indeed, permit an additional metaphysical exposition, but it would allow neither for interference in the immanent aesthetic cohesion nor for intrusion into the
natural sciences. But the issue between Schopenhauer and ourselves depends upon a finer distinction. We can accept that space is an essential
content of a picture, even if this picture is removed from spatial determination. Space is within such a work of art, but the work of art is not
within space. The colored canvas and the piece of marble, indeed, are
within space. But the space that is represented in the picture and the
spatial configuration of a figure that is the content of the object of plas-
tic art are not real space and are not determined by the limits that contain and restrict the canvas and the marble as pieces of matter in real
space. A similar analysis may be applied to the concept of time. The
time in which a drama evolves is purely ideal and, thus, does not contradict the fact that it is completely heterogeneous to time as a form of
real experience. The space and time in which we live surround each
thing and each destiny, individuating existents by creating external
limits. The emphasis on pure content in a work of art places that work

beyond the point at which it still could be limited by other content. Space and time, as they appear in the work of art, are not limited by other spaces and other times, because each work of art forms a world of its very own. Thus, from the standpoint of reality, the work of art is completely outside space and time, though it eventually includes spatio-temporal determinants. Yet, for Schopenhauer, the above determinants exist like all of the others within the sphere of ideas. Schopenhauer's failure to distinguish between the space within a work of art, which is an element of its idea, and the circumambient space, which does not touch the work itself at all, involves him in the hopeless task of a hermeneutic that aims at eliminating as an irrelevent factor space from the work of art.

In order to heal the discrepancy between Schopenhauer's theory of art and a modern interpretation, it is merely necessary to extend his principle gradually to give time and space a meaning in the ideal world that is different from their meaning in actual existence. But there is a far deeper discrepancy concerning the general object of art. Schopenhauer quite definitely rejects the positions that we today call naturalism and impressionism. In brief, he argues that no imitation of reality has any relation to art, because imitation could only provide us with what we already have and not with the redemption and deliverance to another world that are the distinctive creations of art. Also, a mere composition of natural elements derived from a multitude of individual phenomena that exist in reality is as insufficient to represent the object of art as is a specific part of nature that has been severed from the totality. Aesthetic empiricism could not explain its own presupposition of a criterion governing the selection from the individual phenomena of nature of those elements that make up the work of art. The essence of art, therefore, could not be discovered on the pathways of naturalism and empiricism, because art does not receive and transmit something that is given. Art lives by an idea that transcends mere data and that activates deeper levels of our existence than receptivity and experience.

However, the mere rejection of art as subservient to reality does not establish the autonomy of art that is typical for modern interpretations. The problem of the dependence of art is, perhaps, at least as severe with regard to art's relation to the preexistent ideal levels created by the objectification of will. Nobody more than Schopenhauer rejects speaking of art in terms of its utility. Yet for him the attraction and importance of art turn out to be its "use" in interpreting the idea. As long as we remain within the realm of pure aesthetics, "idea" can be merely one of the names for the object of art. But within the metaphysical network of Schopenhauer's interpretation of the world, the "idea" is an independent reality, the presentation of which becomes the function of art. If Schopenhauer were to be consistent he would have to declare art to be superfluous, insofar as mankind had more adequate forms to express the idea. Even if we grant that art cannot be thought of except in terms of an ideal content, the value and meaning of art in modern experience is independent of the value and meaning of the content itself, and concerns the specific way in which art forms its content. Perhaps the object of art is similar to the human body, the attraction of which would be diminished or at least quite different were it not the bearer of a soul, but the configuration of which would retain its value even if the soul could express itself in other and far more adequate forms. It is, indeed, difficult to vindicate the special right of one of two elements that are absolutely united in reality, especially when that right can only be exercised with the cooperation of the other element. It remains the merit of the formula *l'art pour l'art* that it directs us to the unique importance of the form of art itself, regardless of historical, psychological, metaphysical, or other meanings. Subjectively, indeed, there is some reason to postulate *l'art pour le sentiment*, whereas objectively it is intelligible to speak of *l'art pour l'idée*. But the formula *l'art pour l'art* indicates a third domain, in which art's own kingdom is established on the same footing as the kingdoms of cognition, religion, and morals, even if the kingdom of art only appears in relation to values outside its specific realm. The idea has a metaphysical reality regardless of aesthetic parameters and artistic realization. If the value of art is based exclusively on the idea expressed in it—which means that the degree of perfection of the aesthetic object is fully proportionate to the purity and perfection of the idea's expression—then art is just an indifferent tool of the idea, and the separation of art's special meaning from all other meanings has not been accomplished. Schopenhauer's identification of form and essence does not establish a special meaning for art, because matter is radically singular and exists only once, whereas form serves an infinity of essences and still remains self-identical. Even if the artistically indifferent materiality of things is left aside, the constitution of art requires content as well as form. Thus, if in the production of art materiality is stripped away from what appears in human experience, the remainder is a form of mere reality which must then be transformed by specific art forms such as painting, sculpture, or some other mode of stylization. The liberation of the real from materiality provides the work of art with a form which turns out to be a content of the work itself and of the forces that shape it. And now we may pose the decisive question: Is the meaning and value of a work of art constituted by the presentation of *this* content or by *this* presentation of the content? Does the innermost meaning of the transformation of the content of reality into a work of art reside in the degree of success with which an intrinsically interesting content is presented, or is that meaning bound up with an interest in the transformation of the content itself, thereby vindicating the existence of art without having to appeal to any specific content? Schopenhauer did not explicitly raise the above question, but he did provide an answer to it nonetheless: The *raison d'être* of the work of art is its content or idea, and everything else relating to what might be called the functional aspect of art, including style, technical methods, expression of artistic individuality, and the solution of problems specific to the particular work, is only interesting in terms of the idea that constitutes the content of the specific work. I will cite one of his statements in order to show to what degree his viewpoint contradicts any purely artistic interpretation of art. He states that the proper goal of painting is the conception of ideas and our spiritual translation into cognition devoid of will. Yet he also says that "there is an independent beauty that exists in itself by virtue of the mere harmony of colors, auspicious light and shadow, pleasant grouping of figures, and the tenor of the entire picture." This subjugated mode of beauty aids pure cognition and is to painting what diction, meter, and rhyme are to poetry: it is not essential but it provides a starting point. Unfortunately there is no longer any doubt that Schopenhauer has proclaimed that perhaps the most substantial part of the pure form of art, which supposedly follows only its own inner laws, is merely a crutch for subjectivity. In contrast, if art is really considered as art, as an intrinsic goal, and as a specific configuration of the elements of existence, then all of the "subjugated" elements identified above have objective value. They are not merely pacemakers, but congeal with less sensual elements into the absolute unity of artistic structure. Thus, Schopenhauer at first battles vehemently and victoriously for the independence of art from the immediacy of experience and from all content that can be expressed conceptually, but then he forces art to become a mere servant of a metaphysically significant content.

In order to unite the divergent interpretations of art as autonomous and of art as a servant of metaphysical content without changing their opposite directions, we must recur to a motive that is present in Schopenhauer's thought but that his pessimism did not allow him to bring to full fruition. There is, perhaps, a reconciliation between the purely inner artistic norms of a work of art and the capability of that work to bring forth a world-content. One might only have to follow the immanent laws of a purely artistic interest, relieved from other concerns and distractions, in order to reveal ultimately and perfectly the nonvisible meaning of a represented content. It is possible, indeed, that the artistic and metaphysical intentions meet once a certain degree of fulfillment has been achieved, and that neither must be forced to relinquish its own direction. The basic problems of the different arts are similar with regard to the fusion of the artistic and metaphysical intentions. For example, the goal of portraiture is to create an artistically valuable whole by depicting the model authentically, but it also seems to be purely accidental if the model's reality permits the inner requirements of the painting to be satisfied. Similarly, the poem has the double requirement of presenting the meaning, shape, and emotional value of a content through the independent stimuli of form and sound. Architecture, finally, must transform the inner relations of materials—such as mass and flexibility, tension and rigidity, and organic structure and endurance—into inward experience and tranquil harmony through qualities that are pleasing in their own right, such as surfaces, geometrical structures, and distributions of light and color. The deepest happiness created by art resides in the surprising and even unmerited harmony of values that are unrelated to each other in our normal experience of the world. Whereas in immediate existence the various orders of value are sometimes interconnected harmoniously and sometimes dissonant, the artistic viewpoint is the only one that provides the insight and gives the guarantee that these orders are bound together radically and necessarily. Schopenhauer could not assent to the great importance of art for emotion, because his radical pessimism conflicted with the moment of positive and synthetic happiness in the aesthetic emotion. Emotion finds the deepest meaning of art by uniting artistic value and value based on content. But, for Schopenhauer, the happiness

that stems from art must, like all other happiness, be understood negatively as nothing more than liberation from will and its pain. Therefore,
the meaning of art can only be for him mere concentration of interest in
the world as pure imagination, and mere flight into the only world that is
untouched by the reality of will and pain. The only happiness art provides by replacing the world of will and by allowing us to turn away from
will and pain is negation through which we become free of pain. Thus, it
is obvious that Schopenhauer cannot attribute to art any basic and synthetic theme that could effectuate a positive happiness independent of
the negation of will. If happiness is thought to consist merely in not
willing, then the mere fact that in aesthetic experience we are filled with
the content of things rather than having their existence engage our will is
sufficient to bring happiness. Thus, pessimistic absolutism has adulter-
ated the significance of emotion for the will and has hidden the eudaemonistic value of approaching a conclusive goal. Schopenhauer has
concealed the specific meaning of art, which lies in the development of a
eudaemonistic value beyond the silence of will.

It would not, however, be justified to claim that Schopenhauer's aesthetic is some sort of intellectualism, although it is based subjectively
upon the sovereignty of imaginative consciousness, and objectively upon
the content of pure ideas exemplified in things. His conception of art,
which is the most ambiguous element in an otherwise unambiguous
philosophy, allows for an alternative interpretation in which art is not
degraded to the status of a tool for the expression of the idea, which in
itself is deemed the only valuable and interesting thing. The alternative
thesis is that the essential happiness involved in art lies not only in expressing ideas, but in the *expression* of ideas. The above two themes are
correlated in Schopenhauer's thought. Schopenhauer mainly seems to
hold that the only important thing is bringing ideas to consciousness,
regardless of how that is accomplished. But he also indicates that bringing ideas to consciousness in sensual matter and in singular phenomena
is important for its own sake. He might have to admit that the idea is
not in itself "beautiful," but that beauty is what, with varying degrees
of success, makes the idea visible clearly and perfectly, and allows us to
accept it with certitude. We would then call ugly or unartistic a being
or a work of art, the apparent phenomenality of which would not allow
a clear vision of the idea or of the level we suppose should be exemplified in the phenomenon. The negative case of ugliness could possibly

provide a key for interpreting the aesthetic we are now discussing. The fact that the mere nonexistence of an idea cannot be ugly shows that beauty, which is sensual form, is not part of the idea, but is rather an indifferent vehicle for its expression. The ugly object is something sensual that is devoid of an idea, or, to put it more strictly, is something sensual that makes it more difficult to realize the idea that is alive in it, in contrast to the beautiful object that facilitates such realization in accordance with the structure of the particular thing and the structure of our soul. On the face of it, any object should be as beautiful as any other, because all objects are exemplars of ideas. Thus, an intellect directed to the objective structure of things would presumably have neither need nor room for art. However, our human spirit has an imperfect, haphazard, and variable relation to ideas, and beauty is relevant to the degree to which phenomena display their ideas to a specific spirit. An absolute spirit for which everything was equally beautiful would obviously find nothing beautiful, because beauty cannot be experienced and no longer has meaning if it is attached to every point in existence in exactly the same degree. The fact that some animals always appear to be ugly to us does not mean that they are objectively devoid of an idea, but rather that by unavoidable association they impose upon us their similarity to other configurations. For example, the associations of ape to man and of toad to dirt and slime hinder us from accepting purely their ideal essence. Thus, Schopenhauer's statement that art only serves to make ideas manifest can be easily misunderstood, because it is incomplete. Indeed, if the statement were complete, the specified goal would be illusory. If the ideas of all things were equally and completely accessible, which would imply that all things were beautiful, then there would be no differences among aesthetic values and, therefore, no aesthetic values at all. If there are aesthetic values, however, art must contain something that opposes the pure idea, that is other than the idea. In art, that which is other than idea is the material specificity through which the idea is expressed. The idea, then, is important to art in the same manner that the emotional make-up of a man is significant for sexual love, which originates in emotion. Love might take all of its warmth, meaning, and substance from sympathy for a soul, and it might be a reaction to the existence of a certain soul that brings mystery, salvation, and happiness, but love would still not exist, or at least it would not exist in the same way, if the soul were not connected to a body. A body in itself, indeed, might exhibit no erotic attractiveness whatever, diffract and shadow the pure light of the soul, and even appear to be an obstacle to be overcome by the soul in pursuit of the satisfaction of its innermost need. Yet the soul seems to develop its special capacity to be loved only through its demeaning embodiment that creates a veil through which an epiphany never fully bursts. Perhaps we are now discussing a very general sort of human behavior: an interest in an object is exclusively directed at a specific part of or something specially important in it, but that interest would never have arisen had the part in question been considered in isolation. The interest always is directed to the whole object in which a particular value is expressed through its interpenetration and mixture with matter and reality, which of themselves do not exert attraction. Thus, it is not contradictory to say that art borrows its meaning and value from ideas that are visible in phenomena (a phenomenon whose matter we can touch is alien to the idea), yet that the value of art is not attached to ideas but only to singular phenomena that are permeated by ideas. Thus, the category of the beautiful in art is shown to be original and not reducible to components. Once the idea and the phenomenon are separated from one another, neither one of them retains aesthetic value, because the idea can only give and never can have value.

It is important to formulate Schopenhauer's principle in the above manner, because it is an example of purely metaphysical thinking. We do not speak here of a real description or psychological analysis of art, but of an interpretation consistent with any other specific or corrigible mode of thought: the category that comprehends metaphysics can never clash with reality, psychological processes, or the validity of physical laws. It is sometimes said that metaphysics is art because its constructions are derived from the elements of given existence, but express the spontaneous requirements of a strictly ideal urge that is alien to reality, rather than measuring up to existence. The above claim is true, but in a strictly negative sense. Although art is similar to metaphysics, in that it is situated on a level that does not involve analyzing and measuring an object, the levels of art and of metaphysics are not the same. Our soul is not so lacking in categories that every nonscientific image of things must be an artistic image. Metaphysics is a reaction of an individualized intellect to the totality of life and, similarly to art, certainly can be expressed in terms of specific problems. But the metaphysical reaction will be expressed only in the form of very general concepts, because it is directed to the whole of things. One of the main attractions of all significant systems of philosophy is precisely the tension that they keep between the coolly conceptualized and sublimated abstractions, and the feelings, which these abstractions structure, of personal sensibility, the relation of the soul to the basis of things, and the relative worth of reality and irreality. Both exact science and art combine the same elements from experience that constitute metaphysics, but science stresses abstraction and generality at the expense of individuality, and art emphasizes individuality at the expense of abstraction and generality. Only metaphysics attempts to express an individual, though not a subjective, feeling in conceptual abstractions. Hence, we find such metaphysical constructions as the reduction of all existence to matter and form; the ordering of all phenomena in an ideal chain reaching from matter devoid of form at one end to pure form devoid of matter at the other; the image of an absolute inner unity of the world that reduces the contradictory dualism of space and imagination to two languages expressing the same integrity; and the idea that it should be possible, in that the same world spirit is alive within us and in the things external to us, to exemplify the content of the world factually and historically through the logical development of concepts. The interpretation of art, as we have noted, belongs to the province of metaphysics. Thus, the value of art lies exclusively in the transtemporal creative types or ideas it reveals. The idea, however, only gains the aesthetic value it lacks in itself by being exemplified in a singular, visible, and substantive existence, which is heterogeneous to ideal essence. The above description of art is from the metaphysician's standpoint, not from the viewpoint of the artist or of the appreciator of art. Metaphysics only provides one aspect of the answer that a soul with a specific orientation and sensibility might give when confronted with the total impact of existence. In employing the concept of a general world-view, such a soul expresses the meaning and value of the special way in which being becomes phenomenal for it.

All of the themes of the philosophy of art under consideration here reach their culmination in the problems of music. Musical works are different from the objects of other arts, which only express essential ideas, because they do not represent singular things. Objects of the arts other than music retain, through their relation to essential ideas, a singular character, because the idea, which is shaped by form and essence into an infinite number of phenomena, is always itself something singular in contrast to the unity of being. In the human intellect the uniform ray of being is diffracted into a boundless plethora of levels of representations. Hence, although in relation to particular phenomena every poem, every painting, and every drama is not merely a delimitation of appearance, but possesses a generality through the forms of imagination that frees it from the singularity of the here and now, when it is viewed from above, such an art object is a singular realization of just one mode of the expression of metaphysical independence. But in music we immediately feel closer to absolute generality and feel greater redemption from specificity, which encumbers reproductions of the unity of will that are mediated by singular ideas, such as the meanings of words, spatial forms, and depictions of events that characterize the other arts. Music, however, does not represent the inner absoluteness of life in a special form, but transcends ideas by representing life immediately. Music is an image of the will itself and comprehends the tidal flow of its being, its dissonances, its loss and recovery, and its ceaseless movement toward resolution and redemption. Music expresses completely in its own language the inner essence of the will before it congeals into singular forms, which the rest of the world attempts to express through phenomenal representations of ideas. Music does not express some particular joy, sorrow, enchantment, or horror, but expresses joy, sorrow, jubilation, struggle, or peace in an absolute way: it expresses the essential being of will without any excess baggage and independently of the singular themes that incite the will to some particular representation. When the appropriate music is played as an accompaniment to words, scenes, actions, or landscapes, it seems to unlock their most secret meaning and to place that meaning in contact with their one-sided individuation of the general and the absolute. Yet even music is but a picture of the rhythm of metaphysical being in its innermost reality that pulsates within us. Although music is the most complex, fundamental, and general of all realities, it is still distant from reality itself: as the meaning and form of being, it is not being itself and, therefore, is removed from the pain of being. Thus, music remains cheerful even when it sounds the most painful dissonances and the most melancholic tones. In expressing only what is most general and profound, music relieves the spirit of narrowness and cloudiness of mind. Schopenhauer aptly remarks that the ability of music to offer each one the absolute in the measure in which his being is able to penetrate it, allows each one to feel clearly his own worth or what his worth might be. The domain of music excludes everything ridiculous, because only the transcending imagination can contain deception and ridicule. Indeed, music is essentially serious even when it is serene, because its realm is that of will itself, the original of the image prior to its diffraction and reflection. And will is the most serious thing of all because everything depends on it.

Perhaps Schopenhauer's explanation is the most meaningful that has ever been given to music. Our fragmented experience that is conveyed by distinct psychological data indicates, in conformity with Schopenhauer's pure metaphysical statement, that music is something extraordinary that makes all other arts appear to be efforts based on inadequate means. However, the psychological reality of music is not contained in metaphysical description. Psychologically, the uniqueness of music with respect to the other arts is something relative that is mediated, for example, by a glissando. The feeling that all of the contrivances for presenting the ultimate mystery of existence are effaced in the immediacy of surrender to a work is experienced as much by standing in the cathedrals of France or before Giorgione's Madonna of Castelfranco, or by grasping the mystical transformations of Hamlet and Faust, as it is by listening to a Bach cantata, the quartet in F Minor, or the Overture to Tristan. But because we are dealing with its meaning, it does not matter if the specific realities and consequences of music coincide with those of the other arts. By analogy, religion still keeps its metaphysical distance from all other levels of being and of the soul, although specks of the meaning it expresses are interwoven in the psychological phenomena of love, patriotism, morals, and art.

But it seems to me that the thesis can be contested that music "transcends" ideas, and that the hidden idea is only brought forth by putting the totality of being immediately into art, and not by presenting individual things. The above issue is significant enough to merit discussion so that the value of the metaphysical interpretation may be retained, although its content is challenged from an empirical standpoint. I find the starting point of music in the melodic and rhythmic elements of language. Among other observations, those of uncivilized tribes in particular show that when religious, erotic, and martial feelings are intensified, language is transformed into chant. A chant that emerges from such intensification of feeling is not art, but is a natural ejaculation like a cry that belongs to the immediate being of man: it does not in the manner of art resolve anything or crystallize anything into a specific form of being. But music arises from the chant when the development and change of certain feelings are connected to the pitch, rhythm, tempo, and tone of melodies. The relation of music as a form of art to the merely real and natural chant that vents feelings is the same as the relation of visual art to a piece of visible reality: art "imitates" nature in the sense of using it as a point of departure for form and meaning. Music begins on the formal and sensual side of the chant and then, by following immanent laws, works its material up into infinite sublimations, complications, and intensifications, shaping a work of art, in which the specific meaning (the typical significance of the actual correlation between the event within the soul and its musical expression) can be seen purely and is cleansed of any contingent individual causes or influences. The connection between the state of the soul and its musical expression, which is based on deep physical and psychological correlations reaching into an unfathomable past, mediates the emotional reaction to a musical work we call "understanding." However, the reality of such a connection between feeling and sound is less obvious than that between a model and a statue, or the erotic emotions and a love poem, because that connection is attenuated in higher and more differentiated cultures, and it depends upon a fragmentary and obscure essence. Nonetheless, the connection is part of natural reality: musical art isolates and presents in impressive economy and purity of form the inner logic or idea that unites significantly sequences of emotion and their audible materializations. The metaphysical dimension of music is not affected at all by providing music with the genesis discussed above or with some other psychological origin that places it on the same plane as the other arts. Although music is an "imitative" art that contains the "idea" of a specific knot in reality, it is still, as Schopenhauer wishes, able to make the totality of life its object. Similarly, we sometimes feel that our soul embraces the entire soul of someone whom we love, although from an empirical viewpoint we are bound together only by specific relations, beyond which many other interests, thoughts, and feelings remain that are quite definitely part of "our soul." It is also no problem for metaphysics if a saintly person cannot always be thought of as exceptional or if his deeds are not miracles that interrupt the course of nature. From the standpoint of the metaphysical meaning of his existence, such a person could, indeed, claim to be the son of God, and the meaning of his actions could transcend natural causality, just as the meaning of a sentence transcends the psychological reasons for its utterance. Only if one learns to respect the manifold levels of our spirit, which create different meanings, truth-values, and references for the same conduct, can one understand the richness of structure of our spiritual activities. Beyond all of the various ways to derive music psychologically and to label it aesthetically is the right to interpret it in the metaphysical dimension where being is impressed as an image of cosmic fate in concepts of the highest generality, though still remaining only a relative part of the world order, on an individual soul.

But now the question arises of how Schopenhauer's entire aesthetics, and not only his philosophy of music, fits with the pessimism of his general interpretation of the world. How can the pure and deep recognition of things, which is the essence of art, make us happy if Schopenhauer acknowledges only pain? The object of aesthetic recognition is surely not the inanimate object of spatial vision, though restriction to such an object made independent of its context would allow us to expect liberation from will and pain. Indeed, the modern interpretation of the arts as presentation and purification of space provided insurance against being drawn toward the opacity that characterizes the inner space of things. The aesthetically creative soul has the greatest freedom with respect to any object, so long as there is no expectation of finding something like a soul in the object. But the arts transcend optical and acoustical vision, and have as their object a totality including the inner space of life. Schopenhauer draws the logical conclusion when he eliminates the optimistic moment of "poetic justice" from tragedy and retains for it the triumph of evil, the pain and misery of humanity, and the decline and fall of all that is great and just. Schopenhauer's understanding, however, opens up a chasm he cannot bridge between the character of the content of tragedy and the pleasure that results from its presentation. The gap between content and feeling impelled Schopenhauer to cancel out pleasure and to posit only a moral relevance for tragedy involving resignation to and inner liberation from a world and a life-will that are responsible for pain. However, when aesthetic pleasure arises from the presentation of the scenes and emotions of life, the psychological contradiction between content and feeling cannot be annulled: those contents that we have understood deeply and truly bear greater fruit in us and also evoke more and deeper aesthetic pleasure. In Schopenhauer's system, the above problem can be solved only by assuming that the tragic presentation of the pure content of things does not contain any of the pain which is inseparable from those things when they exist or are represented as existing. Logic would not acquiesce in the above conclusion. With regard to quality, something that exists cannot contain anything more or different than that thing as merely imagined, because otherwise one would have to be speaking of two different things. Kant's well-known example that one hundred real dollars do not contain a single cent more than one hundred imagined dollars applies here. However, Schopenhauer's viewpoint contains a psychological depth and truth that is immune to such logical considerations. Factually, any content of thought, whether it be things, fate, personality, or nature, evokes when it is entertained intently a reaction that alters qualitatively, if that content is taken to be real. There is not merely a gradual increase in reaction when attribution of reality is added to the pure and ideal image of the content. The category of being, which is the simplest and most mysterious medium through which content is conveyed, does not change any content in a logical sense, but makes a great deal of difference psychologically. The psychological difference is not only the one Kant acknowledges between one hundred potential and one hundred real dollars, which is a question of whether or not I have property, but something objective, even if we do not consider the influence that reality can have on my situation and that mere thought alone can never achieve. We are, certainly, emotionally moved when we think about something abhorrent or tragic, even when we are aware that our object is only imagined and not real. But we are moved in a different, though not always stronger, way when we know that the very same thought represents reality. The difference between the ideal and the real reference is crucial for pessimism. The category of being, though it does not at all change the content of things logically, allows for content to become the absolute negation of value through the opposition of the metaphysical will and the existence of the world: metaphysical will, which is free in the sense that nothing exterior to it determines it, accuses the world of being responsible for everything pernicious and devoid of meaning. It would be a simplistic misunderstanding of the above doctrine if we believed it to be self-evident that because we can only feel something that really exists, pain can only come from reality, whereas the image of things by itself cannot touch us. The above interpretation is just not correct. Fiction also "moves" us and we respond to the image of the pure content of things with sentiments that include pain. The only difference is that the response to image does not contain the painful irrevocability of being and the dimension of irreconcilability typical of everything real. Art, therefore, might be able to purge reactions to pain from the purely imagined content of things, and in that case Schopenhauer, despite the lack of logical grounds for his thesis, could see the liberation from pain wrought by art as something necessarily related to content. There remains only the question of whether the pure negativity of the absence of pain could be the very positive enjoyment of art in the psychological realm. The above question must be raised even if we accept Schopenhauer's interpretation of happiness as the cessation of pain, the mere filling of a gap, and the extinction of desire.

There is one line of argument that allows Schopenhauer to derive the empirically undeniable positivity of aesthetic enjoyment from the mere negativity of the absence of pain. At one point he remarks that in the realm of art we are removed not only from real pain but even from the "potentiality" of pain. There cannot be any real pain in the aesthetic realm, but at most reflections of pain, because the basic law of that domain excludes will, which is the origin of every pain, by logical necessity. The impossibility of pain that is referred to here is obviously different from the mere irreality of pain, and results in qualitatively different emotions than the latter. The reality of life knows moments in which pain ceases, but the danger of a new eruption of pain always lurks behind the temporary tranquility. As we search the obscure foundation of our momentary liberation from pain, we feel our contingency and sense the operation of heartless laws that have given us peace now but, in adhering to the same nature and direction, will momentarily bathe us in the full flow of pain. No series in the aesthetic world contains the above predicament, because there is no contingency or chance in aesthetics. Thus, in the realm of art we experience a peace and salvation that are deeper than the mere freedom from pain. Even if the content of aesthetic experience comprehends the negativity of pain, our reaction to it is quite different than it is to a real experience. The above difference in the sphere of pleasurable feelings is similar to a distinction in the intellectual domain: causality, interpreted as internally necessary connection among events, is not the same as a merely temporal sequence, even if what is established and what occurs are the same.

It seems, however, that Schopenhauer did not even understand what was basically new and of profound promise in his own thought. Having placed the happiness found in art at a distance from the chain of lived reality, he entangles the two again by comparing aesthetic pleasure to the happiness of sleep. The undeniable qualitative difference between the pleasure of art and that of sleep is obscured by Schopenhauer and cannot be explained by his principles. Even if we granted that all happiness could be basically negative, the differences among kinds of happiness could not be merely quantitative and grounded in various mixtures with pain, but would have to be explained by positive causes that a pessimistic system cannot accommodate. It is a common occurrence that the refusal to make a relative concession leads eventually to making the same concession to a far greater degree, and sometimes absolutely. Hence, Schopenhauer's negation of a specific and positive happiness belonging to the artistic realm leads him to an extravagant optimism in two respects. First, there is his implication that it is sufficient not to be unhappy in order to be happy. The doom of radically pursuing a deduction from first principles is often that reasoning leads to both negative and positive meanings. Although it is deeply pessimistic to declare happiness to be only the cessation of pain, it is highly optimistic to claim that the cessation of pain is already happiness. The claim that a mood is genuine gains substance from the mood and not from the claim. Second, it seems to me to be an optimism, that balances Schopenhauer's pessimism with regard to being, to declare that the content and the purely imaginative side of the world can provide absolute peace and happiness. It would be consistent with radical pessimism if the unreal and imagined world of art were both relieved of the meaninglessness, contradiction, and despair of the real world, and devoid of any joy or pain, indifferent to our fate, and as inconsequential as the clouds reflected in a mighty river are in determining its course. But the contents of the world provide a beauty that rises above indifference, and that beauty becomes all the greater the more truly it is reflected in the mirror of art. Art reveals a structure of the world that is absolutely bent on giving happiness, and it offers a richness of happiness against which the pessimism of world-being, even when it is radically embraced, appears poor and dimensionless.

Over and over again Schopenhauer's pessimism turns into optimism. A clear formulation of one of his basic themes reads: "Without peace there is no real happiness." But doubtlessly he also means in the positive sense that peace is happiness. It does not take much effort to find the source of the error in the above statement. Certainly there is no happiness that does not presuppose the peace that protects one from danger and that allows one to do certain things. The pathway of happiness is bounded by walls, the destruction of which would lay it open to a thousand disturbing and disrupting influences. But by turning the relative peace that gives shelter into an absolute peace, Schopenhauer removes the predication that makes peace a condition of happiness. It is simply an empirical error to view peace not only as the condition in which happiness is not threatened by disturbances, but also as the substance of happiness itself. For example, think of the vacant lives and the ennui of so many retired people who had expected perfect and positive happiness after they had left behind the stress and worry of work. If the statement that pure peace is happiness is affirmed against empirical evidence, it can only be done so on the basis of absolute optimism. The equation of peace and happiness means that happiness is exclusively within us and needs no supplementation or instigation from outside, because were that not the case, happiness could never result from the mere removal or exclusion of obstacles to it. Schopenhauer would seem to have to bind happiness to the essence of our existence, seeing it as something that evolves by parthenogenesis from our depths and that is simultaneously our soul's product and form of existence that immediately arises and takes over consciousness when no other influences obstruct or distract it. Pessimism is turned into radical optimism by assuming that peace is in itself happiness. The doctrine of happiness in art through liberation from will is just a special case of such radical optimism.

The principle that peace is happiness allows not only for optimism but also for realism, which Schopenhauer abhors, and for the subjugation of art to reality. The postulate that the total subjective eudaemonistic meaning of art is freedom from reality makes art dependent on reality, albeit in a negative sense. Art is here judged from the standpoint of reality, just as it is in realism. It lives at the boundary of reality, but not beyond it, and reality becomes part of aesthetic experience just as our enemies and the people whom we try to avoid become parts of our lives. As long as Schopenhauer sees art only for itself, he provides it with the purity and independence of a self-enclosed world, and permits its values and meanings to emerge exclusively in conformity with its own norms. But Schopenhauer deprives art of its sovereignty and independence when his pessimism declares that art must derive its stimulus from the negation of reality. Art's nonreality in a purely negative sense, which places it beyond the question of being and nonbeing, is turned by Schopenhauer's erroneous thought into a nonreality that has the positive relation of denunciation to reality (a relation of liberation from the world to which every relation had previously been rejected) and that embodies a conscious decision not to want to know. The same difficulty always characterizes the structure of Schopenhauer's thought: he mingles at any cost the principle of pessimism with other themes that are derived from quite different insights or impulses. His intellectual approach involves correlating the essentially emotive element of pessimism with other motives, making it impossible for him to draw clear and cogent conclusions. Schopenhauer's difficulty surfaces in regard to a possibility for aesthetic interpretation that would basically solve the problems previously indicated. He alludes to but never develops in theoretical form the argument that if art's subjective significance is to rid us of will by translating us to the realm of the pure idea, then happiness as well as pain must wither away, because both are rooted in the domain of the will. Schopenhauer does not want to deny the above implication: "Neither happiness nor pain is taken beyond this boundary." But he can neither define with clarity what remains of the subjective value of art nor refrain from mentioning innumerable times the "joys" of art. There is definitely an emotional value in the aesthetic situation, which is neither happiness nor liberation from pain, but which is positive and specific, and, in the same fashion as morality, is indifferent to the eudaemonistic opposites. It is, however, more difficult to clarify aesthetic value consciously than it is to elucidate ethical value, because moral value increases in purity when we are unhappy, whereas aesthetic value flourishes when we are happy. Inner tensions that appear as upward strivings, enthusiasms, and guiding lights for existence can be seen more easily against the dark background of pain than against the bright background of happiness. Despite the collaboration in fact between the specific aesthetic reaction and happiness in art itself and their psychological identity, one should not overlook the diversity of their essence. The emotion proper to beauty and art is as primary as the religious emotion, and, like the latter, it cannot be reduced to other conscious values. Both the aesthetic and religious emotions, however, energize the whole person and, therefore, are found in experience to be united to such movements of the soul as loftiness and humility, pleasure and pain, expansion and contraction, and identification with and distancing from an object. There has often been a temptation to reduce the aesthetic and religious reactions to the affirmation and negation, and the fusion and opposition of the great potencies of life. Schopenhauer, who is one of the few German philosophers with an aesthetic nature, obviously has a sure instinct for the originality and positivity of the aesthetic situation. But had he assented to that originality and positivity, he would have introduced into our existence a value which would not have been compatible with a pessimistic trend of thought. Although he is not prey to the kind of intellectual dishonesty that surrenders solid insights in order to save general principles, the inner necessity of his emotional life leads him to the same result. The internal logic of Schopenhauer's philosophy of art should lead to an enhancement of value within the aesthetic situation, which then would be coordinated in the system of life with the value of happiness. Such coordination is a psychological fact of our experience, although the aesthetic and eudaemonistic values are independent of one another. But Schopenhauer changes the direction of his argument, because his pessimism does not allow him to admit that the elements of life have any moments of value other than liberation from pain. Among all of the theories of art expounded by the great philosophers, Schopenhauer's is surely the most interesting, the most erudite with respect to the facts of art and its appreciation, and the most impressive. The zeal of pessimism to usurp the prerogatives of other aspects of life is revealed more clearly and deeply in Schopenhauer's refusal to acknowledge the positivity and autonomy of art and its enjoyment, than it is in any increase he allows to its own domain in order to balance life's measure of happiness and unhappiness.

Whereas Schopenhauer does not give sufficient attention to the definitive subjective meaning of art, he gives too much emphasis to its objective value. However, the depth of his appreciation of art is no less exemplified by this "too much," than the depth of his pessimism is illustrated by the "not enough." He summarizes his conclusive opinion about the objective essence of a work of art by stating: "Every work of art tries to show us life and things as they are in truth, and is fundamentally an answer to the question: What is life?" Here he seems to contradict completely every meaning of his interpretation of art as we have presented it so far. Art, we have been led to believe, should liberate us from life and should only present the bases and laws of real phenomena as they exist in our intellect, not as they exist in reality or as they relate to what life really is. Life is will, the disappointing game without an end in which every achievement spawns a new desire and every resting place launches a new movement. But art separates itself and removes us from the world of will and enjoys a "colorful reflex," of which the essential thing to note is that it is the *reflex* of being and not the reflex of *being*. All of a sudden art is supposed to reveal the essence of things, rather than those things as mere phenomena, and is supposed to answer a question that transcends its realm of surfaces. Here we have a fundamental and glaring contradiction, as well as a transgression of the boundary erected against life that was the meaning and justification of art. But this contradiction, perhaps despite or perhaps because of Schopenhauer's failure to identify it as such, radically reveals an interpenetration of logically opposed values and requirements that is only possible in art. Art treats of exteriors, surfaces, and immediate sensory data, but also expresses through the symbolism of visible things the innermost meaning of existence, the ultimate mystery of things, and eternal ineffability. Art looks for how the elements of things that appear and occur are correlated to their own laws, and does not appeal to the hidden forces that impelled what is obvious into existence and that are a presupposition for its existence in the real world: art searches for the meaning of the *phenomenon*. But as art moves in the above direction it is also drawn in another one which concerns the *meaning* of the phenomenon, the essence of a being without essence, and the spiritual or transcendental meaning that reveals all forms and superficial stimuli to be symbols. It is the foregoing duplicity of art's function that gives art the power to touch our soul from both the depths and the heights. But when we scrutinize this duplicity carefully we see that it remains just a mode of expression that allows us to analyze the unity of artistic impression, which cannot be subsumed under a single immediate concept. It would be completely contrary to the integrity of art to synthesize it by mechanically juxtaposing two partial meanings, each one gaining its value from an independent source, and then putting them together by serendipity. In aesthetic experience we find that the objective unity of a work of art causes a subjectively uniform response that can be felt but that cannot be described adequately in a single concept. Just as in many similar cases, the only possibility that remains is to construct by uniting two opposing specific determinations. But such determinations are only components that express a unitary result later on, and a deeper interpretation of art is aware of causal reciprocity. The clarification of phenomena, the laws governing events, and the sensual attraction of colors and sounds are only tools to reveal the deepest essence and the invisible meaning of the visible. But from the alternative standpoint, the metaphysical values of a work of art, which often are only present as obscure hints and frequently are tied to art's religious or erotic role, are merely tools for making the presentation of phenomena more clear and meaningful, and for rendering something visible more attractive and proportioned for its own sake and not for any ulterior aim. At this point I must, unfortunately, note that Schopenhauer's doctrine of art, and even our own explanation, both suffer from the defect common to nearly all general philosophies of art of insisting that there must be shared determinants for all of the different arts. We leave open the question of whether there are such shared determinants, but it seems doubtful that there are when we consider how difficult it is even to come up with a definition of art. One would prefer to think that the ground for calling by the same name actions so different as acting and architecture, constructing a statue and making music, is a gradual transition within a single chain of meaning, in which two neighboring parts are closely related, and two distant parts only very loosely related. In the chain AB−BC−CD, it is intelligible that the same name can be used to denominate AB and CD through the mediation of BC, though the same name does not indicate a qualitative identity of the two things named. Sometimes one might feel strait-jacketed to have to accept that the metaphysics of tragedy and the art of growing a beautiful garden have a common basis. Schopenhauer does not always accept the above constraint, and his metaphysical explanations of the arts sometimes lead into divergent paths. But he does not make an issue of the differences among the arts, and holds out the postulate of a uniform explanation for art. The above imperfection in Schopenhauer's thought symbolizes the deeper truth that art reconciles opposites that are otherwise irreconcilable, and this might justify our calling all of the particular arts by the same name: art stands for the general, but is limited to singular and self-enclosed phenomena, and is the expression of a decidedly individual, radically differentiated, and incomparable soul; art is supposed to be nothing but form and idea, but its vision is only possible under the conditions of materiality; art is purely intellectual and is a form of consciousness that is removed from the specific and conditioned being of things, yet it must be free from the constraints of causality, which is the basic law of the intellect. And all of the preceding contradictions are encapsulated in a final one: art is expected to show us what life is by letting life dissolve before our very eyes. The attraction and joy of art lie in the impression it gives us that it displays the world as it is, that there is no obscure, obdurate, and unresolved reality beyond the dreamy play of phenomena, and that it expresses reality at its most real, the specific and the basic essence of things and of life simultaneously. From a logical viewpoint such a contradiction of claims would pose a problem. But perhaps art is one of the structures that allows us to have insight into the problems they pose in such a way that we grasp those problems in their purity and see that they are insoluble. Whether or not it was his aim, Schopenhauer's doctrine of art seems to imply this interpretation.

The aesthetic salvation from being—that is, from pain—which is wrought by art, can only occur in moments of aesthetic ecstasy. Within such moments being and pain continue to exist in the depth of our essence, and the intellect, which has been uprooted but cannot exist without roots for any length of time, falls back inexorably into its servitude to the will. In moments of aesthetic pleasure we are like a slave who has forgotten his chains or like a warrior whose enemy is no longer in sight. The warrior has not overcome the enemy but has tried to flee. Soon the enemy will be upon him again and he will not be able to disregard him. Redemption by art is insufficient for the same reason that such redemption is possible at all. We have to be freed from will, but art just turns away from it. Real and irrevocable redemption has to wrestle with will. And that is done as morality and ascesis. Let us move, then, to the practical solution for this obscure problem, which is so typical for Schopenhauer's view of life.

6
Morality and the Self-Redemption of the Will

CHOPENHAUER'S DISPOSITION TOWARD AND HIS explanations of good and evil in the world can all be reduced to one basic thought: metaphysical will as it is perceived in its absolute unity, before it is splintered by human intellect into a specific individual form, is clearly the potentiality of all pain and misfortune, but it is not the realization of evil. The reality of evil is only given through the process of establishing some spurious goals by the individual, by the struggle of individual forms against one another, and by the consequent awakening of individual consciousness to the totality of conflict and to general suffering. But if these individual forms, which are figments of individual imagination that are singularized in space and time, are merely considered in themselves, prior to being infused by wish and thereby called into being, then they are also beyond evil and ill: aesthetics has acknowledged the innocence and joy of the imaginary world that has been liberated from will. Pain, guilt, and inner contradiction can only come into existence where will becomes singular existence, that is, where it assumes the form of imagination. Neither will nor imagination considered singly can account for the realization of evil, but only their coincidence can eventuate in absurdity. The necessarily disappointed appetite of something relative for absolute satisfaction creates the struggle among individual phenomena. Each individual, alive with the totality of will, creates the pain of existence which becomes conscious only in individualized subjects. Consequently, there must be three ways of evading the pain and the horror of life: first, through aesthetic creation and enjoyment, which separates imagination from a will that is bound to life; second, through a will transcending individual division in which the individual subject identifies itself with all of the others and thereby removes struggle, contention, and that consequent reaction of pain that proceeds from the will entering into individual form; and third, by the will's negation of itself, in which the subject uses the will existing in itself to decide to negate it and thereby eradicates the potentiality of struggle and pain, and of greed and disillusionment, leading back into nothingness a world released from will. We have recognized the first path as that of aesthetic salvation, the second way is what we call morality, and the third road is the sanctification of man, who no longer desires, who has acknowledged the essence of the world (though not necessarily in cognized concepts), and who therefore has withdrawn from the disastrous quick march of will ("the disastrous circle dance of willing"). The sanctified man is beyond disillusionment and beyond the experience that things are in vain, that is, beyond evil, because he no longer wants anything. And now it is time to describe the pathways of salvation by morality and by negation of the will and renunciation.

The phenomena of morality are first characterized by their contradictions. The natural and logical consequence of the individualization of will into a specific ego is that this ego wants everything for itself, inasmuch as it owns the total will in the form of being a person. But because there is more than one ego, it follows that one person wants what another desires, and that the more robust ego will interfere with someone else's sphere of will, thereby engendering evil: one will satisfy or assume that one can satisfy one's will at another's expense without any concern for the pain one inflicts. The phenomenon of justice, which defines the sphere of the will according to the boundaries of personalities, arises from this ground. The just man has seen through the illusion which separates individuals radically from each other and which makes one person the natural enemy of the other—makes that person see the other as someone whom he can damage to his advantage. The just man sees himself and the being outside himself as constituted under the same law and, therefore, he does not want to hurt the other being. He respects the boundary between individuals and does not violate it through his egoism, because his egoism senses an independent existence which is not absolutely contradictory to his own, but which is fundamentally identical to his own in its essence.

Justice, therefore, remains within the negative realm and is a mere holding back, a confinement of a will which is limitless in all of its individuations by the fact that there is more than just one individuation. Its positive side is limited to the metaphysical emotion that goes far beyond justice through the compassion that abhors every wound and domination of the other: the subject overcomes the ruthlessness that is almost logically connected to the fact of individuation by putting himself in the other's place and by sympathizing with him, the possibility of which is logically connected to the profound fact of the identity of essence. The radical tragedy of life, that struggle between phenomenal logic and the logic of the thing-in-itself, is dissolved in favor of the latter logic. Here the development of Schopenhauer's ethic is definitively placed on one side of the great potentialities of moral philosophy. For Schopenhauer, the objective, lawful, and imperative necessity of moral norms never exists. These norms are but the expression or culmination of the single fact that will in all beings is one and the same and that, indeed, will should not really be at all. Thus, justice as formulated by the principle *suum cuique* does not, for Schopenhauer, contain the meaning it has for others, that is, that the relation "to each his own" is an intrinsic value that should be realized whether or not it eventuates in someone's pleasure or pain, or whether it be deduced from metaphysical identity or from the radical being-for-itself of personalities. Thus, Schopenhauer does not find any justification for punishment but the preservation of society's integrity through deterrence. He believes that punishment for the sake of retribution is merely meaningless cruelty and revenge. However, even if one rejects retribution as a principle of punishment for whatever reason, one should realize that it contains an objective principle, however imperfectly formulated it might be, that is ethically autonomous and does not require appeal to utility or to a higher metaphysical court. It is at least a possibility that an evil deed is balanced ethically by the pain inflicted on the evildoer, and that the logic of morality demands it apart from social, historical, or theological considerations, just as intellectual logic deduces a necessary conclusion from given premises without recourse to any legitimation that transcends its inner necessities. Perhaps the response of the soul to the ideal meaning of punishment that has just been sketched can be discerned in the frequent desire of criminals to be punished and in their sense of decontamination and purification after they have experienced the pain of punishment. It is, however, foreign to Schopenhauer's thought to assume that deeds and facts could be required just for their own sakes and meanings. For him, ethical necessity resides either in the goal of action or in the metaphysical structure of general being. But the legitimacy of his two modes of explanation does not exclude the third one of deducing the ethical necessity of a deed not from something else, but by recognizing it as something immediate that is legitimate in itself. There should be, of course, a good deal of dispute about the legitimate content of such moral imperatives, but perhaps no more than there is about theological and metaphysical issues such as: Should justice or the will of God reign supreme? Should individuals merge into a societal or a mystical-transcendent unity, or should they value separation and develop to an extreme their identities? Should all essential human traits be educated equally or should some of them—for example, sensuality—be attacked and repressed in favor of rational potentialities? All of the above perplexities are experienced innumerable times, either in their fundamental generality or in individualized and concrete actions or states, as self-contained and intrinsically justified incitements, as "oughts," the values of which are lived through in their realizations without appeal to a before or an after. It really does not matter if individuals, groups, or epochs disagree on the contents of the "ought" and if they fight bitterly about them. The only thing that is important for us is the ethical possibility that every content gaining recognition should be the definitive pacification of a motivating sense of value, that it should be acknowledged in the form of a not-questioning-beyond-itself. By virtue of his pessimism Schopenhauer denies any such solidarity of the "ought" with a positive state. Were he to have affirmed this solidarity he would have had to recognize the existence of positive values. Schopenhauer's many arguments opposing Kant's and Fichte's morality stem from their assumption that certain modes of conduct are simply ethically necessary and are, thus, radically valuable. But if the value of existence can never reach beyond the zero point, then no action or state that is in-itself, for-itself, and with-itself can be ultimately valuable: attributing final value to a singular condition would give a new importance to the world that would be negated by the constituting ground of pessimism. What remains is either to include ethical values in the never-ending chain of relative means and purposes (Schopenhauer does this when he makes punishment a mere social deterrent), or to strip these values of their immediate worth and to base them directly on the metaphysical foundation of existence. In the latter case ethical values can gain no positive significance other than that accorded by Schopenhauer to the feeling of happiness or aesthetic pacification. Schopenhauer argues in this manner that any possible justification of morality, which he defines as altruism, can only be based on egoism. But this confinement of human motivations into egoism and altruism, which assumes that whatever does not stem from one source comes from the other, clearly overlooks a third possibility which is radically connected to the other two. In fact we want quite a lot which is useless either to "I" or to some "thou"; that is, we follow an immediate impulse or some ethical imperative, and even if we are useful, this is not our motivation for acting. We merely act, perhaps because we just want something to happen, or desire the realization of a specific state of affairs, or wish something particular to be created, known, or believed. Such contents of will are suspended before our eyes, in their pure objectivity, as things that should be just as they are, independently of their possible connections to sentimental responses of pleasure or pain, or egoism or altruism. Indeed, a value is created that might satisfy or provide beneficial consequences for the actor and for people at the present or at some future time. Such is the feeling of the researcher gaining knowledge, the artist completing his work, the statesman realizing the victory of his political conviction, or a religious believer intent on the realization of the divine will. But such radiations and reactions from feeling subjects do not exhaust all possible motivations. The goals are presented as objective values independent of sense and experience, just as the truth of a statement is independent of the process of imagining it. Because Schopenhauer's radical devaluation of existence would be threatened by a category of intrinsic values, he declares every value to be relative to someone. Yet even if a value would actually require a subjective consciousness, as is the case for the world of facts in idealist philosophy, it would still be mistaken to assume that value could only exist in subjective states. It is perhaps a miraculous fact, but nonetheless a fact which cannot be reduced to anything else, that our feeling can separate itself from its subjective basis and can experience an existence, a state, or an action as value and as "ought," and that it can do so perfectly objectively apart from any question about the eventual success of "I" or "thou." Schopenhauer believes that we can achieve liberation from the subjectivity of the will within the aesthetic ideal, but not within the sphere of practical ideals. His position follows from his relegating practice to a realm of illusion, which is a fleeting dream of the mere shapes of things, and results in his negating *a priori* any positive value to existence, which perpetually perishes. However, the reality of life is touched through ethical values, and, so, he must negate the possibility that their subsumption under mere relativity, subjectivity, and negation can be avoided. Were he to accept that just one thing was positive, be it a norm, an action, or a state that was good and simply good apart from its predicated interrelations, then he would have to introduce a new cosmic element and a new dimension of values that would radically and permanently rupture the quality of a world justified by absolute pessimism. There cannot, for Schopenhauer, be any existential value beyond pleasure and pain, including their conditions and consequences, because only the summation of these states leads with certainty to a pessimistic result.

Schopenhauer interprets the fundamental fact of morality as the expansion of the phenomenon of justice. In acknowledging the metaphysical identity of "I" and "thou" while respecting the boundary between them, justice halts the natural tendency of the ego to breach this boundary and, therefore, allows the identity established to breach this very boundary. Schopenhauer believes that the essence of an ethically noble person can be exhausted by the statement that such a person draws less of a distinction than is normal between himself and others. The noble person has seen through the illusion of individuation and knows, though not necessarily through ideas of reflection, that someone else's suffering is ultimately his own. He does whatever he can to mitigate suffering, because everything one can do for others and, thus, finally for oneself is to alleviate the suffering that forms our general destiny, from which we cannot escape. The metaphysical significance of all morality is that the absolute and transempirical unity of all being, which includes the unity of "I" and "thou," is realized in the phenomenon, in that metaphysical unity suspends the proper nature of the phenomenon, the division between individual entities. Morality does not negate will, but only negates that which contradicts within the phenomenon the basic unitary predication of the will. Thus, it is superficial to argue that the ethic of essential identity is egoistic by using the transcendent as a mere point of deflection and failing to acknowledge its function for Schopenhauer. If I give my powers, my well-being, and my property to others, because ultimately they are me, where, one might ask, is there a difference from any other egoistic action, which also requires a certain amount of sacrifice and a certain amount of interaction with a nonego as an unavoidable means which does not diminish egoism by a jot? The most definitive scheme of immorality, in which others were used exclusively as tools, could not be effected more radically than on a basis on which everything one did for others was eventually done for oneself. Here, more than in any other relation between "I" and "thou," the exclusivity of the means-character is obvious. There is simply no possibility of interpreting the "thou" as the final goal, for, without exception, all actions aimed at the "thou" are directed back to the "I" through the shared root of metaphysical unity. But, as I have already said, I see this interpretation, though it may seem obvious, as an erroneous one. The absolute unity of essence dissolves not only an independent "thou," but also the "I." It is surely not the meaning of Schopenhauer's doctrine that I would only harm myself if I harmed the other, and that I would promote myself if I promoted the other. His meaning is obviously that the altruistic action radically dissolves the difference between "I" and "thou," and that it benefits an impersonal and absolute being which exists undivided beyond the phenomenality of "I" and "thou." In expressing the most inclusive formula of morality—Do not hurt anyone, but give as much help as you can to everyone—Schopenhauer seems merely to teach the banality of moralism contained in the ideal of the good and helpful human being. But he is really describing only the practical-exterior phenomenon of moral behavior. What matters in depth and essence is not the interaction of "I" and "thou," which presupposes phenomenal division, but the supercession of division by which an action deceives its own presupposition. Thus, the real meaning of Schopenhauer's ethic of identity is directed toward a new dimension that is different from that of the empirical and superficial morality of good deeds. It is aimed at a theme to which we have alluded before and which permeates ethics from its origin: Be what you are. It seems that among the typical sentiments and imaginations of humanity is the idea that all that we should be is already present as a reality, though it is hidden and undeveloped; that, indeed, this is our most proper and certain reality. The ethical task is to permeate the superficial, merely phenomenal, and almost irreal aspects of our being with the deeper reality, and to dominate these aspects by making everything cloudy, exterior, and spurious in our existence into an expression of our real being. There seems to be a logical contradiction within the commandment to become what we already are in our most real reality, but this apparent contradiction results from the conceptual formulation of a strictly uniform conformation of ideals in the soul. Somehow, for example, in the design of a morality of reason the essential substance of man is taken to be rationality, but the ethical necessity is to have rationality really rule in this life and to dispense with the sensual elements which are assumed not to constitute the real human. In a similar, though less obvious, way this is also the design of Schopenhauer's morality: the ethical requirement of altruism, love, compassion, and willingness to help means that the unity in which individuals already exist by virtue of their pregiven essence should appear in the exterior relations among human beings and in the relations among their phenomenal and individual forms, which do not belong to their deepest reality. This morality follows the ideal formulation that human beings should become what they are. If my interpretation is correct, then Schopenhauer's principle of morality shows a grandeur which might, perhaps, be obscured by the feminine charity and compassionate passivity of the phenomenal actions that shape this morality. It is a sublime and grand idea that man in his ethical actions expresses his most profound and proper essence, but that the ultimate is not thereby expressed; that is, that this essence becomes definitive and final only when it reveals itself as identical with the essence of all other beings and testifies in truth to the structure of the metaphysical unity of the cosmos. This is, admittedly, a metaphysical dogma. Another dogma opposes it, which is based on a fundamentally antagonistic temperament: Our actions must express the structures of an unmistakable individuality, because only individuality and not any supra or subpersonal all-unity is the final element of being. The two temperaments have no possibility of making peace or of finding a resolution on the basis of right and wrong. For the one opposed to Schopenhauer's, to be what you are could not mean to be as the others, but must mean to be what others cannot be and what only you alone can be, because the absolute, real, and ideal structure of being rests on the being-in-itself and singularity of individual entities, on their demarcation and opposition. The idea that individuality touches the abyss of the cosmos in phenomenal action and ethical value is unacceptable to Schopenhauer, because the definitive and irreducible value of the personality would introduce a moment of value into his world view that could not be reconciled with pessimism. This concept of individuality is beyond the addition or subtraction of pleasure and pain, and it cannot be touched by any summation of the totality of existential value, retaining its specific positive meaning regardless of the abysses of pain, negativity, or dearth of values into which the world sinks.

Thus, Schopenhauer is beyond the suspicion that his ethic of identity only lays the foundation for a sublime egoism. Altruistic actions do not flow back into the ego, but are directed toward a point which can be reached neither by "I" nor by "thou" in their phenomenal sense of separation. But we may raise here a far more serious problem with his ethical principle from the standpoint of moral sentiment. This problem is exacerbated because Schopenhauer altogether refuses to propound a new and reformatory morality, and only claims to elucidate the foundation and meaning of extant moral concepts. But if one does not, as has normally been the case, look down from the phenomenal actions of moral life to their metaphysical foundations, but instead looks up from the foundations to the actions, then altruism as well as egoism loses its meaning. The significance of morality's content must be viewed in terms of the absolute foundation of the world as the relief of pain. Morality's importance is to realize the metaphysical unity of entities, which is, strictly speaking, negated by their individualization in the relation among singular phenomena. Certainly altruism, which for Schopenhauer is but compassion and soothing of pain, happens in the world of individual phenomena. But the suffering of phenomena is not merely the phenomenon of suffering, but, in that it is the life of our will, also is absolute reality. The intensification and alleviation of pain reach from the peripheral point of existence, where our personality is located, into the very core of the thing-in-itself, in the unity of which all the lines that originate from the periphery meet. If such is the case, there is no reason to prefer my benefit to that of someone else, but also none to prefer someone else's to mine. If all pleasure and pain meet in a central mediating location, and if all of the hedonistic values thereby are lodged in the same place, then it is not at all important if this location is named "I" or "thou." At this locus are placed the specific quantities of all phenomena, and both gain their real importance and lose their independent efficacy. If from the decisive metaphysical standpoint the "thou" is as good as the "I," then the "I" is also as good as the "thou" and there is, thus, no reason why an action that creates a certain amount of happiness for the actor should be less valuable than one that has the same consequence for his neighbor. Here is the radical problem in Schopenhauer's contention that morality only demands that we love our neighbor as ourselves, that is, place him on the same practical level as ourselves: to sacrifice ourselves beyond the measure of self-love would seem to Schopenhauer, according to his premises, to be senseless, in that under certain circumstances I might sacrifice a relatively large quantity of my own happiness for a relatively small quantity of someone else's. Such a sacrifice would be unreasonable, because it would reduce the sum total of attainable happiness on the metaphysical level, where all separate quanta are merged through the annihilation of phenomenal subjects.

It is rather remarkable how Schopenhauer, by being logical and systematic, closes himself off to the evidence of the reality of ethical feelings. If these feelings tend toward altruism, they always deny that the ethical value of an action is limited to the equivalence of sacrifice and gain, and tend to affirm that ethical value increases when the pleasure-pain balance turns against the ego's interest. Had Schopenhauer accepted this evidence, he would have posited a value of ethical conduct independent of any hedonistic summation, which, of course, is necessary for his pessimism. Although Schopenhauer excludes an egoistic interest in happiness from morality, he nonetheless links morality to happiness and suffering as such and to the relation of their quantities in a uniform and transindividual being. When an action takes on ethical value because through conscious intention a small happiness for "thou" is purchased by a greater suffering of "I," the world achieves a category of value which outruns the measuring scales of pessimism and makes its cosmic balance illusory.

It may be permissible to draw a conclusion here, though with great delicacy because there is real danger of abuse and error: Perhaps Schopenhauer would not have indulged in an intellectual power play against a rather common, if deeply ingrained, fact of ethical consciousness had he, subjectively, been of an ethical nature. Obviously I do not mean this to be a moralizing condemnation. For the higher evolution of the spirit, natures of Schopenhauer's aesthetic and intellectual cast are as important as those oriented to ethics. In any case, barring an unimaginable change in our form of life, as a matter of principle one should not usurp the seat of judgment in the case of the most elemental oppositions of our existence. The real opposition to the ethical nature is not the artistic but the aesthetic one. Nietzsche was disposed artistically and ethically, whereas Schopenhauer was disposed aesthetically and nonethically. Whenever Schopenhauer addresses the understanding of art and nature one senses immediate and spontaneous experience, whereas when he speaks of the completion of the moral ideal in the ascetic self-annihilation of the will, one feels that one is beyond the pale, reaching for an otherness with unrequited desire in an impossible dream which is understood to be such. This is probably the reason why Schopenhauer does not take a realistic approach to selflessness and asceticism, but instead pays uncritical homage to impure and pathological versions of these phenomena. His is a typical reaction to a group of phenomena we may appreciate and admire, though we have no real inner relation to them. Whoever is at home in a certain region of values and plays some part in it will carry its meaning scale within him. Thus, even when he admires and adores great realizations of value he will not go overboard, but will have a pure instinct for absolute authenticity that will be lacking in an outsider. Dualism, which is the radical form of the human soul's existence, its rhythm and its many melodies, is exteriorized in a basic opposition in which it succumbs to its own law, the division between unity and multiplicity. This opposition lives in the theoretical problems of reducing phenomena either to a unity or to a plurality of ultimate elements, but it also thrives in the practical realm where the ideal of amalgamation and unification is opposed to the independence and separation of personalities. When ethics posits itself metaphysically, both kinds of opposition combine in many ways. The ideal quest for unity and merger with the other never concedes to metaphysical differentiation and to the deep irreconcilability of entities. Yet, despite any absolute metaphysical unity, the desire, even if it cannot be requited, remains that every human being be a self-enclosed totality, a self-centered microcosm. As we have already seen, Schopenhauer explains all morality as the practical reconstitution of the absolute unity of the thing-in-itself, which overcomes the splintering into separate individualities devoid of essence and perdurance. Yet, even if one recognizes fully the metaphysical depth of Schopenhauer's ideal, I am afraid that he turns his back on the real moral problem. If I am not completely mistaken, the problematic depth of the duality of "I" and "thou" reaches deeper into the abyss of being than Schopenhauer's metaphysical explanation permits. Even if one assumes that the supercession of duality is the task of morality, Schopenhauer places the fulfillment of this task in the infinite so far as phenomena are concerned. Yet in the case of the fundamental reality of man, no leap to a transcendent unity can be permitted without losing all of the rigor and basic importance that the task of supercession has for existence. The procedure of formulating a unity which subsumes duality in itself and negates it seems, therefore, too simplistic to satisfy this task, because it forces the infinite multiplicity of the functional relations that pertain to the ethical sphere into a substantive scheme which cannot do justice to moral tension. The innumerable ethical requirements which must be fulfilled in the reciprocal relations among human beings simply cannot be circumscribed by the assumption that two individualities eventually form something similar to a unity. Even the most supreme expressions of moral value remain dualistic by virtue of the total being-in-itself and firm quiescence in-itself, which constitute the individual value of personality and allow the development and achievement, in feeling and devotion, of ethical values in the relations among human beings. It is, perhaps, possible to acknowledge duality and unity as the poles of our ethical behavior, and to grasp the measure of them both as nearly the form of every singular ethical occurrence. But such an occurrence is surely no more perfect or valuable if it shows less duality and more unity. Indeed, it seems to me that the zenith of morality is reached when relations among human beings evince simultaneously full duality and full unity: a moral occurrence is just that one in which duality is not permitted to disappear in the quest for unity. Here we have the highest form of relation among humans, but one in which the resolution of duality and unity can only be described in terms of contradictory concepts. I cannot deny that all of Schopenhauer's ideas about the essence of morality are imprecise and biased. This holds for the unity of "I" and "thou," the equality of the love of others and the love of oneself, and the annihilation of the difference between oneself and anyone else. Schopenhauer's metaphysical unity, which supposedly reduces the difference of individualization into itself, actually rigidifies the myriad of moral relations into something like a substance. His procedure is similar to that of an earlier time when the innumerable functions and reciprocal relations that constitute the organs of a living being were treated as a substantially unified "spirit of life." Further, love for someone else and love of oneself surely cannot be equated as though the same intimate occurrence only changed its object, here a "thou" and there an "I." The idea of unitary substance, which was passed down through the centuries and has been pushed to metaphysical heights by Schopenhauer, is really extremely crude and psychologically incorrect. Only by extravagant analogy could egoism be described as a division of subject and object in which the subject experiences for himself as object the same love that is directed toward others. Surely there is not only a difference of object but also a totally and fundamentally different process. The idea that in the inner dimension the same act only changes its goal from self-love to love of the other, just as a gun might change direction from murder to suicide, stems from the fact that the same external object can be given to someone else or kept by myself, or can be accepted or rejected. In claiming that psychological questions or queries about the facts of emotion can be resolved only by subjective re-experiencing, I would like to assert that anyone who really analyzed the inner dimension of his egoistic conduct and of his devotion and love for a "thou" would have to grant that the two states were totally different functionally and qualitatively; indeed, that they were two different lives right down to their ultimate foundation, and that as basic emotions they could not be subsumed under a common denominator. The above remarks are fruitless as criticisms, because it is quite unimportant whether Schopenhauer errs here or there: one should take from a donor what one can really use and not what one has to refuse. Schopenhauer's errors, though, show something enlightening because it is so typical of human thinking. All converges to the single point of trying to reduce all of the movements of existence to the two rivers of positive and negative value, which meet one another and flow into the single metaphysical design of the cosmos. This cosmic scheme does not allow for qualitative differences between the two sources of value, nor for their basic irreconcilability, nor for any value-dimension beyond their juncture: everything is summed up to yield a uniform and simple result which forms the foundation of pessimism. This is why the essence of altruism had to be interpreted in so general a way that it lost its specific meaning and was judged only according to its general hedonistic result, which could just as well have been achieved through egoism once the difference between "I" and "thou" had been abolished. This is also why ethical action was not supposed to require a sacrifice surpassing the amount of happiness gained through it for someone else, for such a sacrifice would confer a value beyond the calculus of pleasure and pain. Finally, this is why morality could only exist in the annihilation of personal differences, in the amalgamation of "I" and "thou"; their existence-for-themselves as the unequivocal condition for ethical value would have endangered the all-embracing metaphysical unity which must receive the value-implications of ethical action only to create its absolutely uniform cosmic balance sheet.

Schopenhauer's reformulation of any value-in-itself into a metaphysical continuity which knows basically only pleasure and pain, and, in reality, only knows pain, is expressed most perfectly in the claim that all love is compassion. Inasmuch as the substance of every entity's life is suffering, an act of love could be nothing else but an easing of the other's suffering. Thus, the recognition of the other's suffering—which is equated immediately to one's own by sensing the identity of essence—and the attendant experience of compassion become the themes of any sacrifice and of any submission, for which love is only a special name. Obviously the reduction of logical and psychological facts to a nonindividual unity of suffering is an unfair power play. If love were nothing but compassion, how could we distinguish all of the compassion that we do not call love? Perhaps we would find some deeper meaning if we turned Schopenhauer's sentence into the formula, All compassion is love. Thus, the mystery of love, taken in a sense close to its Christian meaning, could grow into a relation toward enemies, toward people to whom we are indifferent, or toward people whom we despise, and could manifest itself as the potential unifying element of all human relations, inasmuch as no human relation directly excludes compassion. But Schopenhauer had to refute this position unequivocally because it creates a value that cannot be reduced to his cosmic theme. And, so, we may still query how he wishes to divide love which is compassion from compassion which is not love. The former is necessarily different from the latter in a specific way: it contains love as itself and nothing else, as an ultimate element of the world and of value. In my view, then, Schopenhauer, for reasons already advanced, cannot acknowledge the intrinsic value of love and, thus, merely extends into the metaphysical realm an error found generally in the normal idea of love. If love gains response and thereby apparently reaches the perfection for which it is destined by essence and meaning, then ordinary language calls it "happy," indicating by this qualification that love's inner direction and destiny is happiness: only if it turns into happiness has love fulfilled its idea. However, love is "unhappy" whenever the lack of response curtails its development and does not allow for the realization of its inner potential. By virtue of this sort of argumentation, though, the proper meaning of love is usurped in favor of that of a concomitant phenomenon, even where love is understood merely as a subjective experience. In the series of inner destinies love appears as a value in itself, as a meaningful and great occurrence, and whether or not it reaches perfection and supreme evolutionary development does not depend on happiness or unhappiness, but on the individual dispositions of the subjects who confer a large significance on it in particular circumstances. The double meaning of happiness puts love into a false dependence on hedonistic reflexes. Love itself, then, appears as a rudimentary phenomenon when its fulfillment is made contingent upon "happiness": it is thought not to have achieved its proper meaning if "happiness" is lacking. Love's value for the soul and the value it gives to the soul may be shaped in measure and mode by the echoes of its reverberations, and, indeed, love may be furnished with a variety of different sensations of happiness. But beyond all of its consequences, the value of love remains simply unique and independent through a function of life in which it has gained a new and incomparable importance, and which can be combined with all possible modifications such as happiness and unhappiness without losing the significance of its being-for-itself in any combination. Although the shallowness of the popular mind's conception of love that I am criticizing here has little to do with Schopenhauer's theory of love, both ideas are at one on a decisive issue: they misread the irreducible importance of love in the totality of life and its values, which is not reducible to generalities. This misreading is unclear and relativistic in common consciousness, but it is clear and absolute in Schopenhauer's thought. Love, in its total person-relatedness and in its destiny, which is unmoved by happiness or unhappiness, is the ultimate threat to the reduction of all values of life to an absolutely uniform level comprehended by the hedonistic calculus. Thus, Schopenhauer thought of his theory of compassion as the brilliant means by which love could be removed from its relation to the opposition of individuals. He even declared it to be the break point of opposition. But he also posited the purely hedonistic point of amalgamation into suffering, in which all of the specific values of life flow together to reach a common level on a purely quantitative basis. This is the reason why love cannot be allowed to have its own roots, just as pleasure in art and the ethical relations of human beings are not permitted autonomy.

In each of the above cases, Schopenhauer has evinced a sure instinct in following the only path toward a unification of the most heterogeneous and self-existent values of life. He has turned their negative aspect of the annihilation of will, individual existence, and pain into their substance. This tendency runs deep within the human context. Often the only way that persons who are motivated by diametrically opposed tendencies can join in common action is through shared animosity and shared interest in destruction. When it comes time to build things up in a positive way, the directions of practice once again become irreconcilable. Plebiscites, for example, often result in the rejection of the proposal at hand, whereas it is difficult to unite people in unanimous acceptance. Ancient Egypt provides an interesting example of the formal behavior in question. When, during a certain period, the religious unification of previously independent regions was proceeding, it turned out that in one region the eating of one animal was forbidden, in another region a different animal's flesh was proscribed, and in a third region yet a different animal's flesh was prohibited, and so on. In order to create a uniform religious conduct, the eating of meat as such had to be interdicted as a last resort: points of negation within religious customs could turn into points of unification, whereas positive prescriptions could not logically serve the same purpose. Schopenhauer's doctrine is based on this form, which provides its ethical grounding. His pessimism required that he place all values under a uniform viewpoint so that they could flow into one another and be aggregated. Aesthetic pleasure, morality, love, and even all of our mental activity, which he defined as the pushing back of boredom, had to be voided of positivity and, therefore, of specific and incomparable contents. These contents had to disappear completely so that value could serve the single goal of annihilating suffering. The comparability that he achieved made values into factors in a unidimensional and uniform account of life.

It is a highly remarkable fact, which leads us to the ultimate depth of Schopenhauer's ethical mood, that all of the ethical values he explains and roots in the cosmic subsoil do not appear in his writings in the form of imperatives. Not only does he fail to give the moral philosopher, who should seek knowledge though not command, any right or duty to preach morality, but he also denies that in an ethical life the purely moral and unreservedly valuable action should be the consequence of an "ought" or should grow out of a consciousness bound by an imperative. For Schopenhauer, there is no other ought than that which is caused by and grounded in reward and punishment, and no other duty than that which is the reciprocal of a right which has been asserted to gain an advantage. An absolute "ought," a duty valid for itself and freed from every purpose—that is, something categorical such as was propounded by Kant—is, Schopenhauer argues, a construction of self-contradictory concepts that cannot be realized anywhere. I have already indicated above something that should now be clearer in light of the preceding discussion: the rejection of an "ought" that is ideal and valid as such is conditioned by the pessimistic intention. If, as in Kant's interpretation, there were a duty which had to be fulfilled simply as a duty, without regard for the results defined by its content, then its fulfillment would be a value of life that could not be included in the pleasure-pain calculus. The value of an action which is not performed to achieve a goal but for duty's sake is as absolute as the imperative from which it proceeds and cannot be legitimized by a higher court of appeal, in that it is absolute and legitimated in itself. Schopenhauer cannot acknowledge a dimension of value which would destroy the unity of his cosmic design. But his scheme of purification, which represents mostly the merely local interests of pessimistic philosophy, does not exhaust the meaning of the rejection of the Kantian viewpoint. What are at stake here are the most profound and decisive oppositions, which divide among themselves even down to the ultimate foundations, the world of ethics. My task will be to show how a sense and a picture of innermost existence is expressed in Schopenhauer's seemingly superficial concept of "ought" and duty. His vision, along with Kant's, circumscribe the great potentialities of ethical understanding.

In brief, the two convictions opposed here are that our action is the expression of a fundamental and unchangeable being, and that we possess, as bearers of practical values, an unlimited plasticity of response to ethical demands that is not prefigured by a preexisting being. It is not quite adequate to interpret this opposition as the same as that between determination and freedom. The second alternative really only addresses how we come to make a decision. The decisions constitute the final judgments on the quality of our innermost essence: they formulate the irreducible sentiments that accompany our ultimate decisions. The question about whether or not this process follows natural causality is secondary, in that its alternatives bear on a different sphere than what is at issue here. Thus, the ease or difficulty with which causal relations can be established should not divert attention from the fact that a decision is the conceptual fixation of a fact of inner life. Inasmuch as will is the being of man, Schopenhauer is convinced that the individual is at the outset gifted with moral quality and that this quality is that of unchangeable being from which the individual cannot flee, because it is his own being. Our action is determined through and within this being, and is but a means by which we progressively learn to know ourselves. A new act does not proceed strictly on its own account. Contrary to general opinion and to the ultimate argumentation of Kantianism, the will does not initiate each process of choice with a decision that is appropriate only to the specific moment, for Schopenhauer holds that we simply are as we are and, hence, that we must decide in a manner that is prefigured by being-itself. In consequence, the exclusivity of any requirement of duty is denied, and here we find the turning point of our problematic. From whatever depth of the actor's reason or conscience the requirement of duty might come, it always remains exterior to the will, which must decide and face up to its decision with the words: It does not matter what you want, you must. These words are meaningless whenever the composition of the will that is addressed has already been predetermined. When Fichte states that "whoever says I cannot does not want to," he expresses the unlimited malleability of the soul's response to the ethical demand of the moment, whatever it may be. He provides thereby a corollary to the categorical imperative, to the duty that rules reality from the world of values, regardless of whether or not reality obeys, because this duty is legitimation and not reality. In this case any original hindrance to obedience of the law that stems from the individual qualities of the being of the soul is rejected. Yet this doubtlessly creates a difficulty for the normal use of concepts that is difficult to overcome. The imperious ought which lords over our will must somehow be willed by us, for if it were not it would merely be suspended in thin air, devoid of any contact with life: to make this "ought" the norm of our will, we must want it. Kant evidently does not solve but merely verbalizes the problem when he claims that our pure reason presents to our will those imperatives derived from the world of ideas, and our will can follow them or not. I must admit that I am unaware of any adequate and compelling interpretation of the soul's experience of its will abhorring a specific "ought," which is itself a sort of willing, and then acceding to this "ought" without feeling any decrease of resistance. Perhaps this is one of those typical and fundamental processes we cannot perceive as unities but can only describe in a circular fashion. Here the will follows the "ought," but the "ought" must be will from the very beginning. Or, perhaps, there exists in such imaginations of the "ought," which are sometimes overpowering and sometimes of no import for our final actions, a form of energy in the soul that has not yet been understood in its specificity and in its relations with what we call will.

"Lord, not my will be done but Yours," is the religious substantialization of a logico-psychological contradiction: if I want something to be done, then that is my will, and I cannot want, as is the case in this prayer, something to happen that I do not want. Yet the prayer expresses a clear fact of the soul that is deeply true and is apparent in its sentiment, even if that state cannot be described adequately by psychological concepts: it is the ideal demand of the will no longer to be itself within its willing but to become a reality which is not its own but is that of an "ought," the contents of which create a dignity beyond will and its negation. For Schopenhauer this difficulty falls away, because for him there cannot be any imperatives that oppose the will and constitute an independent world of values. Will is unequivocally unique and uniform, it is being, and it develops qualities that are carried immediately to the individual's life of value and nonvalue. The phenomenon of regret is, for him, nothing but the process of becoming aware of actions that do not accord with will and essence as such. Thus, when the intellect is obscured by a passion, to the degree that it does not discern the full range of motives which would interdict the action suggested by that passion, it need only wait until the deed has been done and the desire informing it pacified for those motives to become visible and prominent. This is how we come to realize that we have done what we should not have done according to the major and permanent motives of the will that are within us. Probably nowhere more than here is the uncompromising opposition between the two ethical perspectives more clearly delineated. Wherever an objective "ought" beyond the will is posited, regret means that the will has been following itself instead of the "ought." From this viewpoint regret only punishes a will that obeys itself, that is, it punishes a defect in plasticity of response to objective norms which oppose the given will in ideal space. Such a formulation, indeed, must be made in any psychological interpretation of this question. Here regret is the sentiment that accompanies a total reversal of the will, a reformation of its actual facticity toward the norm that is not itself. Schopenhauer can never admit to such a change in will, because will is what it always was. The only thing that changes is the intellect, which under certain circumstances erroneously projects something as our intention which in fact is not, and then acknowledges the true tendency of will by experiencing pain over dereliction from its factual essence. Both interpretations of regret do equal justice to the facts. The altruistic account also has access to what seems to be explained better by Schopenhauer's interpretation. For example, an evil and mean individual has regrets when he acts fairly and selflessly, because he realizes too late that he has been unfaithful to his own proper willing. For such an individual the ethically negative, the imperative of immorality, is just as much an objective norm, which is opposed as an "ought" to his actual willing, as is the "ought" of a good man who has been derelict in his duty. One must be very careful not to identify with some definite content the category of an "ought" which is valid in itself and is both close to and distant from our willing. Perhaps even within the sphere of ordinary moral conduct the content of the "ought" could be quite special for each individual. The man who is destined to evil and corruption by his very idea and constitution may fill the form of "ought" with a content which, when it is not fulfilled in action, may cause him to regret; likewise, for Schopenhauer, one regrets when one is derelict toward the properly individual direction of the will itself rather than toward a norm outside the will.

There are, however, many ethical facts and consequences which seem to find their deepest interpretation in Schopenhauer's design. An example is his contention that the decisive moment of our morality and, therefore, the point at which responsibility originates, lies deep in our own being, but not in singular actions which are only phenomena of the metaphysical will within us. Schopenhauer's opinion seems to be incomparably deeper than the shallow imaginations we normally use to explain our sense of responsibility; that is, he claims that the objections of conscience are immediately aimed at what we have just done, but are more radically directed at what we are. He thereby explains the irritating quality of conscience when we regret, the feeling that all of the baseness and evil in which we were implicated remains unforgiveable, though we might possibly live beyond it or forget it, and that as we try to escape, the latent terror never ceases. This experience is not really connected to the deed as such, to the singular act of will, or even to the state we were in at the moment of action, but has the elementary and radical meaning that our being corresponds to what we did, is the potentiality of this action, and expresses who we are. The teaching of conventional morality—that in moral conduct it is not the action that counts but the intention of the will that informs it—takes on its full depth and breadth in Schopenhauer's account, in which will is no longer assumed to be merely the singular impulse responding to a specific stimulus, but the fundamental being-as-such of man, subject to neither time nor change. Compared with Schopenhauer's interpretation, the popular back-dating of moral responsibility seems merely to be an initial and perfunctory step beyond a juridical judgment which only takes into account the executed deed. But this ordinary conception leads no further than to a moralism which might provide sufficient motivation for everyday practice, but which does not move far enough back from the external fact to reach the last station, the metaphysical dimension. The whole man in his changeless absolute being is the bearer of responsibility for the specific reality of every single phenomenal being, whether good or evil.

Among all our modes of behavior, fidelity is perhaps the most conspicuous example of a moral evaluation, which is directed toward a being, that is beyond singular values. Keeping an inward faith with someone can at most be only partially and indirectly effected through conscious willing. As time goes on the conditions that grounded fidelity often disappear and one becomes of necessity unfaithful, just as the leaves must wilt when autumn fades into winter. Yet such infidelity is experienced as an ethical default, whereas keeping faith is judged to be an ethical value: one is ethical here if one's evolution does not lead naturally to unfaithfulness or if an emotion of fidelity, which is really beyond one's control, remains constant. Thus, being, the profound and fundamental will within us, decides whatever cannot be determined by its individual and conscious manifestations, and bears the responsibility which could not be shouldered by those manifestations.

There is an even more difficult observation that seems to me to reveal the profound importance of Schopenhauer's idea of responsible being. The mind of which we are conscious as being immoral is not always a cause, but is often the consequence of a conditioning fact. In observing psychological phenomena as best we can, we notice that a deed often occurs without thought and through momentary weakness, seduction, or coercion by circumstance; that is, culpability is somehow shared. Such a deed, however, demoralizes its perpetrator and later engenders an appropriate moral attitude toward itself. Often we do not have a guilty conscience because we are demoralized, but are demoralized because we have a guilty conscience. Especially when we sum up our small faults we find that we have become evil behind our own backs and, as we look at our past in a sweeping way, we suddenly acknowledge that we are on a much lower moral level than we had thought we were in our single moments of consciousness. When we realize we can become evil without ever freely and totally consenting to it, we fall into a deep desperation and feel we cannot help sinking. What occurs in moral tragedies of this kind is probably no different from what Schopenhauer indicates: our singular actions, which seem to emanate from ever-new impulses of the will, are really just occasions in which we learn to know ourselves. All actions, once and always, emanate from the being we are. Their relations with the fates of external phenomena shape them into very different appearances, but in looking back on their aggregation we find they share a common thread and refer us back to the point at which their coordinates meet. Only so long as we give an essential importance to the passing moment or to the beneficence or adversity of our internal or external situation will we be able to think ourselves capable of renewed fresh starts and of novel and radical changes. But when we acknowledge a decisive and uniform stability in all momentary combinations, we see ourselves as chained to the immutability of our being, which refers us consciously to a point on the moral scale that we cannot uproot. Now we feel less responsible for all of the singular acts in which the impulse of will and external influences cannot be neatly separated by cognition, but we also cannot deny the being which makes all the difference and allows for no redress. We must stand for what we are and not for one of our singular phenomena.

It should now be easy to clarify how the "freedom" of our being coincides with the definiteness of our singular actions according to the Kantian preconditions that Schopenhauer accepts. Each of our actions, which occurs in the realm of phenomena that is formed by space, time, and causality, is just as much determined by natural laws as is the form of an ocean wave or of a flickering flame. But the existence of being as such and the reception and individuation of its fundamental essence in the forms of representation is absolutely given and is not explicable in an empirical-causal context. Being as such is in this sense "free," because there is nothing exterior to itself by which it could be determined and because it exists outside the causal nexus of singular phenomena. Once being is given in one of its phenomena all other phenomena are also necessarily determined, but being as such does not itself have to exist, because no law or logical necessity would be breached by its nonexistence. The same conclusion obviously applies to the being which is ourselves. The fundamental will which is our being need not exist and, in its original quality, does not have to be the way it is, because it exists prior to all causal determination. Naturally in this case priority is not understood as being within a temporal dimension, but as a "before" of inner meaning and metaphysical import. The fault of all moral philosophy, as Schopenhauer puts it, is to see our being as something unavoidably given *a priori* and, thus, to treat singular actions as free, so that we are responsible for each one of them, as though any one of them could have been different. Schopenhauer holds that, on the contrary, just these singular actions are determined, but being as such does not and did not have to be as it is. This is expressed in the fact that being is will. Our words are inadequate to this task of metaphysical description and can only hint at the mysterious relation by which we posit our essence in a nontemporal act of will, that we are this metaphysical act of will, and that, consequently, all of our conduct has to develop by necessity, devoid of any further freedom of choice. Freedom and responsibility are removed from doing to being, because only being emanates from or coincides with a self-reproducing willing. This is the motive for Schopenhauer's profound statement that the pangs of conscience following an evil deed are not really aimed at the action in its singular determination, but more generally at the quality of our essence, which we only recognize through the action. Our essential pain proceeds from the realization that our being is such as to do what we did, that such a deed can emanate from our primal qualities. This pain is all the more severe

as we recognize that our original quality is free and is our original willing, and that it must also be experienced as unchangeable and immutable. We might make good on a single deed by changing our action
and, therefore, alleviating or annihilating the evil. In such a case an
inextinguishable regret about the deed would not be intelligible. But
inasmuch as our being is fixed and beyond time, and yet still is responsible, we feel that the evil revealed in us proceeds from the abyss of our
existence, which cannot be reached by regret and by individual willing,
and yet remains the root of all regret and individualized willing.

Schopenhauer has described what is, perhaps, the most tragic ethical
situation: that we are fully responsible for a basic being which cannot
be annulled, but the "freedom" of which, while providing the ground
for responsibility, is also immutable. All of what seems to be a change
in our moral quality is, for Schopenhauer, either a change in external
circumstance, which permits different expressions to an immutably
lasting being (a being, in popular parlance, who was "born that way"),
or a change in the images of perception, which grow slowly and reluc-
tantly from the as-such of our essence. This climax of his interpretation
of the problem of ethics also reveals his distance from the ideal of evolution. The absolute stability of our character, which exists as such,
though surrounded in its timeless and immutable being by variable
phenomena, mirrors a specific rigidity in Schopenhauer's own nature: despite his enormous volatility, there is no development in Schopenhauer's
thought after he completed, in the 1830s, his major work, which offers
the purely original image of his doctrine. But it seems to me that the
idea he takes from Kant of the combination of a freedom attributable to
us so far as we are thing-in-itself, and a necessity that marks us so far as
we can be viewed as phenomena within time and causality, does not
bind us to the absolute immutability of a will directed once and for all
toward an act beyond time. Schopenhauer declares that it is impossible
for a human being to act differently in exactly the same circumstances,
in that external conditions operate according to uniform laws of nature,
and change must proceed from a metaphysical will that is beyond time
and is, therefore, immutable. But why, we might ask, should this ultimate being in ourselves not be aimed at a change in direction? Why
should it not carry in itself a difference which could represent temporal
phenomena of change, alternation, and successive affirmation and negation? Schopenhauer naively identifies the statement that character is

given by birth with the assertion that it is immutable. Indeed, a change could not occur in time, because time is merely a form of perception that organizes and orders phenomena, but does not touch the being-as-such of things. But it is a speculative possibility that this fundamental being-as-such, which shapes phenomena necessarily in its image (any new metaphysical character would be represented in a new empirical phenomenon), contains a quality which reveals itself as a total change in our essence at certain temporal moments. We cannot describe such a structure, but we also must take unity and immutability as symbolic expressions of the mystery and ineffability of the absolute under the passing waves of our phenomenal nature. Thus, a transcendental change in and evolution of our being raises no more of an intriguing puzzle than does the immutability of being.

What is involved in the above discussion is not merely a set of alternative conceptual-speculative possibilities, but also the opposition of ultimate and final sentiments and interpretations of inner life. Schopenhauer merely shares in a widely held prejudice that the transcendent—which is constructed purely on itself and becomes, by metaphysical design, the basis for the changing play of givenness—must be simple and immutable. But why must immutability be the condition of a fundamental and primary existence, and development and evolution require a special impetus, motivation, and destiny transcending the self-evident? The condition of immutability is a dogma derived, perhaps, from a superficial observation of human practice, which discloses that man is only moved to changes and developments by external impetus and by motivations proceeding from beyond his actual situation. In moving beyond conventional wisdom, one encounters another interpretation of our essence opposed to the one that locates it beyond time in immutability. This interpretation, which is based on evolution, holds that to become different is the ultimate and inherent meaning of our essence and is the form of our metaphysical substance. Here there is no fear that temporality can degrade our freedom. We are shielded from such fear by this analogy: if a conclusion follows from two premises, we have a development in which one thing grows out of another but is yet nontemporal, because the conclusion is timelessly valid so long as the premises stand. If we acknowledge such a relation in a psychological sense then, admittedly, one thing comes first and another one follows it. But the meaning of or the truth that becomes conscious in this temporal process is beyond the relation of one-after-the-other: it is the pure development of the meaning of a content, the unity of an idea and of a truth that consists in the ordering of its elements. By a strict and not merely symbolic analogy, one might consider that the deepest layer of our being, in which Schopenhauer finds only rigid immutability, plays an essential part in development by tending radically toward difference. In this case, contrary to Schopenhauer's claim that freedom means the irrevocable quality of will, the ultimate within us—which must be free because there is nothing behind it to determine it—is so by dwelling in the changes and vicissitudes of innermost life. We can see that these metaphysical opposites depict once again the opposition of the pessimistic sentiment and the sentiment that expects the possibility of salvation from progress and novelty, and that makes the ultimate foundation of our being into a radical opposition to its past, which, of course, is formally continuous with its past. Schopenhauer's interpretation of basic moral problems, however, binds human action inevitably and constantly to being, except for shifts in circumstance and insight. The freedom of this being under phenomenal action is negative, in the sense that it is not touched by the causality of phenomena, and gains its positive meaning insofar as every being is will. The singular content of the will is produced by the chain of phenomena, whereas the original and mystical act of our freedom is to will the totality of our life as we will it. And inasmuch as life is but continuous willing, the totality of life becomes a profound moral problem. The discussion of the moral problem leads to a meaning which has not yet been isolated. Up to now the "I" and the "thou" have been mediated by the production of the will, which thereby liberates itself from the predicament of a being which is given with the facticity of the world. Thus, though only to a limited degree, contradiction and self-consummation are annihilated as ways in which the will produces itself by its own division into individual phenomena. But we may call this process symptomatic, because, as we have shown above, we cannot completely overcome separation as a form of consciousness. Perfect salvation and liberation, therefore, cannot be reached on this road. At best we can make good on some of the terrible oppositions created by the expression of will in special forms, but the source of these contradictions within and outside us, and all of the pain that they cause us, have not been removed. Therefore, Schopenhauer judges that moral virtue is not the ultimate goal but only a step toward it. The final goal can only be the annihilation of the will. Morality could be the highest stage for Kant because he acknowledged a norm behind the will that conferred absolute value on it. But moral virtue, which is always a positive act of the will, cannot be given definitive value by Schopenhauer, in that he acknowledges only will and not any norm. If we follow the path of moral altruism and tear down the wall of separation between "I" and "thou," we find at the end of this path the unity of the "I" with the totality of existence and the sentiment that, in truth, we are not individuals but are the one and indivisible cosmic will. Thus, we discern that the suffering, meaninglessness, and contradictions of the world are all brought together in the single willing ego. We need not cognize all of this in reflective concepts, for we are dealing with a state of mind that is only expressed in conscious representation. We could say that the soul in question displays characteristics and behaviors as though it were determined by this insight. And this determination can only result in the total distancing of the soul from will, because why should the soul cling to the will if it is nothing but pain, aimlessness, and despair over existence? The instinctive force of a will that lives within us is broken at the moment that we know, not only rationally but in our entire being and essence, that this will cannot be satisfied and that its meaning is meaninglessness. Whoever realizes this cannot be disturbed any longer by his will: the phenomena of this world, which once were motivating incitements, become invitations to quiescence, and will-in-itself dies. Through a process which cannot be completed within the span of the empirical existence of life, will removes the phenomenon of existence by removing its ground.

The meaning of the above becomes more clear when we note that Schopenhauer considers suicide to be in absolute opposition to the internal self-destruction of the will. The suicidal man does not negate the will to live, but desires life with passion, only not under the circumstances in which it is presented to him. The one who really has renounced will suffers every pain because there is no longer anything in him that is opposed to pain. Indeed, for such a man pain becomes the desired means of decisively cutting off the deep roots of the will within himself. He despises hope and enjoyment because they carry the danger of creating new ties with life. In contrast, the suicidal man intensely wishes to live, but with more satisfaction and less suffering: he renounces life because he cannot renounce clinging to will. Thus, suicide can win neither liberation nor salvation. In suicidal man, metaphysical will is not dead but is so virulent that it destroys its own phenomenal ego in order to achieve freedom from the suffering that entraps it, and would destroy the phenomenal other were it to turn outward. Will in man must annihilate itself, not its individual phenomenon, for in negating the phenomenon the thing-in-itself retains its undisturbed existence and with it, as Schopenhauer expresses this mystical fact, all the suffering of being from which the suicidal man seeks to flee. But we must say that this rational construct does not hit its mark. We can easily admit that one who really despises life has no reason to take it and that whoever takes life does so not out of hatred for life but from unhappy and unrequited love. But Schopenhauer would also have to admit that whoever destroys his individual-empirical life annihilates along with it the possibility of experiencing pain. Only when will has created the organ of a sensitive brain is its essence reflected in the form of pain. The annihilation of will does, indeed, remove the possibility of suffering, but this procedure is unnecessary if the annihilation of the phenomenon completely cuts off the reality of will. Schopenhauer contends more stringently here than he does in any other concern of practical morality that the arguments of civil and theological morality are inadequate: suicide, for him, should be rejected only because it is metaphysically useless. The weakness of Schopenhauer's argumentation in this case is obvious, especially as it pertains to life's suffering, because in the instance of suicide alone, the treatment of the symptoms is as radically potent as is the internal annihilation of the will to live. But still he has provided a formulation for a profound sense of value in which suicide, by virtue of its degradation, is differentiated from a real negation of will. One, such as the ascetic, who has overcome life and wants nothing general or specific from it need not annihilate it violently, because life has already turned into a nullity for him. One who takes his own life only proves that he has not overcome it. The justification of the decision against suicide, however, is only applicable when the ultimate and radical meaning of life is addressed. Another approach must be used when life is considered as a series of empirical destinies and facts that includes death. In this case suicide may be justified by incurable physical suffering or by the loss of any possibility of filling existence with worthwhile activities. Here the rational comparison of individual life-values would apply, as it does in the decision to amputate a limb.

Though it may seem paradoxical, suicide might seem to be justified in less radical cases, whereas it would not be a proper remedy for a profound and total distaste with life. In the case of radical ennui Schopenhauer is correct and shows profound perception, though weak argumentation, in claiming that an external annihilation of life would be a totally useless and contradictory expression of an inner separation of life from itself. Schopenhauer's concentration on the values of pleasure and pain, which was unfortunate but was entailed in his system of thought, forced him to argue in favor of something that was far more superficial than what he really meant and to leave gaps in his arguments and to assert them far too forcefully. His interpretation of the liberation and salvation of will by renunciation and denunciation of all willing aims at creating in the subject an abhorrence of this world through an absolute, superindividual, and infinite sharing of the experience of suffering in the world. Thus, he rejects existence, that is, the will, which makes pain real and confers suffering on reality. In rejecting suicide while affirming the motivation to negate the will, Schopenhauer must evade the fact that suicide removes the individual organism, which is the only tool for producing suffering, without any trace or potential for further suffering. In reality he means something far more profound than he can express within his dogmatic calculus of pleasure and pain, just as he lived aesthetic enjoyment and ethical value more truly and deeply in his real thought and instinct than he could formulate them in his system. The renunciation of life and ascetic resignation from all desire that Schopenhauer proposed as the perfection and sanctification of the soul are too comprehensive and fundamental to be motivated merely by suffering, even if the metaphysical unity of the world translates all suffering into the personal soul. We rarely find that this is the motivation for renouncing the will by the holy penitents and ascetes of all religions, who Schopenhauer deems to be the embodiments of his ideal. And though Schopenhauer is quite correct and incisive when he urges us not to accept all of the superstitions and the childish and fantastic reasons ascetes use to explain their deeds in superficial reflection, the discrepancy between the being of their souls and their ideas about the ground of their being should not be abused to justify any interpretation of their motives. Schopenhauer's fertile idea that the real motivations of men have a rather accidental relation to consciousness has led to extravagant psychological ruthlessness, of which he has provided a prime example. We have no right to assume a special hedonistic justification for the renunciation of life by an ascetic saint. The phenomenon that occurs in such a saint is far more general and original than pessimism permits, and can be expressed in an incomparable way through the metaphysics of the will as long as it stays clear of pessimism. The resurgence of the will to live is without foundation, but so is its dissipation: that the will turns toward a goal as such is motiveless, because only the change from one singular goal to another requires motivation; but, similarly, there is no identifiable incentive for the will to turn against itself. A gaze from a point beyond optimism and pessimism reveals that both phenomena are equally miraculous, just as the attraction of the jet of a fountain resides no more in the victorious power of its upward thrust against invisible force than in the no less mighty energies of the downward fall of the water to its source. The fading of the will in ascetic resignation is totally different from weakness of will. Someone whose will is weak is not lacking in will but usually pursues many goals, often with desperate violence. What he lacks is continuous concentration on a single goal: his will flickers and never achieves an efficacious form. The will of the ascete, however, possesses the highest concentration and the most acute efficacy, because it is not directed at exterior objects which are always at the periphery of the ego, but makes itself its own object, subjugating only itself and not the world. Thus, the aspirants to this kind of sanctity often come out of a life filled with passion and even with violence. The power of the will, which had been without peace and had reached out for one thing and another, is now enclosed in itself and dies not to things which cannot be overcome, but to itself. The value of the holy purity and perfection of a life that returns to itself and transcends the world because it no longer wants it cannot, however, be demonstrated. And Schopenhauer, who is profoundly aware of this value, foreshortens the greatness of his thought by deducing it from suffering and its annihilation. The metaphysical turn as such possesses the measure of this value, not in its successes, but only in itself and in its contradictions, that is, in the taking over of the world by a positive will to live.

With a breadth and depth worthy of admiration, the metaphysics of the will circumscribes the inner meaning of ascetic renunciation by having the world of phenomena proceed from will as its creature, mirror, and space of play. Thus, the fact that the world disappears for the saint is explained in its ultimate metaphysical depth, in that it becomes a phantom devoid of substance and reality. It had been accepted as allegory that the world becomes nothing for the saint and the penitent, but now this saying gains immediacy and truth. By overcoming his will he has overcome the world, which is nothing but the product and reflection of will, a place he created through his imagination when he wished to expand outwards. The affirmative will possesses the world, whereas the negating will possesses it no longer because it does not need it, and only need had created it. Beyond morality as such and beyond the question of pleasure and pain, life here finds perfection in itself, leaving no trace of the world behind: with liberation and salvation from itself the will has dissolved all of its outside-itself into nothingness, because it is no longer created, permeated, and maintained in existence by externality. Schopenhauer has found words for the state of the saint, whose will has annihilated itself and, therefore, also the world. These words could only have been found by the desire of the unredeemed for redemption and will be valid for all times:

> Quiet and smiling he looks back to the phantasms of the world which once had the power both to move and to torment his mind, but which now stand indifferent before him as do the pieces in a game of chess after the play has been completed, or as do the discarded costumes, which once teased and disquieted, on the morning after the carnival. Life and its figures are still suspended before his eyes as fleeting phenomena, as morning dreams are to the man who is already half-awake and who sees reality shining through them, knowing that they will no longer deceive him.

7

Human Values and Decadence

UST AS SCHOPENHAUER RECOGNIZES ONLY THE negation of life as an absolute value, so Nietzsche acknowledges only one thing: Life. Schopenhauer utilizes values acknowledged as independent by others—such as beauty, sanctity, metaphysical meditation, or ethics—as means toward his final goal. But for Nietzsche, these and all other perfections and goods of life are only means to a total acceptance and maximization of life. The definitive value of the negation of life allows Schopenhauer to unite the dynamics of life in an ideal unity, which itself is not a goal. The goal of life would not be its own negation, which is a unique and definite predication of sense, separate from any teleology. Indeed, the negation of life permits the exclusion of relative goals as well as an absolute end, thereby disposing of the idea of evolution. Life is turned back upon itself and its meaning is a dead end. Thus, Schopenhauer's aversion to all kinds of history becomes clear. His special justification for depreciating history is that all knowledge, especially philosophical knowledge, treats of the general, which is beyond temporality. Thus, history is not an object worthy of the spirit, because it deals only with the unique, the individual, and the accidental. Yet this justification is only a logical construction that hides a deep-seated aversion to history. If the summation of facts excludes any evolution of values according to a design, then these facts can never be integrated in the way that we call history. One may be skeptical of any speculation that the history of humanity leads to a final goal and to the realization of a single dominant value, but each separate epoch gains integrity only through goals and values, which, on the one hand are seminal, rudimentary, and in the process of active evolution, and, on the other hand, are achieving reality, fuller existence, and greater meaning. Perhaps history as a totality does not evince meaning, progress, and genuine "evolution," but if these categories did not order the sequences of moments, we would not have history but only events. The profound opposition between Nietzsche and Schopenhauer is thereby evident: whereas Schopenhauer's need for redemption freezes him in a mere negation of life, Nietzsche's similar need is satisfied in the infinite historical evolution of our species. Nietzsche's thinking is shaped by historical notions. His concepts of value, which indicate by their ebb and flow the cosmic process borne by man, are of a specifically historical nature. Whereas Schopenhauer formulates a division between the singular, accidental, and individual occurrence of historical material, and the value-laden and extratemporal general idea, Nietzsche transcends this division by transposing values—which have been developed as the culmination of historical life in the evolution of our species—into the sphere of the absolute and into the regions of the ought. Nietzsche's thinking is marked by extraordinary combinations, which are profound in their concrete applications rather than in their logical abstraction. All of the human qualities in which life affirms itself—such as energy of will and nobility, rational power and benignity, and greatness of conviction and beauty—are not mere tools, but gain their value by leading humanity upwards. Although these values realize a general end, their character as value is not conferred on them by an end for which they are used. They have independent meaning and are absolute values. The growth of humanity, which is the higher level for which these values are preparations, is but their ever more intense manifestation. One may grant that life is an original fact (*Urtatsache*) not composed of more primal elements, that the same applies to life's value, and that life can only be experienced in an undivided way. However, as an historical phenomenon, life is but the abstract name and the unifying dimension for all of the singular energies and valuable states. The existence of these states and energies is life itself and the motive force of its increasing intensity. Everything we call small and cowardly and stupid and ugly is merely a depreciation of life and its future promise. And insofar as there is no limit to the fullness of life, the valuable states are in the unique position of being at every moment not only goals, but also way stations toward our realization of value. This formulation of Nietzsche's doctrine is the purest manifestation of the idea of evolution, because it integrates absolute value into the process of evolution rather than leaving it outside this process. For Nietzsche, specific aspects of the historical dynamic of life can be of absolute value and can be independent of their consequences, even if this dynamic is one of development, condensation, and relativity, and is a stairway to the future overman. The valuable states possess their value by virtue of being themselves, because the future results that flow from them and supersede them comprise only their increase and not an instantaneous and historical transformation of existence, such as that proposed by Kant, the mystics, Schopenhauer, and Christianity. Thus, for Nietzsche, the historical process tends toward the infinite, and the absoluteness of value is transformed into its relative stages, through which it can be related to transient and lapsing phenomena without losing its definitive dignity, its self-sufficiency. Through its play with the forms of historicity and finitude, life can be the absolute value. Thus, the cosmic process does not need a final goal or even the idea of one.

The basic image and impression of the meaning and value of our existence that Nietzsche presents seems almost to have been spiritually prefigured in him. The special situation of culture during his lifetime precipitated that impression into a specific theory which dominates the totality of his thought. Or, perhaps more precisely, because Nietzsche was dominated by the mood (*Stimmung*) expressed in his theory of value, he could explain the historical world he encountered as such: In the course of history, especially since the advent of Christianity, the majority, which naturally consists of the weak, the mediocre, and the insignificant, has gained external and internal dominion over the minority of the strong, noble, and exceptional. This is Nietzsche's fundamental theme. As a consequence and expression of this historical process and also as its cause, the original moral values have been completely transformed. The history of language shows that originally it was "good" to be victorious, to dominate, and to express power and perfection successfully, even at someone else's expense. The loser, the weakling, and the ignoble one were "bad." This original contraposition of values has been altered by the democratic-altruistic tendencies, which gain ascendancy in Christianity: the good person is the one who negates himself, who renounces the success of his will, and who lives for others—the weak, the poor, the inferior. Just these lowly ones, who suffer, who are starved for everything, and who never received their share, are the truly "good"; they are the blessed who will inherit the kingdom of heaven. The intelligible consequence of Christianity is that the strong, those who seem ordained by nature to give commands and who are internally and externally independent, are no longer able to live freely and according to their natures, but must live with a guilty conscience. They try to avoid guilt by pretending to be the executors of superior commands and of authority, be it of law, constitution, or even God. Thus, they gain power by pretending to the virtues of those whom they overpower. Moral dignity is altered and ethical interest is inverted: no longer are they oriented toward the increase, plentitude, beauty, and specificity of life, but instead are geared to the submission of the higher to the lower, of resignation to the weaklings and the defeated. The unavoidable consequence of this alteration must be a lowering and levelling of the general human type. The herd animal has achieved victory over the higher and superior specimens of its species through the demand that its herd mentality, the mentality of the suppressed and retarded majority, become the general norm and goal. Whereas vital and healthy instincts are dedicated to growth, increased strength, and the will to power, all of which are the only guarantees of the higher evolution of the species, in the Christian era obedience to these impulses has been stunted by bending them downwards. The Christian, democratic, and altruistic notions of value are intended to make the powerful serve the weak, the healthy minister to the ill, and the mighty submit to the lowly. Insofar as this ideology succeeds, leaders degenerate to the level of the mass. What seems to be moral benevolence, humility, devotion, and abstinence reverses ascending values and increasingly debases the human type.

The crucial point in the above chain of ideas is that Christianity intends to give a religious legitimation to corrupt and declining life. Although Nietzsche obviously was not familiar with it, there is a phrase of St. Francis in which the Christian sanctification of the negation of value seems to be accepted without reservation:

Do you want to know why people follow me? Because the eyes of the Almighty have willed this. Because they did not see among the sinners any more lowly, incapable, and sinful man than I, they seduced me to perform the wonderful work of God. He has seduced me because He could not find anyone more lowly, because He wanted to make nobility, greatness, power, beauty, and the wisdom of the world useless.

Nevertheless, we encounter here a great misunderstanding on Nietzsche's part. We can see that his nature was by no means transcendental, but remained completely within the confines of life, history, and morality. He was unaware that in great measure his own values and those of Christianity could be subsumed under the same standard, so long as the transcendental structures and relations of Christian belief are noted, and Christianity is not viewed solely in terms of its earthly dimension. The point here is that both Nietzsche's thought and Christian belief are exclusively concerned with the quality and structure of individual being, which for Nietzsche is expressed and fulfilled in the concept of life and in Christianity by a divine and higher order, within which the double status of final goal and element of a transcending totality is retained for the individual, just as it is in Nietzsche's concept of life. By transposing Christian values totally into the sphere of altruism, Nietzsche overlooks the Christian emphasis on the value of one's own soul. Jesus is not concerned with those who will receive or those for whom life is sacrificed, but with the giver and the one who sacrifices his life. The parable of the rich young man who is supposed to give all of his possessions to the poor is not a lesson in how to give alms but a commentary on how giving is a means and support for the liberation and perfection of the soul. These distinctions are subtle and invisible to the practical eye, but they are absolutely decisive for the inner value experience of life. The alternatives are those of an activity that gains rectitude and value by influencing objects, and of one that has rectitude and value in itself by realizing a state of being. The latter is not aimed at success, but may be understood as a tendency of the soul that operates regardless of results, a good will. What is decisive here is that work on an object, whether it aims at the well-being of another person or at the construction of something, is itself the bearer of the meaning and value of a moral existence, even when activity is strictly internal to the soul. Such is the decision for value of Kant, of democracy, and of a social ethic. But Christianity and Nietzsche's thought take a decisive turn when they posit all of the value of the soul in its inner qualities, in a completely internalized state. In its activity the soul may and, indeed, must and ought to extend itself, but the value of its action resides in its centripetal direction, which reveals or maximizes its inner state, and not in its centrifugal direction, even when that is characterized by high moral value. Within the Christian tradition the Calvinist theme

expresses this point in a strange and paradoxical way: Every soul is pre-
destined by divine decision either to beatitude or to damnation, and no
earthly action can ever influence this fate. But no one knows his destiny, and the only educated guess about it is based on the hypothesis
that those who are called to beatitude act morally on earth and that
those who are damned act immorally. But these behaviors do not determine the soul's future fate, which has already been decided: action is
irrelevant to the state of the soul. If human beings act virtuously and
well, they do not do so because such action has religious value. They
merely activate a mechanism that allows for recognition of a religious
value situation which has already been established.

One might find the above relation between ethical conduct and value
rather strange, but it shows that the ultimate Christian concern is not
with the negation of self, with giving oneself, or with humiliation, but
solely with the internal quality of the person, which resides in itself.
In his failure to look beyond differences in content and of validation to
the ultimate meaning of Christian valuation, Nietzsche completely
misinterprets Christianity. Even if Christian altruism is distant from
Nietzsche's ideal of evolution and power, the former is still opposed to
the construction of merely moral or social ideals: ultimate value resides
not in the altruistic action itself, but in the sanctification and beatitude
of the soul, which is the inner core of this action. Nietzsche judges life
to be valuable in terms of what it can reach, but yet to be independent
of the web of external relations that defines its own quality. Life, therefore, partakes of the category of danger: the steeper the ascent, which
alone makes existence worthwhile, the greater the danger of slipping
before the summit has been attained, and, if attained, the greater the
danger of losing one's balance. Nietzsche's form of valuing life thereby
becomes synonymous with the depreciation of all democratic ideals.
The masses view the good life through their desire for security, warmth,
and peace. And where there is no urgent need for strength, no one will
grow stronger. Whereas the superior person wants to struggle, the
weaklings, for obvious reasons, want "peace on earth." Perhaps this is
true for broad masses of the bourgeoisie, but it is certainly not so for
Christianity. In light of its great decisions with regard to eternity,
Christianity, more than any other religion, is under the sign of danger.
None of the other classical religions, not even Hinduism with its doctrine of rebirth, is analogous to Christianity in this respect, because for

the Hindus even the worst consequences of a period of existence can be ameliorated and reversed in the next one. Nietzsche did not notice the uniqueness of Christianity because he looked only at its earthly side. Christianity, indeed, preaches peace on its earthly side, but not from fear of danger and not, as Nietzsche understands it, as some sort of insurance policy. It does so only because the earthly dimension is not, on the whole, taken very seriously by it and should be disposed so that it eventually interferes the least with the infinitely dangerous struggle for an eternal future. We find here a negative cause for the quest for peace and security. The incitements to communism that form part of this quest are not, as in the case of modern communism, motivated by interest in property, but, on the contrary, by disinterest. Even though Nietzsche cannot understand the transcendence of Christianity, he testifies conspicuously to the success of that transcendence, which blinded him to the close relation of his own thought to Christian doctrine.

Traces of the truly transcendent essence of Christianity are apparent in Nietzsche's thought when the growth of personality through the relativity of the historical process touches the absolute. No God can exist, Nietzsche says, because if He did how could I bear not being God? As fantastic and extravagant as this may sound, it only gives a form of supreme personalism to a feeling that in other forms is close to Christian tendencies of the inner life. In Christianity, beside all of the infinite distance from and humility before God, there lives the ideal of becoming one with God. This desire for union with God and, in its daring expression, to become God, permeates the mystics of all religions and times. Scholasticism speaks of a "deificatio," and Meister Eckhart holds that man can renounce his creaturely nature and become God again. As Angelus Silesius expressed it:

> To find my final goal along with my origin,
> I must find myself; and I win God in myself
> This way; and transform myself into what he is . . .

This is the same passion which fills Spinoza and Nietzsche: they cannot bear it not to be God. Both of them share with the early German mystics the presupposition that individuality, being-for-itself, and specificity cannot be reconciled with universality, totality, and Divinity. Starting from this distinction, Spinoza concludes definitively, in the mystical tradition, that there is no specificity. If there only is God and if the individuality of other beings is a mere negation, a nothing, then there is nothing. And, thus, the human being is made into God. The defining finitude and exclusivity of the "I," which seemed so divisive, has no reality or genuine being, and, so, we merge with the undivided unity of the divine. Whereas Spinoza resolves the incommensurability of God and self by dissolving the "I," Nietzsche reaches the same result by denying God. Thus, the opposition is annihilated regardless of which of its poles is sacrificed. Even the ways of the mystics or of Spinoza do not allow for a unification of the individual "I" with God, because they terminate individuality by introducing "deificatio." Just as Nietzsche, they cannot bear it that individuals are not God and, so, they give preference either to the individual or to God, thereby liberating themselves from the pain of distance from God. Only Schopenhauer could bridge this gulf, because he did not acknowledge the presupposition that to be something special and to be divine universality are mutually exclusive. He taught, instead, that specificity is the form of expression of universality, not merely as representation, but because the mode of existence of the universe is indivisible from the form of personality and uniqueness. Thus, the entire universe, the divine, lives in and as every individuality. Once the dichotomy of universal and particular is resolved, there is no reason why one of its poles must be negated as incompatible with the other. But if the unmitigated opposition of God and the individual is maintained, then Spinoza's solution, which is analogous to that of the Christian mystics, and Nietzsche's negation of God merely respond to the same difficulty according to different mentalities. Someone who is eager to become one with the universe at the expense of his specific personality is inclined to sacrifice the individual in order to retain God, whereas one whose ideal is individual existence will tend to sacrifice God to save the personality. In light of the above, Nietzsche's thought is obviously less paradoxical than is his mode of expression. He is merely forced by his basic theme of personality as the ultimate value of existence to reach conclusions that seem to be different from those of less eccentric thinkers, but that are actually based on the same presuppositions of feeling and thinking as are theirs.

In both Nietzsche's thinking and in Christianity, the aim is to integrate the full and mature personality—who is the absolute bearer of value in this world—into a transcending meaning and goal structure of existence. Christianity achieves this end by introducing the idea of a

kingdom of God to which the soul belongs both in the world and beyond its earthly limitations, whereas Nietzsche does it by using the idea
of a humanity which evolves through more and more perfect individuals, these individuals constituting the evolution itself. The historico-
philosophical significance of Nietzsche's concept is displayed by how the
concept of "humanity" stands against that of "society." Whenever the
quest of modern men for value looks beyond the individual, it generally
stops at "society" as the ultimate form and defining instance of value,
perhaps because a special group (estate) has become the bearer of substantial and real power, and the object of ethical interest, and the members of the upper classes find solidarity only in their belonging to the
same society. But the concept of "society" is no more clear than was the
concept of "nature," which played a similar role in the eighteenth century. Both of these concepts function as the idea of God did previously,
that is, as reservoirs into which are drained manifold perceptions of
fundamental realities and ideal norms. It seems that each era needs
such a concept for its spiritual systematics, one that must be sufficiently flexible and undefined to serve all possible interests and needs
for explanation, and which must exhibit just the correct mix of mys-
tique and immediacy so that the various movements of thinking and
feeling can meet and pacify one another for a time. Initially the concept
that provides the ultimate form of value for an era functions strictly as a
dogma, and criticism of its dignity seems to be pure heresy, even to
more independent spirits. So closely is the concept associated with the
most elementary and permanent human demands, thoughts, and emotions that to doubt it seems to be to doubt the ultimate essentials of the
inner world. In reality "society" is but one of these forms through
which humanity plays out its power, its vital contents, and its interests, and it could do the same through the forms of individual existence, objective spiritual contents, "natural" existence, and the relations between religious and metaphysical fundaments. The realization
that human life is social at every moment and, therefore, must be observed through the categories appropriate to society with the expectation that individual instances can be determined through interactions,
goes along with the primacy of the concept of "society." This realization
has seduced our age to identify the form of social existence with the fact
of humanity. By the end of the nineteenth century, the social viewpoint
(socio-historical, social-psychological, socio-ethical)—which though it

reveals that one of the great motive energies of humanity is but one perspective among others—had developed into the only acceptable one. Because the spatial and substantive boundaries of humanity coincide with those of socialization, it has been deemed possible to understand all of the other aspects of content through social distinctions. The most general significance of Nietzsche's historico-philosophical doctrine of values is that it is a breakthrough beyond the modern identification of history and humanity. Nietzsche discovered values in the life of humanity that in their fundamentality and importance are independent of social formation, even though they are obviously only realized through socially formed existence. This is the same approach that Goethe took to the major ethical problems. His interest in things generally human led him to acknowledge a unity that permeated all oppositions and breached the barriers dividing the human world, and that had to be enhanced or expressed. Thus, the ethical-social projects that ceaselessly grow up between the "I" and the group, or between groups, were made strictly provisional and undeserving of serious concern. It is not trite, then, even if it appears to be so today, for Goethe to criticize the followers of Saint-Simon by saying that each one should care first for his own happiness, and from there that the happiness of the whole would follow necessarily. The different forms of society and their specific values and conflicts are secondary in comparison with the two basic concepts of humanity and the individual. The entire higher history of the spirit, from the cynics and stoics to Rousseau and modern cosmopolitanism, correlates the concepts of humanity and the individual, making them mutually necessary and opposing them to the mediating structure of society. Thus, Nietzsche views the life of a humanity to which he is passionately devoted as exhibited only in individuals. He liberates human values and interests from the limitations and determinations imposed by social forms of relation, and, perhaps, in so doing he underestimates the importance of social formation even for the development of individual values. The only definitive realities in humanity are individuals, yet societies are so self-sufficient that from a socio-ethical viewpoint one could claim that the individual, like the atom, is but a fiction. But even Nietzsche formulates a synthesis that is borrowed from the history of evolution, which gives greater importance to the individual by overcoming his pure isolation. For him, too, the "single person, the individual, is but an error and is nothing in himself, not an atom."

But Nietzsche does not dissolve the individual into social relations and into the functions of giving and receiving within a group: "Man follows a single line to oneself." Society cannot exist as a totality in one individual; and for a social conceptualization, society exists for itself and the individual can only exist in a society. But humanity can exist in the individual, which allows Nietzsche to state: "Through its evolutionary line of development general life makes a step forward in the individual." There are deep variations in both the meaning of existence for individuals and in the meaning of values. The social concept of the individual usually needs to be mediated: each individual is merely a point at which the lines of society intersect; and insofar as such a point is nothing in itself and, therefore, does not effect any inner change in the societal configurations that impinge on it, justice demands that these configurations be considered as equal in regard to their essence and value. In consequence, the many must dominate the individual. If all are equal in principle, then many are more valuable and important than a single one, and the plurality or society is the essential goal and the individual is irrelevant, because he does and should exist only as one-among-many and as one-for-many. This distinction does not apply to the ideal concept of humanity. Humanity is not a special form that is beyond individuals and yet composed of them, but each individual represents the entire chain of evolution up to himself. Here we find the connection between Nietzsche's construction of a curve of values in history and his ideas about humanity and the individual. Humanity degenerates when the quality of the individual, which is its own quality, is displaced from the center of its interests and is replaced by the social and altruistic diversion of the individual away from itself and toward the others, the many. And this diversion is bound to occur if the human synthesis is expressed in the concept of society rather than in that of the individual. Society is a formation of human material that dominates individuals and dissolves them into itself, making the ideal of equality into a mere aspiration for multiplicity.

It is evident that Nietzsche's liberalism is not of the familiar kind. It espouses, certainly, a social ideal, but one in which the technique of orientation toward social goals is based on individual freedom and on the accentuation of individual being. The content of the norms of this ideal is the perfection, power, and happiness of the individual, who, along with the others, constitutes society. And, in contrast to classical liberalism, Nietzsche's specific individuals are unequal *a priori*. Rather than taking sides in the quarrel between socialism and individualistic liberalism, Nietzsche takes a stand beyond their opposition. He is concerned neither with society as such nor with individuals *qua* individuals. He wishes to accentuate the individual neither as an element of society nor as a bare individual who is the same as all the others. He treats exclusively of singular individuals through whose values and qualities the specific human type can progress to higher levels than were previously occupied.

It is not yet clear why an opposition of content must exist between the two ideal constructions that have been discussed, why the altruistic-moral ideal could not be the evolutionary perfection of the individual. For Nietzsche that opposition is based on his presupposition that there is a natural distance between people. The cornerstone of Nietzsche's thought is that differences between individuals are a natural fact, which makes all ethical ideals of democracy and socialism unnatural because they must presuppose relative differences in the goal of being itself. This is the polar opposite of the Socratic assumption that there is only one virtue which is the same for everyone. In Nietzsche's view Christian-social evolution is perverse because the virtues of a certain class, such as humility, obedience, surrender, and selflessness, are made general virtues. That the same demands are made to very different people rankles him, just as would the attempt to compose an organism out of the dissected members and parts of various species. He has learned that what might appear to be the strength of the weak may really be the weakness of the strong. The differences between human beings do not only reside in the real contents of their inclinations and actions, but also in the values they create: individual qualities are not merely different, some are actually more valuable than others. Factual distance creates the opportunity which is the hope of evolution. It is an unfounded utopian idea to expect humanity on the whole to march forward in the same measured step, because upward evolution can only occur if there is value differentiation which enables one person or a few to do what everyone in concert cannot achieve. Two paths originate from the fact of distance. The democratic-altruistic way denies any justification for the distance that does, but should not, exist. Its ethical task is to level—whether crudely through mechanical communism, or in the more refined form of giving everyone an equal chance to acquire the values of life by according equal pay for equal work, compensating only the quantity of work and not its quality, and equalizing the effects of differential potential and skill by utilizing the treasure of social acquisitions or the altruism of the powerful. In contrast, distance between individuals can be understood as the very meaning and bearer of all human evolution: whereas the immense masses move slowly onwards, only the pioneers of humanity, who are not chained to this slow pace, can make noticeable progress and push their limits outwards. And it is inevitable, along Nietzsche's path, that the distance between the leaders of an era and the masses will grow ever greater. For a position based purely on social ethics, every individual development that does not include reference to the past, inclusion of the followers, and provision for the potential of the multitudes is a crime. But for a theory of evolution which measures progress by the most advanced members of humanity, every hindrance to the florescence of individual qualities and every retardation of the ascent, even if it is actuated by concern for those left behind, is a sin against humanity. On the first path the human shall overcome himself for his contemporaries who have not progressed as far as he has, whereas on the second path he shall overcome himself to achieve a higher type. To go beyond the present man, to overcome, is one of the most fundamental human desires, because there is a very deep animosity in us toward all real existence. This desire calls upon us, with more or less clarity, to struggle against ourselves, creating thereby an ideal that is somewhat negative. Man feels that he must develop beyond himself whether by renouncing his sensuality, humbling himself before God, annihilating his empirical ego and replacing it with an ideal one, or negating the will to live. Nietzsche was the first thinker to view this process as an exercise of power which strictly increases the positive elements of life by assuring that the individual does not turn back to lower levels and become socially inferior. We must go beyond the present man, not because there is too much of him or because something must be bred out of him, but because he is not sufficient: the positive element in him must be intensified to the point that he is able to leave all of the previous levels of development, all that he is now, behind. Schopenhauer also wants to go beyond the present man, but, for him, man himself must be overcome. Nietzsche claims that man must overcome and remain the victor.

The difference between Schopenhauer's and Nietzsche's morality is concentrated on one point: in Schopenhauer's view, compassion, the immediate inner form of solidarity among human beings, bears all substantive morality, whereas, for Nietzsche, compassion must be vehemently condemned just because it secures that solidarity. Aside from some rare and transcendent instances, social ethics is always hedonistic and grows out of the misery, deprivation, and gloomy existence of the overwhelming majority. It is the partial consequence of the suffering of the downtrodden masses or, perhaps, of suffering itself. As will be shown later, Nietzsche finds no ethical element either in suffering or in good fortune. Suffering, for him, is but a means to the growth of being through reaction, anger, and struggle, and only the human being, not hedonistic or subjective reflexes, has value. He accuses the compassionate of preferring to abolish suffering when the evolution of humanity is urgently necessary. More than anything else he loathes a solidarity of beings in which compassion grows and the independent existence and distance of the personalities of both giver and receiver evaporate. The compassionate man divests the suffering of others of its personal character, making the sufferer easy prey. For Nietzsche, compassion is the virtue of whores, who excel in it, because they replace self-control and personal reserve with promiscuity and indiscriminate giving. Compassion makes man descend and become depraved, a weakling and a loser. Whereas such might seem worthwhile for those taking a social-ethical attitude, Nietzsche deems it to be the most radical negation of distance between men. And distance nourishes the ideal of evolution for power, beauty, freedom, and security.

The two opposed convictions just discussed cannot defeat one another by argumentation, because each is grounded in an axiomatic program that the other rejects. For Nietzsche, humanitarian care for the many and ministration to the poor and downtrodden is not a genuine affirmation of value, whereas, for his opponents, the evil and damnable character of Nietzsche's position is as obvious as is a logically contradictory proposition. Nietzsche would not even deign to argue with someone who held that the quality of an individual or the height of evolution reached at some specific time was not important in comparison with the misery of the masses, the retarded development of the average human being, or the unjust distribution of goods. Argument and counterargument are only possible when interlocutors share a certain truth and when they acknowledge their shared acceptance as decisive. Under these conditions the dispute is of an intellectual-theoretical nature and is amenable, in principle, to a resolution, because both sides adhere to the same axiom. The division between Nietzsche's theory of values and the social-ethical theory is, however, fundamental. There is no shared ultimate principle to which an appeal could be made by one side that would convince the other that his opponent's position had greater consistency. Here we do not have a duel of reasons and facts, but of two human modes of existence where persuasion does not count; what counts is only psychological unmasking or brute force. Nietzsche's hatred of Christianity is fundamentally a hatred of the idea of equality under God, which is the real source of directing the practical interest toward the spiritually poor, the mediocre, and the failures. The watershed of ideologies is the assumption that the soul of every poor bastard, small-time crook, and knucklehead should have the same value as the soul of Michaelangelo or Beethoven. And although neither of the two positions needs to advance arguments, it is still quite obvious that Christian equality must be particularly odious to those in the camp of the history of evolution. If we agree that the human soul is a product of evolution, then, whether there is a continuous development leading upward from animal to human, or such a development occurred in some historical period, one cannot draw a line determining where the "soul" is present. And even if such a line could be drawn we could not distinguish clearly between animal and human souls. And if we could clearly demarcate animal and human souls, we would find gradations on the human side between lower levels that were closer to animality, and higher, more developed, stages. If there is evolution toward humanity, then there must also be evolution within humanity. In contrast to the idea of a permanent fixity of species, the essence of evolution is that each singular being is in some way a specific step on the evolutionary path. What we call "species" is merely a practical and useful summation of beings which approximate each other but nevertheless vary in innumerable ways according to their harmonies and tensions and their advantages and drawbacks. This is the fundamental reason why a fanatical evolutionist such as Nietzsche must be an unmitigated opponent of "equality under God," which is a concept that consecrates the negation of the ideas dearest to him.

Perhaps the idea of equality under God places an overemphasis on the fact that there is a soul, which makes all differences of content and of singular modifications as negligible as the difference in usefulness and cultural importance of a document that is written more or less clearly. Or perhaps the idea that every soul is called to an eternal beatitude is a reflection of an inherent megalomania in this principle of the soul. Even if it appears that this principle is moderated by judgments of damnation, grace, and election, such judgments still spring from the affirmation of the infinite importance of the soul and betray the same accent and uniqueness of valuation, just as the magnitude of a sum remains the same whether it is charged as a credit or a debit. The most perfect philosophical expression of the absolute evaluation of the soul appears in Fichte's idealism, where the ego not only produces the world out of itself through its own imagination and abolishes the thing-in-itself, which becomes a product of imagining, but also produces the world, because it is action and action needs an object—that is, the formation, penetration, and mastery of an object—in order to become real. Christianity also holds that the world must be overcome. Indeed, it must do so from the moment that it values the soul so highly. But it does not give compelling answers to such questions as: Why is the soul so implicated in the world? Why did God fail to call the soul immediately into his beatitude? The world remains for the soul a dark and unintelligible reality. But by defining the soul as action and productivity, and, thus, in need of an object, Fichte made the reason for the world intelligible: the soul must create the world in order to have something to confront or, more precisely, to act upon; to have something to penetrate, to overcome, and to negate in its independent existence. A theory of evolution must oppose the absolutism of the soul's value and its corollary of equality under God, because the absolute knows no distinctions. Evolutionism connects the human being intimately with the rest of nature rather than opposing the human to the natural, and thereby creates relativities and mixtures that call attention to the high points in the series of souls instead of to a fundamental equality.

Here we find the ultimate difference between the two opposed modes of valuation. For one party the value of humanity resides in the equality of its members, whether this equality be interpreted as real or ideal and normative. For the other party, value rests in the high points of humanity: by inner distancing, individuals gain the opportunity to grow and develop beyond any existing level. One can assume that Nietzsche's position involves some kind of intensification of the psychological need

to be different. The structure of our body and soul requires bombard-
ment by stimuli, each one somewhat different from the others. When a
chain of stimuli activates responses in us, the sensations lag behind
those stimuli. If the sensations are, for example, to be doubled, then
their causes must not only double, but they must become far more intense. We are not, therefore, receptive to the absolute magnitude of a
stimulus, but to its difference in intensity from the preceding one. We
are constituted so as to become dulled, and are affected not by the absolute magnitude of a cause or content when we react to an impression,
but by our general condition and our environing circumstances. Thus,
we hear many noises in the quiet of the night that escape us because
they become part of the undiscriminated hum of the day. We may also
verify our general observation by citing the fact that a material victory
which might make a poor person happy might not have any impact on
a rich one. The more complex and the more supersensual a content of
the soul is, the more the complexity and singularity which are responsible for its inward effect will function in relation to the degree of individual sensitivity. As the individual becomes duller, the difference and
distinction of stimuli must increase in order for any impression at all to
be made. Dullness does not always indicate a primitive state of natural
or cultural being, but usually results from an extremely refined sensibility that has become jaded. The modern differentiation of personalities, and the individualization of doing and being that has been created by the social division of labor, have by now entered into reciprocal
relation with increased sensitivity to the pictures of the human world
that envelop us. In some strata of our culture this individuation and
differentiation becomes extreme, making the personality fragile and
fostering an experience of absolute isolation and being-for-oneself in
which the individual no longer even understands the other person's
speech. When this occurs two divergent psychological responses result.
First, sensitivity to difference can become so acute and overworked by
one's own conduct and that of the social world that an opposing need
develops for a minimization of extreme and unbearable individualization. The more-or-less serious tendency toward socialism that appears
in these layers of culture might be explained psychologically through
the need for a moderation of sensitivity, and through the desire for a
state in which the individual's own sense of life and his own image of
the human world do not make great demands on his sensibility. Second,

the nourishment of the sensibility by a profusion of distant stimuli may activate a need for ever more diverse and titillating stimuli in order for the individual to sense anything at all. Nietzsche's insistent appeal to the singular high points in the history of mankind and his quest for greater distance may be interpreted here as the expression of a sensibility that has been dulled by the impact of modern individualization and that needs more and more powerful stimuli just to feel its own life. Thus, the radical opposition of socialism and Nietzsche's thought may be formulated in terms of the responses of two contrary mental dispositions to the same cultural and psychological fact. If such an example be granted, we have here an analogy to the case in which a palate that has been dulled by stimuli of taste eventually must flee either to primitive and rustic food or to refined cuisine that surpasses anything previously tasted.

If we compare Nietzsche to his polar opposite, Maeterlinck, whose soul is saturated with democratic values, we will see how the difference we have been discussing is a distinction between formal elements of life that influences all of life's contents. When Nietzsche stresses the value of humanity by pointing to the singular and towering personalities, he also emphasizes the value of singular hours within a life. For him, life gains meaning through its high points, at which heaven and hell are polarized. In contrast, Maeterlinck incorporates the supreme values of existence into each moment of everyday life and finds no need for heroics, catastrophes, or exceptional acts and experiences. He remarks, with uncommon sensitivity, that abnormal and excessive occurrences are always somehow accidental and external: even if they express moral grandeur, profundity of temperament, or excellence of achievement, they contain additional elements that proceed from the world and from destiny. For Maeterlinck, the myriad elements of an uninterrupted existence secure the real ego and the totality of the soul. We might experience every great passion, every sort of wild exuberance, and every unheard of pleasure, but such experiences would count only for what they left us in those quiet and normal hours that have no special names. Extravagance has use only for opening our eyes to the depth and beauty of the quiet hours. Maeterlinck's appreciation of everyday happenings as the only confirmations of a human interiority that transcends accidentality, and his devaluation of the abnormal into a means of spiritualizing the usual, is the most profound philosophical turn of the democratic tendency. Our happiness and our dignity are at home in the sphere of our continuous life and in the shared dimension of all of our experiences and actions; just as in socialism, what is essential is what is shared by all people. The real dwelling of our soul, where we are independent of all external things, random accidents, and momentary stirrings, is the sphere of the normal and the reliable, not the realm of the extraordinary and improbable. We mention Nietzsche's opponent, Maeterlinck, here with reference to Schopenhauer's and Nietzsche's general discourse on modern attempts to understand the value of life. Maeterlinck does not view the democratization of inner and, as a consequence, of external and phenomenal life as implying the renunciation of special qualities, of depth, and of development; conversely, Nietzsche finds value only in aristocratic differentiation, distancing, and the incomparability of a pioneering mission. The democratic sensibility is also what makes the figures in Meunier's work so convincing: the individual, though he is presented in his identity with the others in the mass, does not lose individual, aristocratic, and aesthetic value. Maeterlinck and Meunier have at least by intention succeeded in giving the democratic impulse a metaphysical and artistic form, whereas social-democratic praxis is effective only by renouncing the values of life, which, for Nietzsche, provide life with value in the first place.

The fundamental opposition between social and human values that is posed by Nietzsche may be formulated in a basic manner: the value of a human group has normally been equated with its spatio-temporal realization of individual values of a hedonic, cultural, and characteriological sort; thus, the significance of any form, action, or institution has not included the excellence of the values realized through it, but only the quantity and extension of the values actualized. In contrast, Nietzsche views only the elevation of the highest point achieved by a human group as decisive for the value of that group. It does not seem valuable to him that a thousand people attain an average measure of happiness, freedom, culture, and power: the meaning and final goal of our species is for a few or even for one person to be able to realize an extreme measure of these values and powers for themselves, even at the expense of a low level of realization for thousands of others. The vanguard of humanity is of importance to him, not the average individual. There is no way to compromise or unify the two opposing modes of valuation, because they dispute the standard of valuation and not some special value or specific reality. There is no logical means for deciding which state of mind is correct when one of them derives the value of the elementary unit from the average of the values achieved by each individual component, and the other derives it from the highest values manifested, regardless of how many components attain them. Any attempt to unite the two views—by assuming that a social structure aimed at maximizing distance between ranks and at favoring its most gifted elements would maximize the average value of the group—is doomed to failure. This viewpoint is that of a social aristocracy, in which an aristocratic order is interpreted as a means to the common good. But to accept such a standpoint to be Nietzsche's principle would involve the most crass misunderstanding. For Nietzsche, achievement of the height of human qualities is not a means to any social good or progress, but an end in itself and, not, as we will note later, a way of bringing selfish benefits to some persons, but of elevating the human type. And even the maximization of personal values, is, for him, not a means that is somehow independent of these values: humanity moves forward immediately through these values. Thus, a social aristocracy is not the medium through which the two units of valuation could be reconciled, one of them appropriate to the sum or average, and the other relevant to the excellence of any element.

The Nietzschian mode of valuation is in some ways a reversal of the theory of marginal value (*Grenznutzen*). If there is a specific quantity of a commodity on the market, a specific price for each of its units results from the dynamic of supply and demand. Thus, any added supply that reaches the marketplace must be sold at a somewhat lower price because the most urgent demand has already been satisfied. If there is no interference with the normal process of buying and selling, then the first parcel of the commodity must be more expensive than the second, the second more expensive than the third, and so on. It has been observed that the price of any parcel of an entire quantity that is offered for sale at a given time is not higher than the price that its least expensive parcel can command. Thus, in general, the price for the totality of a commodity is no higher than the price of its least expensive parcel. Value here is not determined by an average, but by an extreme. This extreme, however, is the opposite of that employed in Nietzsche's valuation: in the economic case, the desire of the evaluator, the buyer, is for a low price, whereas in the case of human value, what is sought is the highest level of value.

The complexes of religious, sociological, and ethical value have mixed criteria of valuation, some of them utilizing extreme standards and others averages. Israel would have been pardoned for a single man. The importance and honor that are accorded to a single family or group because it contains an outstanding member is often strangely independent of the value and significance it would otherwise have had according to its average value. In contrast, a solidarity that unifies social groups, particularly on a primitive level, takes on a pessimistic dimension: in cases of punishment and revenge, all members of the group are made culpable for the wrongdoing of one of them. In consciousness and action, the group is tainted far more by the sin of one of its members than it is ever enhanced by a good deed. When something about an individual becomes ethically problematic in relation to the group's values, there are different ways of seeking resolution. A typical sentiment is symbolized by the scales of judgment, in which our good and evil deeds are weighed in the balance, and a determination is made about whether we are saved or damned. Here evaluation is made according to an average: the sum of positive and negative elements determines the value of the whole. But even in this case, evaluation is based on certain key elements. In judgments about individuals it is common for the image of the person to be determined by a single and impressive good or bad deed, so that all of the other activities of that person fail to count, even those of a lower grade that would support the primary valuation: the one very good or very bad deed is sufficient to place the whole person into a high or low rank, regardless of any other considerations that might seem relevant. The individual may even evaluate himself according to some extremity on the scale of values and thereby gain undisturbed security from his best deed, or insatiable despair from his worst one. Surely, scales of valuation are not determined generally and abstractly, but concrete judgments are nonetheless based on the following principles: the value of the whole may be derived from the sum of its elements or, perhaps, less frequently, obviously, and openly, from the value of its most extreme element, be it positive or negative.

The best analogy to Nietzschian principles can be found in art. The value of a period in the history of art, in which a genius of the first order exists alongside a multitude of rather mediocre or less than mediocre talents, will be judged as superior to a period in which there are many talents, even if their average level is quite impressive and their number is remarkable. We can also apply the same mode of valuation to the productions of individual artists. The meaning for us of Titian and Rubens, of Shakespeare and Goethe, and of Bach and Beethoven is not determined by the average quality of their works. Each of them produced a large number of uninteresting and often surprisingly mediocre works during their extended periods of creativity. If we combined their lesser efforts and their great contributions into a sum total, their importance would probably decline. The significance of these great masters for us stems from their greatest works, and that significance then spreads to all of their productions. The same holds for personalities of all kinds: their importance depends on what they have done, on their contributions to the independent spirit and not on their personal lives. There are many historical forces that operate continuously to consign to oblivion the less important aspects of the life and work of great individuals, and to equate the value of these individuals with their best performances, even when these efforts have a restricted scope. I mention all of this to make it clear that it is not always mistaken to follow Nietzsche in placing the decisive accent on the highest examples of human excellence. He has, for the first time, merely extended a widely used method into a principle for evaluating social and human existence as a whole.

Once Nietzsche had made his fundamental commitment, it is obvious that he had to interpret the democratic-socializing tendencies of the nineteenth century as leading to the decadence of values. His standard of value is but the passionate expression of the human need to grow and to ramify, which blinds him to the importance of evolution on a broad scale and makes him a fanatical partisan of qualitative evolution. Any attention to the broad spectrum of human life seems treasonous to him, because it drains energy from the pure ascent. The democratic proclivity to decrease the distance between the lowest and the highest levels of human life seems to him to be a failure of the evolutionary process, if one might use such terms, because the crowd develops more slowly than the select and, in a democratic society, the latter must wait on the former. The logical consequence of combining the idea of evolution with the principle that every human being should attempt to realize his highest potential is the evaluation of all genuinely social movements of a democratic character as decadent, as deprived of the instincts impelling growth and exaltation.

What Nietzsche calls the will to power, and what he terms decadence when that will dissipates, is merely the expression of his doctrine of values at its climactic point. One may express the specificity of this doctrine abstractly by saying that the absolute level of a human's ascent depends upon his relative level of ascent: an individual can only represent a substantial step forward on the scale of human evolution if he occupies a rank within a social group that is superior to the standings of others, keeping in mind that rank here is not coextensive with its traditional and external social meaning. Nietzsche is convinced that the growth of life means the continual increase of the forces necessary for influencing the world around us and for integrating, utilizing, and dominating it. One who gathers power and soars over, dominates, and even tramples on other beings is the bearer of the individual qualities of power and nobility, and of intensity and significance of personality. Thus, we find an inner and positive reason for what until now seemed to be an external condition for upwardly surging life and for the theme of distancing: the many, who are inevitably mediocre and weak, cannot evolve as rapidly as can the pioneers, those of genius who are born to leadership. The level of the masses or of a socialist society may remain static or move in some way or other, but by their very natures neither one can contain the values of a concentrated life that surges to surmount others. The unavoidable expression of life is the accumulation of forces through struggles, victories, and the consuming exercise of power: the more life there is, the more the will to power is evidenced and the more consciousness arises of external and inner distance, resulting in culminations of domination and providing a self-referential standard for the progress of value. If Nietzsche's concept is utilized beyond the domain of brutality where at first blush it seems to apply, one cannot deny its profound meaning for the interpretation of the ever obscure, fragmentary, subtle, and continuous processes of life. Just as it is the nature of love to grow constantly so long as its foundation is secure, allowing us to say with paradoxical brevity that love is more love, so, for Nietzsche, life is more life and thereby it fulfills its deepest function as a form of evolution. But Nietzschian life must be lived on life's accounting system: height is achieved at the expense of breadth. This relation does not indicate a painful necessity that might be remediated by more favorable socio-historical circumstances, but is the inner essence of life itself: life is such or is not at all. Nietzsche's interpretation of the essence of life reveals why he obviously has no sense for the immense tragedy which for any other sensibility would be contained in such an image. For him, by logical necessity, interest in society is destroyed by interest in mankind: the value of the individual is bound to a dominating, surging, and all-consuming distance.

It is only because Nietzsche's view of life is a logical deduction from axiomatic premises that he fails to be aware that his commitment is inconsistent with the idea of the obligations of nobility, which, as we shall see, are of such eminent concern to him. If individual life has so many needs and demands, then it follows that it is not self-sufficient and that its own powers need to be supplemented. Nietzsche should at least have made the boundary lines clear between his will to power and the base desire for possession, showing that there is value only in the qualities of individual souls expressed in social relations, and not in the external realities of domination and force. Only a metaphysical concept of life—that derived a unitary standard of value from the concentration of all forces on the tip of a perfect pyramid in formation—could properly respond to the ethical objections against a doctrine of rapine. For such a metaphysical interpretation, individuals would only be containers and forms, deprived of any real significance, inasmuch as the essential process of life as a whole would occur within and beyond them. Starting from organic life, which is propagated by successive acts of procreation from a hypothetical original seed, we may derive a speculative image of life in which life flows constantly through all individual beings, giving meaning and significance to accidentally adapted forms so long as it permeates them. Thus, by a metaphysical justification, life would be the vehicle of form and of the perfection of value, and individual bearers of life would not have the right to make any special demands.

The comparison of Nietzsche's ideals to others that are widely recognized shows that, in marked opposition to Kant and Schopenhauer, Nietzsche does not restrict the philosopher's task to codifying operative moralities or even prevailing moral beliefs, but that he calls upon the philosopher to be a lawgiver who must provide "new tables" of values. And it is equally clear that the "immoralism" he proclaims is anything but a negation of morals. He merely fills up the "ought" with a different content, retaining a form that is even more immediate and forceful than Kant's. Nietzsche's positing of values carries its imperative character within itself, whereas the Kantian imperative is merely a formulation of the fact of human reason made by an objective theoretician who places his ideal outside of time and is even indifferent to its practical acknowledgment. Nietzsche, the practical and preaching moralist, does not posit a new ideal, but demands a new quest. He makes, however, a very dangerous and misleading association between the content of previous moralities and morality itself, which leads him to call his negation of the earlier contents "immoralism." This laxity in formulating his thought is responsible for the horde of his followers who find in the liberation from traditional moralities an excuse for being libertines, and not a challenge to create a new law. For Nietzsche, however, as we shall see later, the need for a new, positive, and relentlessly demanding "ought" was self-evident. For him, the interpretations of his followers would have been as decadent as democratic thought was, or as would be any decline of the will into weakness. The instinct to pursue the great goals of humanity is violated as much by no laws at all, as by perverted and life-denying laws that sap the strong. A lucid and resplendent morality springs from the negation of historical altruistic-democratic morality and even from the promulgation of "immoralism": "Morality in Europe today is the morality of herds of animals. As we understand it, this is a kind of human morality, and there is plenty of room alongside, before, and after for many others and, above all, for higher moralities as possibilities and as necessities."

8
The Morality of Nobility

IETZSCHE'S LIFE HAS BEEN DESCRIBED AS: A REPE-
tition of Greek sophism, which already had evinced a radical opposition against all historically established and recognized morality; a general acceptance of nature as the guide
to conduct; preference for individual spontaneity over objective norms; and an affirmation of the right of the strong to override
equality under the law, which was taken to be a groundless protection
for the weak. But this analogy inverts the actual relation. Sophism's essence is to substitute the value of the subject for the objective value and
meaning of being and conduct, whereas for Nietzsche the subject gains
importance only by virtue of its objective value; sophism measures objectivity on a subjective scale, whereas Nietzsche does just the reverse.
For Nietzsche, however, objectivity does not inhere in some palpable
work or in some overtly successful conduct, but in the degree to which
the quality of a human type realizes an evolutionary advance. Nietzsche
clearly does not subsume the worth of the person under any utilitarian
category: the person remains the definitive bearer of goals and values,
but his being and conduct are significant in terms of his specific subjectivity. Nietzsche's method of arriving at values presupposes an acute and
subtle conceptual distinction. He does not define humanity apart from
individuals in the way that sociologists sometimes define society, but
holds that individuals exist in humanity, which yet is made the standard of their value. In sophism, the subject finds only himself through
an inward look, but, for Nietzsche, the subject discerns himself in the
advance or decline of humanity and is determined by the value criteria
of human evolution. Thus, the definition of the subject is fully objective whether or not there is agreement on what contents are progressive

and on how those contents should be graded. Here we grasp the distance between Nietzsche and Max Stirner, which cannot be bridged despite superficial indications of the sort that made Nietzsche appear to ally with the sophists. As did the sophists, Stirner holds that all objective standards and values are imaginary and inessential, ghostly shadows confronting subjective reality. Stirner would find it meaningless to claim that the ego referred to anything beyond itself or that it should be graded according to a scale of values. He represents the renaissance of sophism, whereas Nietzsche writes: "We find abominable any decadent spirit who says: 'Everything only to me!'"

Nietzsche's difference from Stirner gives his doctrine a certain aura of nobility. In the realm of the spirit, there is unanimous agreement that objectivity means nobility: the hallmark of a noble spirit is to treat an opponent's opinion objectively, to argue fairly, and not be drawn into the tempests of subjective passion. Therefore, nobility must be described, and we will examine this more closely below, as a formal conduct which characteristically unites a resolute personality and a lucid objectivity. As an approach to the quality of personal value, nobility denotes the acknowledgment of the individual's objective value. A genuine aristocratic sentiment demands severity toward oneself and the measurement of the value of one's existence by the dignity of one's life as a whole, and not according to the accidents of one's position or the harvest of gifts and pleasures one has accumulated: the noble person has "dignity." Dignity is an inherently relational concept: one is worthy of something according to an objective criterion, whether or not one receives his due. One gives the impression of being worthy and of having dignity by demanding no more and no less than is due to him for his being and conduct in terms of an objective standard. An aristocrat may believe that human beings and things should serve him, but he is to be distinguished from those who are guided by egoistic illusions and carry with them a secret insecurity. The aristocrat has the firm conviction that he deserves service on the basis of objective justice, his personal quality, and the conduct that follows from this quality. His duty, which is the consequence of his right, is directed first upon himself and not upon some task: his duty is to form and conserve his being so that it remains the source of his rights. Both the system of ranking that is so obvious in Nietzsche's thought, and his interpretation of the value of the individual in terms of the development of humanity, stem from the sentiment of nobility.

It is but a consequence of the structure of the ideal of nobility that rank is not determined by overt deeds but by the closed and inward dimension of the individual. A valuable person will evidently act in a worthy manner, but emphasis should not be placed on success—which is always conditioned by the impact of being on circumstance and by the powers of the environing world, and which involves a step from the interior to the exterior. Nietzsche calls those actions which are judged by their results "epidermal." What counts for him is the superiority of the person; all else is accidental. Action may be one of the means assisting humanity in its ascent, but it is not growth itself, which is only evinced in humanity through its highest representatives. Thus, Nietzsche attacks those who oppose hero worship and who beg the question by comparing deeds of great men to those of the masses. The equation of the essential value of a great man with his overt effects involves, for Nietzsche, a profound misunderstanding: "But the higher nature of a great man resides in his being different and in his distance in rank, not in any impact he makes, even if it were to move the world." Here Nietzsche's unmitigated opposition to any social interpretation again becomes obvious. Society is only interested in what an individual does, and his being is of concern only as a guarantee that his conduct will always be directed along specific lines. If society nurtures pure morality and the ethical power of self-transcendence, it does so merely to prevent adverse external consequences. The social principle, which is the influence of each on the others, defines individuals solely through their effects. Society leaves the inner dimension, what the individual is in himself, what his quality is, to each one, and is indifferent to any ranking other than that based on external consequences. For Nietzsche, social morality is merely the residue of the old teleology that has fundamentally been overcome: though man is no longer the meaning of the world, he is still retained as the meaning of others. Even the most sublime form of moral action, in which all value resides in the "good will," overlooks the most profound and purely human dimension. Though the ethics of intention admit that the moral value of a personality cannot be predicated on the degree of success of a conduct, whether it influences real life or is blocked by the forces of reality, this view still presupposes that the effects emanating from the personality are the essence of value. The soul remains centrifugal here, even if the point at which value is assessed is no longer external to the active individual and placed in the social world, but is fixed within the person. If, as for Schopenhauer, the

total human being is not identified with his will, then, despite the impossibility of making distinctions based on overt acts, there will be a
profound decision in value experience: individual value is determined
either by the pure quality of being or by its exterior impact on practical
relations.

Thus, to use Schiller's expression, aristocratic natures pay with what
they are, and lower natures with what they do. Aristocratic morality
raises the individual quality of being—which is subjective for a social
interest and for a morality of the will—to the status of objective value.
But we are now faced with the most grave and consequential question:
Where do individual human qualities gain their objective legitimation
as values? As I have shown up to this point, Nietzsche's response is
that natural breeding generates specific human qualities. Through the
occurrence and growth of these qualities, humanity has reached the
level it presently occupies, which constitutes a criterion that is independent of any subjective and merely personal evaluation. But this conclusion, though it may seem to be compelling, is logically faulty. The
evolution of our species has actually produced not only beauty and purity, greatness of conviction and honesty, and value and power, but also
their opposites. The degree to which one of the two series has prevailed
over the other cannot be determined empirically and is irrelevant to the
nature of value. Thus, it is necessary first to define those traits contained in factual historical evolution that are the core of human value,
because they are the imperatives for our actions and the proof of our
value itself. Natural evolution cannot decide the value of our essential
qualities through an objective standard. Indeed, the basis for any selection of high and low qualities from the evolutionary process must be
based on prior ranking, even if evolution is defined normatively. It had
seemed that a concept of life given new meaning by evolution could
provide what everyone wanted, that is, a logical deduction of the content and meaning of the "ought" from a given and verifiable reality. The
great difficulty of every doctrine of ethics and values has been that
within the realm of the verifiable and real, taken in an inclusive and not
in a crudely materialistic sense, what is valuable and morally necessary
could not be deduced. The sphere of value had to be ceded, it seemed,
to the nonrational individual will, which was left to decide according to
strictly personal convictions. Most metaphysics attempted to elude
these consequences by a mystification that transposed the good and the

"ought" into the realm of the most eminent reality. By positing the concept of life as an all-inclusive form that includes everything essential to man, and by assuming that life is constituted by the urge to grow intensively and extensively and to become more noble, Nietzsche could view the life-process as one of increasing value. Thus, the creation of ideals could be interpreted as proceeding along the innermost direction of human reality, which might not always be observable but was ever present. But now the lack of relation between the evolutionary process and progress toward ideals has been revealed: real evolution produces the negative with the same disinterested necessity as it generates the positive. Put another way, not only noble exalted qualities help individuals to gain power, open up their lives, and develop all of their potentials; innumerable victories in life's struggle are also won by people who lack honesty and conscience, and who are motivated by lust for property and by crass practical materialism. Thus, the selection of the elements that Nietzsche recognizes as values in concrete existence is not predetermined by the structure of life, but must arise from a sense of value that is independent of this structure. Only an optimistic and enthusiastic belief in life that, similar to Schopenhauer's pessimism, can be neither verified nor falsified can regard values constituted by other sources as forming the nerve center of life and of its actual development. Nietzsche, therefore, is finally unable to develop a scale of qualitative individual values from a principle of value based on the increase of life. This is why there must be a split in his account between the principles and forms of human values and qualities as they appear within real contexts.

The objectivity of values in Nietzsche's thought does not follow from their origin or cause, but, as has just been explained, from the ideal of nobility. The existence of certain people and human qualities is valuable not because of their relations to other people or their effects, but by virtue of a "higher law" that makes their existence an end-in-itself. This end-in-itself is not a subjective and specific sense of life or an intrinsic pleasure, but is objective: the totality of things is more meaningful, distinguished, and valuable the more such noble existences are found in it. The objective essence of the values of nobility entails that the price that must be paid for their realization in individual life— subjective suffering, sacrifice of energy, and subjugation—is completely without importance. A noble person does not ask after the price. Therefore, the style of aristocratic life is diametrically opposed to that of the money economy where the value of things tends increasingly to be so identified. Taine observes that the aristocracy of the *ancien regime*, which enjoyed great luxury, regarded it as a mark of nobility not to take money into account at all. This is clearly the opposite of the luxury of conspicuous consumption, which is based on extreme esteem for money. Nietzsche's deep aversion to all of the specific phenomena of the money economy must be traced to his fundamental value commitment to nobility: in the money economy one weighs benefits and sacrifices, and regards something as a value when it is not purchased at great expense; whereas, for Nietzsche, one dissolves the relation between value and price by remaining indifferent to expense. The principle of nobility is brought to its extreme in the assumption that the objective value of humanity is represented only by its most advanced individuals and that the suffering, oppression, and retardation of the masses do not matter because they are but the price of ascent. Nietzsche's law of history and philosophy is that the human being could not develop to his greatest power and sublimity without the most severe process of selection and trials, and without much recklessness and cruelty. Although it appears to be paradoxical and seems to be plausible only if the basic and elementary ethical forms are purified and intellectually freed from all sentiments related to their contents, it is just by such purification that Nietzsche transforms Kant's basic sentiment from an individual morality into an ethics of the species. For Kant, morality is only intelligible as the overcoming of the lower and sensual parts of our essence. In his view, the human being is naturally sensual and lustful, and is not good by nature, but rationality fights an ongoing struggle for liberation against the earthly elements that weigh it down: spoliation of the lower man by the higher man is not possible without pain. This is one of the fundamental themes of the history of the human soul: the essential elevation of our being is effected through pain, and the basic differences in world views are related to how this fact is viewed and understood. Kant has condensed the connection between pain and overcoming in the extreme point of subjectivity so that the value of a person is acknowledged only in self-sacrifice. Nietzsche transfers this connection beyond the individual to mankind: only discipline attended by great pain has brought forth "all elevation of humanity." Thus, it becomes possible to dissolve the self-evident identity of the one who ascends and the one who suffers pain: the pain, oppression, and sacrifice of innumerable people create in one person the conditions for the power, productivity, and potential of the soul whereby humanity conquers a new plateau on the evolutionary path. The Kantian value of the individual soul is expanded to include the totality of historical society, and the tension between value and suffering is no longer centered in the individual soul but in a diversity of subjects who are contained in the unity of humanity.

It is, indeed, peculiar to base the formation of values solely on their objective existence and simultaneously to claim that these values are realized in an absolutely personal way in the individual existence of the soul, so that only the height of evolution matters, regardless of its cost in terms of sacrifices and subjective conditions. But this is just the counterpart of the aforementioned indifference to the effects of the worthy individual. The value of the individual's being is as independent of its conditions of origin as it is irrelevant to its consequences. The value of great men is not determined by what others receive from their eminence or by the benefits they themselves derive from it. Therefore, the personalism of an objective formation of values is not at all common egoism or hedonism. The representation of being in subjective sentiments of pleasure and pain is quite different from the value of being, whether one refers to oneself or to someone else. I shall quote some important passages, because Nietzsche has been more seriously misunderstood on this point than on any other:

'Do I ask for happiness?' Zarathustra queries. 'I ask for my work. . . . Freedom means becoming more indifferent to stress, hard work, deprivation, and life itself; having the masculine instincts, such as the instinct for happiness. Liberated man tramples on the despicable kind of well-being dreamed of by merchants, Christians, cows, women, Englishmen, and democrats. . . . One should not wish to enjoy when one has not given. And, one should not wish to enjoy. . . . My deep indifference toward myself; I do not wish for any advantage from my insights and I do not avoid the disadvantages that stem from them. If one wants happiness then one must join the company of the poor in spirit. . . . Be it hedonism, pessimism, or utilitarianism, each way of calculating the value of things according to pleasure and pain, according to circumstances and external things, is naive and fixated on the foreground: everyone who understands creative forces will view them with both derision and compassion.'

The struggle of the church against sensuality and the joy of life is intelligible and justified in relative terms, only on the understanding that the church deals with degenerates who "are too weak-willed to impose on themselves a limit to their concupiscence." Thus, "lust is only a sweet poison for the weakling, but for those who will with a lion's heart it is the reverently reserved wine of wines." And Nietzsche judges the disposition to "love thy neighbor" to be a poorly disguised expression of the impulse to love oneself: "Higher than love of one's neighbor is love for those farthest away and still in the future—those who are far away must pay for your 'love thy neighbor.'" But let me add that love for those who are distant could denote an extension of a more clear-sighted means for the Christian love for the neighbor. There is no more severe judge of everything anarchic, undisciplined, and soft than Nietzsche, who finds the reason for the engulfing contemporary decadence in the disappearance of strict discipline, piety, and authority in the face of the ignoble tendency toward equalization and universal happiness. Certainly he preaches selfishness, but his exhortations to the elevated and select, the leaders, to retain themselves are meant to save the permanent values, from which they derive their eminence, from momentary impulses that would spoil them and soften their hearts. Thus, he requires an inner distance from the lowly so that the great man will not exteriorize himself and be dragged down to their level, and, thus, destroy the highest values. But none of this is a matter of illogical will or the quest for pleasure. As he says, the noble man must accept "his privileges and their exercise as a duty," and, therefore, he would not "lower his duties to make them everyone's duties." The meaning of what is called Nietzsche's selfishness is the preservation of the highest personal values. Thus, he must demand unbending severity toward himself and others: "The prime will always be sacrificed and we are this prime. But that is what our species wants, and I love those who do not try to preserve themselves." Certainly Nietzsche preaches recklessness, harshness, and even cruelty, but only because these seem to him to be the only school and discipline through which strength—which is endangered by the reduction of our ideals and our reality to the interests of the average and general public—can once again grow: "There will be ever greater hardship and duress for you, because only in this way can man ascend, where lightning strikes him and breaks him into pieces: Upward to lightning!" One of the strangest mistakes in the history of morals is that Nietzsche's doctrine could have been understood as a frivolous egoism and as a sanctification of Epicurian laxity. This error was essentially possible because the new synthesis in which Nietzsche united the elements that form value was not understood. Old associations were still operative and these were joined to single elements of Nietzsche's synthesis. Nietzsche made personalism into an objective ideal, placing it definitively apart from strict egoism, which always returns to the subject. Egoism aspires to have something, personalism to be something. Thus, personalism posits itself beyond the opposition of hedonism and moralism, and thereby subsumes the Kantian morality under itself. Hedonism asks, What can I get from this world? Moralism queries, What can I do for this world? For Nietzsche even the question of what to give is excluded. Although he is concerned with a quality of being naturally evinced in actions and in "giving virtue," for him, value does not depend on phenomena and consequences, but is immediately given with the quality of being, to the degree that it represents a specifically higher level in the evolution of humanity. Similarly, the quality of being may contribute to subjective happiness, but unless happiness reflects depth of growth and animation of existence, the accent of value is placed on being itself, which is the basis for what is expressed in sentiments of pleasure and pain, and not in its emotional consequences.

Thus, Nietzsche continually stresses that life becomes more disciplined and severe the more it ascends. Nobody would have been more disturbed than Nietzsche by the abuse of his concept of the overman, which transforms the liberation from democratic-altruistic morality and concern into a justification for libertinism, rather than into the duty to move onward to an objectively higher level of humanity. From the standpoint of Nietzschian duty, the poorly masked and subjectivistic hedonism of the so-called Nietzschians is only a reversion to a lower level, to the laxity of pessimism, and to a barren use of power, inasmuch as a life that follows the subjective conditions of pleasure and pain must run into a dead end. Thus, the hedonism of the Nietzschians is decadence and declining life, which transfers its objects from the lower elements of society to the baser elements of the subject.

Nietzsche's synthesis of the factors of value into the ideal of nobility should have made it clear that the specificity of his ideals is indivisibly linked to an essential and necessary mood of responsibility. Every proper aristocracy is saved from the pure enjoyment of its prerogatives by acknowledgment of its self-responsibility, not of its responsibility to others or to an external law. Nietzsche's interpretation of this responsibility, which springs from the depth of one's own being, is in terms of the concept of a humanity which achieves the height of evolution through its most progressive individuals. The existing aristocracy appears to him to be false and decadent, not ideal at all. It seems to me that the sense of responsibility that resides in a morality of nobility is the ultimate theme of one of Nietzsche's most peculiar doctrines, that of the eternal recurrence. If, as he teaches, the cosmic process occurs in infinite time and within an infinite mass of forces and matter, then all resultant combinations of elements will occur within finite time, no matter how long this time lasts. After that finite time is over, the game must begin anew and, in light of causality, the previous combinations must be repeated in the same way, and so on *ad infinitum*: given the continuity of the cosmic event, every moment can be viewed as a point at which one cosmic period ends and another begins. Thus, the content of every moment and of the entire life of each human being has already appeared an infinite number of times in exactly the same sequence. The real meaning of this doctrine is evident in its first expression:

> What will happen if one day a demon follows you to your most secluded solitude and says: This life that you are living now and that you have been living you will have to live again, innumerable times again, and there will not be anything new in it, but all the unspeakably small issues and great issues of your life will have to be faced by you again, and all of them in the same order and sequence. The eternal hourglass of existence will be turned around and around, and you will be turned with it from dust to dust. If this thought won power over you it would change the you who now exists and perhaps it would crush you under the grave weight of questioning at each time and in each situation: Do you want this once again and for innumerable times? How good to yourself and to life would you have to be in order not to ask for anything else than for this final and eternal confirmation and seal!

Thus, for Nietzsche, the endless repetition of our conduct becomes a criterion for conscious decision about its worth. A momentary action that normally seems to be inessential and easily banished from consciousness with the feeling that "whatever has passed away has passed away," takes on a formidable weight and can no longer be brushed aside when one knows that it will be infinitely repeated. Eternal recurrence means that every existence is eternal. If there is infinite repetition, then the duration of an existence is synonymous with its eternal continuation. We are responsible for our conduct in a new way, or at least we understand our responsibility differently, if we know that no moment of our life is ever over once and for all, but that we and humanity must experience it innumerable times just as we shape it now.

Thus, one of Kant's basic themes is transported into a new dimension by Nietzsche. Kant finds the ground for an action done according to duty in the possibility that the acting person could wish the principle that guides his action to be a universally valid law. The temptation to lie, to steal, to be adamant against the needy, or not to develop one's own personal potential can be countered on the moral basis that nobody would want a human world in which such temptations held sway as laws of nature: such a world would destroy itself by inner contradiction. The very egoistic interest of the person would declare against such actions being generalized, because they would also be directed against himself. Indeed, the character of an unethical conduct is not altered by its incessant repetition, but in light of such repetition, as under a microscope meanings become visible that are overlooked in a fleeting world of the only-once. But this is the practical meaning of the Kantian norm. The expansion of our actions into a general law does not lend any significance to them that is not already present in each of them taken singly. But the specific quality of our mental apperception is such that an isolated action is frequently not judged according to its full weight: its consequences are blended with the innumerable cross-cutting strands of social life, and its pure effects are distorted in their emphasis. The real import of an action stands out only if the practical milieu is attuned to it, if there are no contrary actions or effects overshadowing it, and, in sum, if it is not an accidental singular case within a chaos of other cases, but a norm without exception, a general law. Kant places action into the dimension of infinite repetition in the one-alongside-the-other of society, whereas Nietzsche has action repeat itself in the infinite one-after-the-other of the same person. Here Kant is consistent with his emphasis on the consequences of an action, and Nietzsche with his stress on the immediately manifest being of a subject. Both multiplications of action serve the same goal of getting beyond the accidentality that colors representation in their only-now and only-here. The inner value of an action, or that for which we are responsible, is in itself beyond time and number, where and how often; but we are chained to these categories and can only be impressed with the real weight of an action by appeal to them.

Fichte's development of the Kantian formula already comes close to the transposition into formal time that is accomplished in the doctrine of eternal recurrence. "The empirical ego," as Fichte puts it, "has to be tuned in the way in which it could be tuned forever. Thus, I would express the principle of morality in the following formula: Act so that the rule of your will could be imagined as an eternal law for you." The extension of the moral criterion into the dimension of time rather than into that of society makes the individual the basis of that criterion, just as for Nietzsche individual duration is decisive and not the multiplication of individuals. But in Kant, Fichte, and Nietzsche, the same proclivity is shown for gaining a reasonable basis for the values to which we are responsible in terms of their realization.

If the doctrine of eternal recurrence had only the importance expressed in the previous quotation of showing tangibly the infinite responsibility of individuals for what they do, then we would not have to broach the question of objective truth. That doctrine would be a symbol, similar to Kant's categorical imperative, which would function as an idea but not as a reality. But insofar as Nietzsche does not stop at that point and insists instead on the reality of eternal recurrence, we cannot be silent about the difficulties of his thesis. Even if we agree that the cosmic process occurs among finite elements in infinite time, there is no proof forthcoming that any configuration of elements must be repeated at any time or even in infinite time. Such repetition might occur, but a combination of cosmic elements which were not repetitive can be imagined.[1] But this argument can be left aside, because reality

1 I refer to the proof of the problematicity of eternal recurrence outside the text itself, because it is a specialized concern. I will argue here in terms of the most simple case of a system consisting of only three elements. Imagine three wheels of equal size rotating around the same axle. There is one point marked on each one of them so that the three points are aligned on a straight line at a certain moment, which may be indicated by a thread straightened across the wheels. Now the wheels start to rotate, the second wheel at twice the speed of the first one. The two marked points

can add nothing to the importance of the eternal recurrence as a regulative idea of ethics. The deep emotion and devotion with which Nietzsche sometimes speaks of his doctrine can be explained, in my opinion, only in terms of his imprecise logical conceptualization. From a logical viewpoint, there is no inherent importance to repetition, because no synthesis is possible of successive repetitions. If an experience is repeated within my existence, this repetition can be of enormous importance for me, but only because I remember the first instance and only if I have already been altered by it. But if we assume the empirically impossible case in which the second instance finds me in exactly the same state as I was when the first instance occurred, then my reaction the second time would be the same as it was initially and, therefore, the repetition would have no importance for me. The importance of repetition depends upon the persistence of the ego, which finds a new meaning and new consequences in the first instance in light of

---

on the wheels will be aligned under the thread when the first wheel has finished one revolution and the second wheel has completed two revolutions. They will be aligned again after the second revolution of the first wheel and the fourth revolution of the second wheel, and so on. In short, both wheels return to their starting positions after n revolutions of the first one and 2n revolutions of the second. Now let us suppose that the speed of revolution of the third wheel is $1/\pi$ of that of the first wheel. Then the $1, 2, 3, \ldots , n$ rotations of the first wheel are expressed by $1/\pi$, $2/\pi$, $3/\pi, \ldots ,$ n/π rotations of the third wheel. According to the nature of the number π, none of these fractions can be a whole number. This means that the third wheel will never have finished a whole number of rotations when the first wheel has completed a whole number of rotations. But because the instantaneous position of alignment, under the thread, of the points marked on the first and the second wheels will occur only after the first wheel has made a whole rotation, the marked point on the third wheel never can pass under the thread at the same moment that the marked points of the two other wheels pass under it. In consequence, the starting position of the three wheels cannot be repeated through eternity. So, if there exist anywhere in the world three motions that are identical to the motion-relation of these three wheels, the relative positions taken by them could never return to their original relations. The finitude of the number of elements in the system, even if one grants infinite time for their motions, does not, therefore, necessitate the repetition of any specific momentary relation. Of course, things might not be as I have described them. Cosmic motions could be structured in such a way that they passed again and again through a recurring cycle of combinations. But the possibility just sketched is sufficient by itself to render this so-called proof for the eternal recurrence an illusion.

the reappearance of the same contents a second time. And the case is no different when it is the whole of existence that returns. The second instance would only have significance if it were compounded by the first one, that is, if the same ego were present in both. But in reality I do not return, but a phenomenon appears which is identical with me in all of its traits and experiences. If the qualitative reality of the second instance referred to the first one and thereby acknowledged itself to be second, then it would not be an exact repetition of the first, just by the virtue of that acknowledgment. I think that Nietzsche has been tempted by an imprecise concept of the ego to see a resurrection of the previous ego when there is only a recapitulation of the same phenomenon. Therefore, he grants significance to the successive egos, none of which is the first ego and each of which is merely qualitatively of the same type as the others. In light of the foregoing discussion, it is clear that not even the first ego has the importance ascribed to it in Nietzsche's doctrine. If many absolutely identical worlds exist in space, but there is no communication among them, then the content of my ego would be repeated identically in each of them. Yet I would not be entitled to say that I live in each of these worlds. And it is obvious that these identical persons living alongside one another would behave in the same way as persons living successively, as they do according to the doctrine of eternal recurrence. The eternal recurrence only has import for someone who watches, reflects on, and unites the many returns in his consciousness; it is nothing as an external reality. The ethical-psychological import of the doctrine lies in referring to it at specific moments in given cosmic epochs. But the reality of recurrence does add a thing to the imaginative function of the idea.

I do not believe, however, that it is sound to argue that the ideas of eternal recurrence and of the overman are opposed to one another. Both of them are norms of and challenges to our conduct. The overman is just the crystallized thought that man can and ought to develop beyond his present state. Why should man stop on the way that has led him from a low animal form to humanity? Just as the present form is above the animal, so the future form will be above man. The overman is a task that grows with the progress of humanity: once the task posed by a particular present is fulfilled, a new one posed by the ideals of this present arises immediately. As long as man is a being who can evolve, the task that is inherent to the concept of the overman can never be definitively fulfilled. This task dogs the steps of mankind as a demand which remains unsatisfied by any of the attempts to fulfill it and as an expression of the fact that, in every moment of his empirical existence and even at the highest imaginable levels, man is still a path and a bridge. There appears to be a contradiction between the ideas of eternal recurrence and of the overman only insofar as the infinity of the over-man's task cannot be reconciled with the finitude of cosmic periods: within each period, humanity could be vested with only a limited number of forms of evolution, which could be constantly repeated, whereas the ideal of the overman demands a straight line of evolution heading toward the infinite. But in reality there is no contradiction if the overman is understood not as a rigid structure with an absolutely determined content, but as a functional ideal indicating the human form that is superior to the present real one. It is quite irrelevant that humanity might not be able to transcend a level of evolution that had been reached in a certain cosmic configuration. Whichever the ideal might indicate, whether something high or low, something that could really be improved or something that could not, something singular or some recurrence, that ideal would be transcendent over every moment of reality and would be independent of all of the limits typical of reality. We can formulate this point in terms of one of Kant's categories: thus we shall live in every moment, regardless of the character of its reality, as if we wished to develop toward a goal which transcends our present reality in an ideal projection of evolution; that is, we should live in such a way that we would will to live that way forever, as if there was an eternal recurrence.

The importance of the idea of recurrence is rather questionable on the level of reality. But on the level of ethical regulation that has already been discussed, and on the metaphysical level, it has a significance that makes up for its defects. Through the thought of recurrence Nietzsche has brought together into a strange union two fundamental and opposed themes of the soul: the need for the finite, for concrete limits, for definite forms in everything given, and the need to lose oneself in the limitless. In the realm of logic these needs might seem to be contradictory and negate each other. But in psychological reality they are found side by side, working together and replacing one another. This peculiar coexistence, which transcends pure logic, is reflected in the structures of metaphysics. For metaphysics, concepts and images appear in such a way that the question of truth cannot be posed in a concrete and logical sense, because these objects are so distant from individual phenomena and on such a high and abstract level that they lose the sharp contours that are so necessary for practice, logic, and science. Thus, the objects of metaphysics are as differentiated from those of other studies as are the objects of art from those of science or action. Metaphysics has its own requirements and norms which cannot reasonably be expected to meet the demands of other scientific approaches. The "unity" of many elements achieved by metaphysics does not result from the application of the norms of all of the other studies, but is often the objectivization or conceptual expression of the spiritual unity in which we experience the diversity of logically disparate elements and melt them into one. Thus, the idea of the eternal recurrence is the synthesis of the need for the infinite and the need for the finite. It teaches that finite contents and phenomena that are limited in form and number take on the form of an infinite through endless succession. It is not a matter here of the accidental conjunction of determinations, but of the same causality which is at the root of concrete and finite facts, and which pushes these facts beyond themselves and finally leads them back, through the exhaustion of possible combinations, to their starting point. Thus, there is infinite repetition, because the only-once retains a finite form that is limited by new configurations. The most meaningful symbolization for this idea is that of a ring with an infinite circumference which allows infinite and limitless movement within itself, and progress from sector to sector and yet continual return. There is the firmest of statements in Nietzsche's unedited papers: "Acumen of meditation: the eternal return of everything is the closest approach of the world of becoming to the world of being." Here is the justification for my interpretation of the doctrine of recurrence as a synthesis of the need for finitude and the need for infinity on the highest metaphysical level. Ever since the dispute occurred between Heraclitus and the Eleatics, the metaphysical process has been lodged between being and becoming. The whole of Greek philosophy is a history of attempts to unite into a noncontradictory picture of reality the substantial rigidity and closure of being—which allows the soul to find peace, realization, and finality—and flux and change, the diversity and vitality that are found in both soul and world. Being and becoming are the most general, formal, and inclusive formulations of the basic dualism that patterns all human beings: all great philosophy is engaged in founding a new reconciliation between them, or a new way of giving decisive primacy to one over the other. Nietzsche's eternal recurrence also has the function of mediating between being and becoming, and in this concept the two poles move toward each other simultaneously. On one side, the empirical chain of finite and individual events forms an uninterrupted becoming that ebbs and flows ceaselessly. Here, in the river of Heraclitus, everything that seems to be substantial is dissolved. But, through their infinite return these events gain being and inevitable continuity: everything finite becomes a fixed point through which the river of becoming passes endlessly. All content is thereby liberated and removed from the flux: finitude wraps itself into the form of the infinite, and becoming into the form of being. On the other side, within the doctrine of recurrence it is just being which seems to be finite, defined by a form, and concrete. The contents of being only gain infinity through the causality of becoming. What we are is limited at any moment; our real action can be inspected, and our need for finite limitation is satisfied by the real content of our existence. But by placing the contents of being under the causal principle of becoming, which necessitates all possible combinations and, therefore, their infinite repetition, the infinity of becoming integrates the finitude of being: the need for boundlessness and measureless transcendence quenches its thirst in the river of becoming. Certainly, only abstract concepts such as finitude and infinity, and being and becoming, can be extended to form diverse combinations that sparkle with different meanings. But metaphysics thrives on just this constitution of concepts. Here our task is only to show how these concepts are related in the idea of eternal recurrence. The infinite repetition of a being that is limited by finitude, and the causality through which phenomena that surge up and then disappear like waves in a continuous river win a durability and an eternity of being—which was stolen from them by their temporal destiny—make the eternal recurrence into a synthesis or, as Nietzsche would say, into an "approximation" between being and becoming. This approximation is expressed in an ambiguous relation among concepts: they transform the finitude of becoming into the infinity of being, or the finitude of being into an infinity of becoming. It does not matter from which point the line that connects the metaphysical poles is drawn, so long as the idea of recurrence is retained. And if one looks back to the historico-philosophical basis for the doctrine of the eternal return, which

Nietzsche's thought shares with Schopenhauer's, but which also contains their differences, we find that this doctrine negates an absolute goal of being. And we also find here a hidden and profound reason, which is not otherwise easily detected, why Nietzsche felt that recurrence was an absolutely essential and central element in all of his thinking. Nietzsche replaces a final goal with an evolutionary process that contains diverse goals and values: instead of one absolute level that is intended by the cosmic process, any level that supersedes the actual one gains significance. But the evolutionary process still contains the disquiet of boundlessness and fosters an insecurity based on the impossibility of any overview of the whole. In the notion of eternal recurrence, however, Nietzsche retains any perspective and any conclusion that being can still exhibit after an absolute goal has been eliminated, because, although each cosmic period is limited, there is still a regulative idea demanding the growth of values toward the limitless. The thought of recurrence includes infinity through the way that the finite appears in installments: endless becoming achieves form and secure boundaries through contents that are formed by definite combinations of numbers and types. For most people the thought that life returns endlessly and changelessly would be abhorrent and chilling, but Nietzsche finds it comforting and beneficial. The infinite drifting that results from the restlessness of his nature and his negation of a cosmic goal are placed within the limits of the circumference of the "ring."

Among all of Nietzsche's doctrines, that of eternal recurrence has the greatest metaphysical import, even though its moral intention is evident in his emphasis on the enormous responsibility of man in light of the eternalization of action by its continuous repetition. Despite his self-proclaimed immoralism, his thought is far more ethically oriented than that of Schopenhauer, who incessantly asserts that morality is the fundamental value of life and the meaning of all meaning. Nietzschian morality is a morality of the base which does not grow to the summit, as do the doctrines of Plato, Spinoza, Kant, and Schopenhauer, which infuse transcendent being into human volition. The ideal of nobility, which through the theme of responsibility places recurrence in its service, has an earthly and empirical nature: it is the final point of a deeply rooted evolutionary process, which lacking a sacred atmosphere does not encounter the difficulties of values and norms that originate from above in a transempirical sphere. This is, perhaps, the reason why nobility has not been recognized until the present time as a special value-quality of the soul. It is to Nietzsche's credit that he was the first one to teach the specificity of this ideal unambiguously and through rich applications, though not abstractly and systematically. Indeed, the idea of nobility cannot be subsumed under the traditionally fundamental categories of value, even though it touches the aesthetic as well as the ethical dimension. The metaphysical tones that resonate beauty and morality are clearly missing here and, thus, indicate a disjunction. The limits of morality might be drawn as naturalistically and empirically as they could be, but any thought that is more profound than is Nietzsche's meets a boundary of interpretation beyond which extends the empire of mysticism, religion, metaphysics, and even skepticism. The transition across this boundary is often barely perceptible. In the same way, the interpretation of aesthetic pleasure extends its roots and branches into this same empire, though in a different direction. As a consequence of its lack of relation to the transcendental, the content of the idea of nobility, though not its bearers, is deprived of genuine depth. Despite all of the human values they evince, the infinite and profound significance and meaning of human beings in the religious paintings of Rembrandt or in the novels of Dostoevsky lack nobility, just because these values somehow spring from transcendence or grow into it. The essence of nobility is the logical cope-stone of Nietzsche's entire doctrine of values, because it postulates the exclusion of the majority, the rejection of all comparison, and the seclusion of essences in opposition to the continuity of sharing. What counts in the Nietzschian image of human value is not quantity but the qualitative level of evolution that has been achieved. The specific nature of nobility resides in the fact that the noble being in his own lonely existence is an absolutely valid representation of the meaning of evolution. The idea of nobility has a biological character: the noble man is a product of breeding, just as are the historico-social aristocracies. Nietzsche's passionate desire to liberate morality from transcendence is consistent with this biological tendency of his morality. His demand for the infinite growth of all given empirical and earthly qualities of value is counterbalanced by his understanding that this growth should only occur on an empirical and historical ground, and that infinite increase must remain in touch with this ground.

It has frequently been stressed that Nietzsche's doctrine is in opposition to his personality: a rude, warlike, and yet bacchantic cry erupts from an extremely sensitive, quiet, introspective, and lovable man. Certainly this does not constitute an argument against the doctrine's validity. Often a philosopher expresses in his doctrine the opposite of what he is, supplementing his shortcomings in a personal dialectic and compensating for the desires he has never realized, thereby striving for full humanity. But nobility is the point at which the ideal Nietzsche teaches and the reality of his nature meet: it is the high-water mark of his personal being from which he floats into the empire of human desire.

Many misunderstandings of the overman result from overlooking the absolutely earthly nature of this ideal, which is fundamental to the opposition between the doctrine of Nietzsche and that of Schopenhauer. Nietzsche dogmatically proclaims the absolute and indisputable value of life. The life-process itself, this mysterious form in which the cosmic elements appear, has exercised an evident intoxicating and overpowering influence on Nietzsche. It appeared absurd and completely contradictory to him that there could be an imperative against life and an order of value inimical to it: a judgment against life could only be a symptom, he contends, of a specific mode of life, and the right to make such a judgment could only proceed from beyond life. But life *is* the empirical, the historical phenomenon. Even if the soul and its contents, life's mysterious blossoms, have an import beyond their earthly limits, life remains an absolute captive of the earth, its child; the ideal of nobility is but the most sublime of the sublimations achieved by the life-process through evolution, selection, and breeding. With an unerring instinct, Nietzsche, who finds value only in life, turns his love toward the idea of nobility, because it is the only ideal element of the soul that does not force life to go beyond itself into the transcendent realm or, at least, to take account of that realm. Thus, his doctrine rests on the dogmatic imperative: Life shall be! And here we find the reason why Nietzsche ultimately regards Schopenhauer as his real philosophical opponent, an invincible opponent, because he negates Nietzsche's presupposition and replaces it with the antithesis: Life shall not be! By arguing from the position that life is and shall be valuable, which was self-evident to him, Nietzsche declared victory over Schopenhauer on the basis that pessimism destroys life. But one can probably say that Nietzsche did not understand Schopenhauer's profound metaphysical dimension, because for Schopenhauer the negation of life and all that that implies is a demonstration of truth and not, as Nietzsche had it, the grounds for refutation.

We meet here the limits of the logical understanding. Nietzsche did not realize that he was trying to refute Schopenhauer on the basis of a dogmatic value-presupposition which was exactly the presupposition that his opponent rejected. This indicates an opposition of being which cannot be bridged by the intellect, just as one cannot reach a point on a line that is parallel to another one by staying on the latter. To search for peace between these two adversaries is the same as any other meritless venture: it is worse than useless because it falsifies the meaning of their opposition and, thus, the meaning of each one of them. On one hand, we have the conviction that life is valueless, which is based on selecting from all of the diverse and nonobservable meanings only monotony, the preponderance of suffering, and failure. On the other hand, we have the belief that life is value and that every deficiency is but a step toward a new attainment, every monotony but an interplay of infinite vitality, and every pain inconsequential in light of the surge of values in the process of realization in being and action. Such convictions are not theoretical knowledge but the expressions of fundamental states of the soul. They cannot be reconciled in a "higher unity," because there is no identity between them. The value of what might be called their synthesis consists precisely in the fact that humanity has developed such a magnitude of tensions in life-experience and sentiment that it can include both of them. There can be no unification based on objective content, but only one achieved by a subject who can regard both positions. By sensing the reverberations of spiritual existence in the distance opened up by these opposites, the soul grows, despite, indeed, because of, the fact that it does not decide in favor of one of the parties. It finally embraces both the desperation and the jubilation of life as the poles of its own expansion, its own power, its own plenitude of forms. And it enjoys that embrace.

INDEX